ATTORNEY GENERAL OF TEXAS
GREG ABBOTT

ECONOMIC DEVELOPMENT 2013

The material herein was obtained from Texas Attorney General Sources. This Texas Economic Development Handbook is reprinted directly from the original government document as an exact facsimile of the original document.

ATTORNEY GENERAL OF TEXAS
GREG ABBOTT

Dear City and County Officials:

Fostering a vibrant, thriving economy is critical to the future of our great state. All across Texas, cities and counties are working to nurture small business, encourage entrepreneurship, advance commerce, and create jobs.

Fortunately, Texas law offers many tools for local leaders seeking to generate economic development and opportunity. As a service to those leaders and other interested parties the Office of the Attorney General publishes this Economic Development Handbook, which compiles the state's economic development laws. This Handbook is intended to inform Texas cities and counties about the wide-range of legal tools that are available to local communities.

Thank you for your interest in economic development and the laws that help foster financial growth and opportunity. Together, state and local leaders can ensure our great state is ripe with economic opportunity for all Texans.

Sincerely,

Greg Abbott
Attorney General of Texas

Acknowledgments

A number of individuals made this publication possible by contributing their time, expertise and support. First, the members of former Attorney General John Cornyn's Municipal Advisory Committee provided the oversight for the original handbook. The mayors, council members and appointed city officials from across Texas who volunteered their time to serve on this committee played an invaluable role in the production of this publication and in the ability of this agency to address the concerns of Texas cities.

This publication was developed with substantial assistance from many sources inside and outside of the Office of the Attorney General (OAG). The OAG would like to specifically recognize the following people and organizations:

Office of the Attorney General
Zindia Thomas, Julian Grant, Stephanie Leibe and Marc Druck

Texas Comptroller of Public Accounts
Roger Wood, Russell Gallahan, Sarah Hall and Ty Myrick

Texas Hotel & Lodging Association
Scott Joslove

Texas Association of Regional Council
Jennifer Storm

Attorney at Law
Jeff Moore

Table of Contents

I.   The Economic Development Sales Tax

Using Sales Tax to Promote Economic Development

The use of the sales tax for economic development purposes has been one of the most popular and effective tools used by cities to promote economic development. Since the authorization for the local option tax took effect in 1989, more than 583 cities have levied an economic development sales tax. These cities have cumulatively raised in excess of $538 million annually in additional sales tax revenue dedicated to the promotion of local economic development. Of these cities, 108 have adopted a Type A economic development sales tax, 361 cities have adopted a Type B economic development sales tax, and 114 cities have adopted both a Type A and a Type B sales tax.

History of the Economic Development Sales Tax

In 1979, the Texas Legislature passed the Development Corporation Act of 1979 (Texas Revised Civil Statutes Article 5190.6). The Development Corporation Act of 1979 (the "Act") allowed a municipality to create nonprofit development corporations that could promote the creation of new and expanded industry and manufacturing activity within the municipality and its vicinity. The development corporations operated separately from the municipalities, with boards of directors that would oversee their efforts. These corporations, in conjunction with industrial foundations and other private entities, worked to promote local business development. However, prior to 1987, the efforts of these entities were dependent on funding from private sources, which was often was difficult to obtain. At that time, development corporations could not legally receive funding from the state or local governments because of a Texas constitutional prohibition against the expenditure of public funds to promote private business activity.[1]

In November 1987, the voters of Texas approved an amendment to the Texas Constitution providing that expenditures for economic development could serve a public purpose and were therefore permitted under Texas law.[2] This amendment states in pertinent part:

> **Notwithstanding any other provision of this constitution, the legislature may provide for the creation of programs and the making of loans and grants of public money . . . for the public purposes of development and diversification of the economy of the state.**

Pursuant to this constitutional amendment, the Texas Legislature has enacted several laws that would allow state and local government funds to be used to promote economic development.

First, in 1989, the Texas Legislature amended the Act by adding Section 4A, which allowed the creation of a new type of development corporation. The legislation provided that a Section 4A development corporation could be funded by the imposition of a local sales and use tax dedicated to economic development. The tax could be levied only after its approval by the voters of the city at an election on the issue.

---

[1]   *See* TEX. CONST. art. III, § 52.
[2]   TEX. CONST. art. III, § 52-a.

The proceeds of the Section 4A sales tax were dedicated by statute to economic development projects primarily to promote new and expanded industrial and manufacturing activities. This authority became popularly referred to as the Section 4A economic development sales tax. The Section 4A tax was generally available to cities that were located within a county of fewer than 500,000 and that had room within the local sales tax cap to adopt an additional one-half cent sales tax.

In 1991, the Texas Legislature made a number of changes to the Section 4A sales tax authorization. The new law allowed the tax to be adopted at any rate between one-eighth and one-half of one percent (in one-eighth percent increments). It additionally allowed cities to offer a joint proposition to be voted on that would authorize both a Section 4A economic development sales tax and a sales tax for property tax relief.

Also in the 1991, the Legislature authorized a new type of sales tax, a Section 4B sales tax. This legislation authorized a one-half cent sales tax to be used by certain cities to promote a wide range of civic and commercial projects. The legislation authorized 73 Texas cities to propose a Section 4B sales tax. Between 1991 and 1993, 19 cities adopted the new Section 4B sales tax.

The popularity of the Section 4B sales tax led the Texas Legislature in 1993 to broaden its availability to any city that was eligible to adopt a Section 4A sales tax. In other words, most cities in a county of less than 500,000 could adopt either the Section 4A or the Section 4B sales tax if they had room in their local sales tax. Until recently, only cities within El Paso County and Travis County were ineligible by statute to adopt either the Section 4A or the Section 4B tax. Now, cities located within El Paso County and Travis County are authorized to adopt a Section 4B tax.[3] As of this publication, at least 583 cities have either a Section 4A or a Section 4B sales tax for economic development.

Historically the Act had been located in the Texas Revised Civil Statutes Article 5190.6, and the identification of "4A" and "4B" sales tax structures were in fact references to sections 4A and 4B of the Act. In 2007, the 80th Legislature authorized the recodification of several civil statute provisions by topic, including those pertaining to planning and development. Under H.B. 2278 (80th Leg., R.S.), the Act was codified in the Local Government Code and was renamed the "Development Corporation Act."[4] As of April 1, 2009, which was the effective date of this change, economic development corporations adopting what was formally known as a "4A" or "4B" sales tax have come to be referred to as "Type A" or "Type B" corporations, as appropriate.

Differences Between Type A and Type B Sales Tax

There are a number of important differences between Type A and Type B sales taxes for

---

[3]   TEX. LOC. GOV'T CODE ANN. § 505.002 (West Supp. 2011).
[4]   *Id.* § 501.001.

economic development.[5] In broad terms, Type A and Type B taxes can be distinguished on the following grounds: 1) the authorized use of the tax proceeds; 2) the oversight procedure regarding project expenditures; and 3) the means for adopting and altering the tax by election. These general differences are outlined below. Further distinctions are covered throughout this chapter of this handbook.

Differences in the Authorized Use of the Tax Proceeds

The Type A tax is generally considered the more restrictive of the two taxes in terms of authorized types of expenditures. The types of projects permitted under Type A include the more traditional types of economic development initiatives that facilitate manufacturing and industrial activity. For example, the Type A tax can be used to fund the provision of land, buildings, equipment, facilities, expenditures, targeted infrastructure and improvements that are for the creation or retention of primary jobs for projects such as manufacturing and industrial facilities, research and development facilities, military facilities, including closed or realigned military bases, recycling facilities, distribution centers, small warehouse facilities, primary job training facilities for use by institutions of higher education, and regional or national corporate headquarters facilities.[6] The Type A sales tax may also fund business-related airports, port-related facilities, and certain airport-related facilities 25 miles from an international border,[7] as well as eligible job training classes, certain career centers and certain infrastructural improvements which promote or develop new or expanded business enterprises.[8]

The Type B tax also can be used to fund the provision of land, buildings, equipment, facilities, expenditures, targeted infrastructure and improvements that are for the creation or retention of primary jobs for projects such as manufacturing and industrial facilities, research and development facilities, military facilities, including closed or realigned military bases, transportation facilities, sewage or solid waste disposal facilities, recycling facilities, air or water pollution control facilities, distribution centers, small warehouse facilities, primary job training facilities for use by institutions of higher education, regional or national corporate headquarters facilities,[9] eligible job training classes, certain career centers and certain infrastructural improvements that promote or develop new or expanded business enterprises.[10] However, unlike the Type A tax, the Type B tax can additionally fund projects that are typically considered to be community development initiatives. For example, authorized categories under Type B include, among other items, land, buildings, equipment, facilities, expenditures, and improvements for professional and amateur sports facilities, park facilities and events, entertainment and tourist facilities, and affordable housing.[11] Also, the Type B tax may be expended for the development

---

[5]   *But see id.* §§ 504.101, 505.101. Section 505.101 states that a Type B corporation "has the powers granted by this chapter and by other chapters of this subtitle and is subject to the limitations of a corporation created under another provision of this subtitle. To the extent of a conflict between this chapter and another provision of this subtitle, this chapter prevails." Section 504.101 contains similar language that applies to Type A corporations.

[6]   *Id.* § 501.101.

[7]   *Id.* § 504.103.

[8]   *Id.* §§ 501.102-.104, .162.

[9]   *Id.* § 501.101.

[10]   *Id.* §§ 501.102-.104, .162.

[11]   *Id.* §§ 505.152-.153.

of water supply facilities or water conservation programs. In order to undertake a water supply facility or water conservation program, the facility or program has to be approved by a majority of the qualified voters of the city voting in an election called and held for that purpose.[12] Additionally, certain Type B development corporations are allowed to do projects that promote new and expanded business development.[13]

Differences in the Oversight Structure and Procedures

Although both Type A and Type B monies are overseen by the development corporation's board of directors and by the city council, they differ in the structure and type of oversight required for each.

With regard to structure, the Type A board has at least five members with no statutory criteria for their selection[14], while a Type B board consists of seven members with certain statutory requirements.[15] For instance, Type B board members have a residency requirement in the Act. A city council may place certain individuals who are not city residents onto Type B boards in two (2) very limited instances:[16] first, in a city of fewer than 20,000 in population, a Type B director may either be a resident of the city, a resident of the county in which the major part of the area of the city is located, or reside in a place that is within 10 miles of the city's boundaries and is in a county bordering the county in which a major portion of the city is located.[17] Second, a person may serve on a Type B board if that person was a Type A director at the time that a Type A corporation was dissolved, and the Type A corporation was replaced with a Type B corporation.[18] Also with respect to Type B structure, no more than four of the seven Type B directors may also be city officers or employees.[19]

Regarding oversight procedures, both Type A and Type B boards pursuing projects are required to obtain city council approval of the project. There is no requirement for additional public notice or a public hearing on individual projects undertaken by the Type A corporation, but Type B corporations are subject to certain additional procedural requirements: they must provide public notice of the project and hold a public hearing prior to pursuing a project and the public has 60 days to petition for an election to be called on whether to pursue the project.

Differences in the Means for Adopting and Altering the Tax

Finally, there are differences in how Type A and Type B taxes may be created or altered by election. A Type A tax is authorized by an election that has mandatory statutory wording for the

---

[12]   *Id.* §§ 505.154, .304.

[13]   *Id.* §§ 505.156-.158.

[14]   *Id.* § 504.051(a).

[15]   *Id.* § 505.051.

[16]   *Id.* § 505.052.

[17]   *Id.*

[18]   *Id.* § 505.052(d). (Since the directors of a Type A corporation are not required to be residents of the city, this change in the law would allow a non-resident to serve as a Type B director in this limited circumstance. However, in a city with a population greater than 20,000, the Type B board member must be a resident of the city.)

[19]   *Id.* § 505.052(c).

ballot proposition. There is also authority for a Type A tax to be adopted in conjunction with a sales tax for property tax relief under one combined proposition at the same election. Once adopted, the Type A tax continues in existence until repealed by action of the voters. The Type A tax can be increased, reduced, or repealed at subsequent elections within the statutory range provided for the tax.

Conversely, the Type B tax has no required statutory wording for the ballot proposition. It can be adopted by a general ballot proposal for the adoption of a Type B sales tax for economic development. In most cases, however, cities place a long list of the authorized categories for expenditure in the ballot wording that adopts the Type B tax. Before the 79th legislative session, there was no authorization for a Type B tax to be combined onto one ballot proposition with a sales tax for property tax relief. If the voters wanted both taxes, they had to approve the items as separate ballot propositions. As of September 1, 2005, a Type B tax can be combined into one ballot proposition with a sales tax for property relief or any other special purpose municipal sales tax.[20]

However, there is no authorization for a Type B tax rate to be increased or reduced at subsequent elections. For corporations created on or after September 1, 1999, the Type B corporation may also be dissolved by petition of the voters and an election on the issue.[21] In that case, the Type B tax would continue until the prior debt obligations of the Type B corporation had been paid in full.

Type A and Type B Economic Development Sales Tax

Eligibility to Adopt a Type A Tax

A city is eligible to adopt the Type A tax, with voter approval, if the new combined local sales tax rate would not exceed two percent and:[22]

- the city is located in a county with a population of fewer than 500,000; or

- the city has a population of less than 50,000 and is located within two or more counties, one of which is Bexar, Dallas, El Paso, Harris, Hidalgo, Tarrant, or Travis; or

- the city has a population of less than 50,000 and is within the San Antonio or Dallas Rapid Transit Authority territorial limits but has not elected to become part of the transit authority.[23]

It should be noted that participation in a rapid transit authority does not invalidate a city's ability to adopt a Type A tax if adoption of the tax would not place the area within the city above its statutory cap for the local sales tax rate.[24] If a city is not certain whether it fits into one of the

---

20   TEX. TAX CODE ANN. § 321.409 (West 2008).
21   TEX. LOC. GOV'T CODE ANN. § 505.351 - .352 (West Supp. 2011).
22   *Id.* § 504.254.
23   *Id.* § 504.002.
24   *Id.* § 504.259. *See also* TEX. TRANSP. CODE ANN. § 452.6025 (West Supp. 2011). (Allowing a city located in a county in which a chapter 452 regional transportation authority has territory to call an election to be added to the transit authority provided a majority of the votes cast in the election favor the proposition. If the

above categories, the city can call the Economic Development and Analysis Division of the Comptroller's Office at (800) 531-5441, ext. 3-4679, for a confirmation of its eligibility.

If a city is eligible to adopt a Type A tax, it may propose a sales tax rate equal to one-eighth, one-fourth, three-eighths, or one-half of one percent.[25] The city may not adopt a sales tax rate that would result in a combined rate of all local sales taxes that would exceed two percent.[26]

Cities That Have Adopted a Type A Tax (108 Cities)

Abilene	Crowell	Hillsboro	Nash	Seguin
Alton	De Kalb	Hitchcock	New Boston	Shamrock
Amarillo	De Leon	Hooks	Odessa	Sherman
Athens	Decatur	Hutto	Olney	Silsbee
Baird	Denison	Jarrell	Ore City	Slaton
Belton	Denver City	Jasper	Overton	Snyder
Big Spring	Early	Kaufman	Palmview	Sour Lake
Booker	Eastland	Kilgore	Panhandle	South Padre Island
Borger	Edgewood	Kountze	Paris	Stamford
Brady	Edinburg	La Marque	Penitas	Sulphur Springs
Bridgeport	El Campo	Lamesa	Perryton	Sweetwater
Brownfield	Fairfield	Lindale	Pharr	Tatum
Brownwood	Gilmer	Longview	Plains	Taylor
Burnet	Gladewater	Lubbock	Port Arthur	Terrell
Canadian	Graham	Marshall	Princeton	Texas City
Childress	Greenville	Maud	Prosper	Tolar
Clarksville	Hale Center	Memphis	Quanah	Vernon
Comanche	Hamlin	Menard	Ranger	Waller
Commerce	Haskell	Mercedes	Raymondville	Wellington
Copperas Cove	Henderson	Monahans	Rockwall	Weslaco
Corpus Christi	Hereford	Mount Pleasant	Rotan	Wills Point
Crockett	Hidalgo	Muleshoe	Rusk	

Eligibility to Adopt a Type B Tax

A city may impose the Type B tax, with voter approval, if the new combined local sales tax rate would not exceed 2 percent and if the city fits into one of the following categories:[27]

- the city would be eligible to adopt a Type A sales tax (see earlier section on Eligibility to Adopt a Type A Tax);

- the city is located in a county with a population of 500,000 or more and the current combined sales tax rate does not exceed 8.25 percent at the time the Type B tax is proposed; or

- the city has a population of 400,000 or more and is located in more than one county, and the combined state and local sales tax rate does not exceed 8.25 percent.

---

proposition is approved, the Type A sales tax can be reduced "to the highest rate that will not impair the imposition of the [regional transportation] authority's sales and use tax.")
25 TEX. LOC. GOV'T CODE ANN. § 504.252(b) (West Supp. 2011).
26 *Id.* § 504.254.
27 *Id.* § 505.002.

An eligible Type B city includes a city "that is located in a county with a population of 500,000 or more," and the Act also provides that an eligible city includes a city "located in a county with a population of 500,000 or fewer." Consequently, every Texas city appears to be eligible to adopt a Type B sales tax provided the city's combined local sales tax rate does not exceed two percent.[28] Further, it should be noted that participation in a rapid transit authority does not invalidate a city's ability to adopt a Type B tax if adoption of the tax would not place the city above its statutory cap for the local sales tax rate.[29] If the city is not certain whether it fits into one of the above categories, the city can call the Economic Development and Analysis Division of the Comptroller's Office at (800) 531-5441, ext. 3-4679 for a confirmation of its eligibility.

If the city is eligible to adopt a Type B tax, it may propose a tax rate equal to one-eighth, one-fourth, three-eighths or one-half of one percent.[30] The city may not adopt a sales tax rate that would result in a combined rate of all local sales taxes that would exceed two percent.[31]

Cities that have Passed a Type B Tax (361 Cities)

Alamo	Columbus	Haltom City	Lockhart	Paradise	Snook
Alba	Conroe	Hamilton	Lockney	Pasadena	Sonora
Aledo	Converse	Hart	Lorena	Pearland	South Houston
Alto	Coppell	Hawkins	Los Fresnos	Pecos	Southlake
Alvarado	Corinth	Hawley	Lott	Pflugerville	Spearman
Alvord	Corral City	Helotes	Lufkin	Pilot Point	Spur
Angleton	Cotulla	Henrietta	Luling	Pittsburg	Stafford
Archer City	Crandall	Hickory Creek	Lumberton	Point	Stanton
Arcola	Crawford	Hico	Mabank	Ponder	Sterling City
Argyle	Cross Plains	Higgins	Malakoff	Port Aransas	Stinnett
Aubrey	Crowley	Highland Village	Malone	Port Isabel	Stockdale
Avinger	Cuero	Hill Country Village	Manvel	Port Neches	Stratford
Balmorhea	Cuney	Hollywood Park	Marble Falls	Portland	Strawn
Bandera	Dalhart	Hondo	Marfa	Post	Sudan
Bangs	Dalworthington Gdns	Howe	Marquez	Poth	Sullivan City
Bartonville	Dayton	Hubbard	Mathis	Prairie View	Sundown
Bastrop	Dickinson	Hudson	Maypearl	Presidio	Sweeny
Bay City	Domino	Hughes Springs	McAllen	Princeton	Taft
Bedford	Douglassville	Huntington	McCamey	Queen City	Tahoka
Bee Cave	Driscoll	Hurst	McGregor	Quinlan	Teague
Beeville	Dublin	Hutchins	McLean	Quitaque	Thorndale
Bellmead	Dumas	Idalou	Meadows Place	Quitman	Throckmorton
Bellville	Duncanville	Industry	Meridian	Rankin	Tomball
Benbrook	East Tawakoni	Ingleside	Merkel	Redwater	Trenton
Benjamin	Eden	Iraan	Mesquite	Refugio	Trinidad
Bertram	Electra	Italy	Mexia	Richland Hills	Trinity
Big Lake	Elgin	Itasca	Miles	Richmond	Troup
Big Sandy	Emory	Jacksboro	Mineola	Rio Grande City	Turkey
Bishop	Encinal	Jacksonville	Mission	Rio Vista	Tyler
Bonham	Ennis	Jefferson	Montgomery	Rising Star	Uhland
Bovina	Euless	Jewett	Morgan's Point	River Oaks	Universal City
Breckenridge	Everman	Junction	Morgan's Point Resort	Robstown	Van

---

28   *Id.* §§ 504.002, 505.002.

29   *Id.* § 505.257. *See also* TEX. TRANSP. CODE ANN. § 452.6025 (West Supp. 2011). (Allowing a city located in a county in which a chapter 452 regional transportation authority has territory to call an election to be added to the transit authority provided a majority of the votes cast in the election favor the proposition. If the proposition is approved, the Type B sales tax can be reduced "to the highest rate that will not impair the imposition of the [regional transportation] authority's sales and use tax.")

30   TEX. LOC. GOV'T CODE ANN § 505.252(b) (West Supp. 2011).

31   TEX. TAX CODE ANN. § 321.101(f) (West 2008), TEX. LOC. GOV'T CODE ANN. § 505.256 (West Supp. 2011) (Making Chapter 321 of the Tax Code applicable to a Type B tax).

Brenham	Fate	Karnes City	Morton	Rocksprings	Van Horn
Brookshire	Flower Mound	Keller	Mount Vernon	Rollingwood	Venus
Brownsboro	Floydada	Kemah	Muenster	Roma	Victoria
Buda	Forest Hill	Kemp	Nassau Bay	Ropesville	Wake Village
Buffalo	Forney	Kenedy	Navasota	Rosebud	Wallis
Buffalo Gap	Frankston	Kennedale	Nederland	Rosenberg	Watauga
Bullard	Freeport	Kerens	Needville	Round Rock	Waxahachie
Burkburnett	Friona	Kerrville	Nevada	Round Top	Webberville
Caddo Mills	Fritch	Krum	New Braunfels	Royce City	Webster
Cameron	Gainesville	La Grange	New Deal	Runaway Bay	Weimar
Caney City	Galveston	La Joya	Nolanville	Sachse	West Columbia
Canton	Ganado	La Porte	North Richland Hills	San Angelo	West Tawakoni
Canyon	Giddings	Laguna Vista	Oak Leaf	San Benito	Westlake
Carmine	Glen Rose	Lake Jackson	Oak Point	San Juan	Westworth Village
Centerville	Godley	Lake Worth	Oak Ridge	San Saba	Wharton
Chandler	Goldthwaite	Lakewood Village	Oak Ridge North	Sansom Park	Wheeler
Chico	Gonzales	Lampasas	Odem	Santa Anna	White Deer
Cibolo	Gordon	Lavon	Old River-Winfree	Santa Fe	White Oak
Clarendon	Grand Saline	League City	Olmos Park	Savoy	White Settlement
Clear Lake Shore	Grapeland	Leon Valley	Olton	Schertz	Whiteface
Cleburne	Grapevine	Leonard	Orange	Schulenburg	Windcrest
Cleveland	Groesbeck	Lewisville	Ovilla	Seabrook	Windthorst
Clifton	Groom	Lexington	Oyster Creek	Seagoville	Winnsboro
Clute	Groves	Liberty	Palacios	Sealy	Winona
Clyde	Gruver	Liberty Hill	Palestine	Seminole	Wolfforth
Coahoma	Gun Barrel City	Lincoln Park	Palmer	Seven Points	Yantis
Coffee City	Gunter	Live Oak	Pampa	Shepherd	Yoakum
Colleyville	Gustine	Llano	Pantego	Silverton	Yorktown

Cities that have passed both a Type A and a Type B Tax (114 Cities)

Albany	Cedar Park	Fulshear	Knox City	Newton	Somerset
Allen	Celina	Georgetown	Krugerville	Nocona	Southmayd
Alton	Center	Goree	La Feria	Northlake	Sugar Land
Anna	Cisco	Gorman	Lake Dallas	Orchard	Sunnyvale
Anson	Coleman	Grandfalls	Lancaster	Paducah	The Colony
Aspermont	Collinsville	Grandview	Levelland	Pottsboro	Tioga
Atlanta	Crystal City	Groveton	Linden	Primera	Tom Bean
Balch Springs	DeSoto	Hallettsville	Little Elm	Progreso	Trophy Club
Beasley	Donna	Harlingen	Littlefield	Red Oak	Tye
Bells	Edcouch	Haslet	Magnolia	Rio Hondo	Van Alstyne
Blue Ridge	Elsa	Hearne	Mansfield	Roanoke	Von Ormy
Bowie	Escobares	Heath	Matador	Roaring Springs	Whitesboro
Bremond	Fairview	Hempstead	McKinney	Robert Lee	Whitewright
Bronte	Farmersville	Iowa Park	Melissa	Roscoe	Wichita Falls
Brownsville	Ferris	Joaquin	Miami	Saint Jo	Willis
Burleson	Floresville	Joshua	Midland	Sanger	Wilmer
Calvert	Fort Stockton	Justin	Midlothian	Seagraves	Wolfe City
Carthage	Franklin	Keene	Munday	Simonton	Wortham
Cedar Hill	Frisco	Knollwood	Murphy	Sinton	Wylie

Economic Development Corporation Projects

The Development Corporation Act provides a wide variety of purposes for which Type A and Type B tax proceeds may be expended. Some of these projects require the creation or retention of primary jobs.[32] Other statutory provisions require that the Type A and Type B corporations

---

[32]   The definition of "project" was significantly amended in the 78th Legislative Session. Changes made applied only to projects that were undertaken or approved after June 20, 2003. Any projects undertaken or approved

meet the requisite revenue amounts, population, and other requirements specified by the Act without having to create or retain primary jobs. A few projects do not require either the creation or retention of primary jobs or that certain criteria be met. It is important to emphasize that any activities of an economic development corporation must always be in furtherance, and attributable to, a "project".[33]

Type A and Type B Projects Which Must Create or Retain Primary Jobs

In 2003, the Texas Legislature amended the definition of "project" to require that certain projects result in the "creation or retention of primary jobs".[34] Accordingly, most Type A and Type B projects must now create or retain primary jobs. Yet, not all projects contain this requirement. "Primary job" is defined to mean a job that is "available at a company for which a majority of the products or services of that company are ultimately exported to regional, statewide, national, or international markets infusing new dollars into the local economy" and that meets any one of a specific list of sector numbers of the North American Industry Classification System (NAICS).[35]

The enumerated sector numbers are:

111	Crop Production
112	Animal Production
113	Forestry and Logging
11411	Commercial Fishing
115	Support Activities for Agriculture and Forestry
211 to 213	Mining
221	Utilities
311 to 339	Manufacturing
42	Wholesale Trade
48 and 49	Transportation and Warehousing
51 (excluding 512131 and 512132)	Information (excluding movie theaters and drive-in theaters)
523-525	Securities, Commodity Contracts, and Other Financial Investments and Related Activities; Insurance Carriers and Related Activities; Funds, Trusts, and Other Financial Vehicles
5413, 5415, 5416, 5417, and 5419	Scientific Research and Development Services

---

[33] before June 20, 2003 are governed by the law that was in effect on the date the project was undertaken or approved.

Op. Tex. Att'y Gen. No. JC-0118 (1999) (Ruling under the former statute, Sales and use taxes levied under section 4B of the Development Corporation Act of 1979, Tex. Rev. Civ. Stat. Ann. art. 5190.6 (Vernon 1987 & Supp. 1999), may only be used for project costs; they may not be used for "promotional" costs unrelated to projects).

[34] Tex. Loc. Gov't Code Ann. §§ 501.101, 505.155 (West Supp. 2011). (Section 505.151 incorporates Type A projects under Chapter 501 as authorized projects for Type B corporations.)

[35] *Id.* § 501.002(12).

551	Management of Companies and Enterprises
56142	Telephone Call Centers
922140	Correctional Institutions;
928110	National Security and for corresponding index entries for Armed Forces, Army, Navy, Air Force, Marine Corps, and Military Bases.

For more information on the North American Industry Classification System, please visit: http://www.census.gov/eos/www/naics/.

Section 501.101 of the Act specifically allows funding for the land, buildings, equipment, facilities, expenditures, targeted infrastructure, and improvements that are for the creation or retention of primary jobs that are found by the board of directors of the Type A and Type B corporation to be required or suitable for the development, retention, or expansion of the following eight types of projects:

Manufacturing and industrial facilities. A primary purpose of the economic development sales tax is to promote the expansion and development of manufacturing and industrial facilities which create or retain primary jobs.

Research and development facilities. Economic development corporations can help provide research and development facilities which create or retain primary jobs.

Military facilities. Economic development corporations can help promote or support an active military base, attract new military missions to a military base in active use; or redevelop a military base that has been closed or realigned.

Recycling facilities. With the recent federal and state statutory encouragement of recycling enterprises, a growing number of businesses are emerging to meet these needs, and cities will be competing to attract these businesses. Recycling facilities which create or retain primary jobs are permissible projects.

Distribution centers. In cities with access to major airports or ports, and in areas that have passed the Freeport exemption, the environment is often favorable for the location of distribution centers. Funding distribution centers which create or retain primary jobs is allowable under the Act.

Small warehouse facilities. Again, in cities with access to major airports or ports, and in areas that have passed the Freeport exemption, the environment is often favorable for the location of warehouse facilities capable of serving as decentralized storage and distribution centers. Small warehouse facilities projects which create or retain primary jobs are permissible projects.

Primary job training facilities for use by institutions of higher education. The Development Corporation Act allows the funding for "primary job training facilities for use by institutions of higher education". The term "institution of higher education" is defined under Section 61.003 of the Texas Education Code to include any public technical institute, public junior college, public senior college or university, medical or dental unit, or other agency of higher education as defined under Section 61.003.

Regional or national corporate headquarters facilities. "Corporate headquarters facilities" is defined to mean "buildings proposed for construction or occupancy as the principal office for a business enterprise's administrative and management services."[36] Accordingly, Type A and Type B corporations may fund corporate headquarter facilities, provided the facilities create or retain primary jobs.

Additionally, only Type B corporations may provide land, buildings, equipment, facilities and improvements found by the board of directors to promote or develop new or expanded business enterprises that create or retain primary jobs, including a project to provide:

- Transportation facilities (including but not limited to airports, hangars, airport maintenance and repair facilities, air cargo facilities, related infrastructure located on or adjacent to an airport facility, ports, mass commuting facilities and parking facilities)[37],

- Sewage or solid waste disposal facilities[38]

- Air or water pollution control facilities[39],

- Facilities for furnishing water to the public[40],

- Public safety facilities[41],

- Streets and roads,

- Drainage and related improvements,

- Demolition of existing structures,

- General municipally owned improvements,

- Any improvements or facilities that are related to any of those projects and any other projects that the board in its discretion determines promoted or develops new or expanded business enterprises that create or retain primary jobs.

---

[36] *Id.* § 501.002(4).

[37] *Id.* § 501.101(2)(D). *See also id.* § 504.103 (Section 504.103 limits Type A corporation from doing certain projects.)

[38] *Id.* § 501.101(2)(E). *See also id.* § 504.103 (Section 504.103 limits Type A corporation from doing certain projects.)

[39] *Id.* § 501.101(2)(G). *See also id.* § 504.103 (Section 504.103 limits Type A corporation from doing certain projects.)

[40] *Id.* § 501.101(2)(H). *See also id.* § 504.103 (Section 504.103 limits Type A corporation from doing certain projects.)

[41] *Id.* § 505.155.

Type A and Type B Projects Which Are Not Required to Create Primary Jobs

The following categories are authorized Type A and Type B projects that are not conditioned upon the creation or retention of primary jobs.

> **Job training classes.** Certain job training required or suitable for the promotion or development and expansion of business enterprises can be a permissible project. Type A and Type B corporations may spend tax revenue for job training classes offered through a business enterprise only if the business enterprise agrees in writing to certain conditions. The business enterprise must agree to create new jobs that pay wages that are at least equal to the prevailing wage for the applicable occupation in the local labor market area, or agree to increase its payroll to pay wages that are at least equal to the prevailing wage for the applicable occupation in the local labor market area.[42]

> **Certain infrastructural improvements which promote or develop new or expanded business enterprises.** "Project" also includes expenditures found by the board of directors to be required or suitable for infrastructure necessary to promote or develop new or expanded business enterprises. However, the infrastructure improvements are limited to streets and roads, rail spurs, water and sewer utilities, electric utilities, gas utilities, drainage, site improvement, and related improvements, telecommunications and Internet improvements, and beach remediation along the Gulf of Mexico.[43] Accordingly, Type A and Type B corporations may assist with limited infrastructural improvements that the board finds will promote or develop new or expanded business development.

> **Career Centers.** Certain career centers can be provided land, buildings, equipment, facilities, improvements and expenditures found by the board of directors to be required or suitable for use if the area to be benefited by the career center is not located in the taxing jurisdiction of a junior college district.[44]

> **Commuter Rail, Light Rail or Motor Buses.** A Type A and Type B corporation, as authorized by the corporation's board of directors, may spend tax revenue received under the Act for the development, improvement, expansion or maintenance of facilities relating to the operation of commuter rail, light rail, or motor buses.[45]

In addition, there are three categories that are not required to create or retain primary jobs, but for which there are revenue amount, population and other requirements specified in the Act:

> **Airport Facilities.** Type A and Type B corporations located wholly or partly within twenty-five miles of an international border, in a city with population of less than 50,000 or an average rate of unemployment that is greater than the state average rate of unemployment during the preceding twelve month period, may assist with land,

---

[42]   *Id.* § 501.162. *See id.* § 501.102.
[43]   *Id.* § 501.103.
[44]   *Id.* § 501.105.
[45]   *Id.* § 502.052

buildings, facilities, infrastructure and improvements required or suitable for the development or expansion of airport facilities.[46]

Infrastructure for Airports, Ports, and Sewer or Solid Waste Disposal Facilities. Type A and Type B corporations located in a city wholly or partly in a county that is bordered by the Rio Grande with a county population of at least 500,000, and having wholly or partly within its boundaries at least four cities that each have a population of at least 25,000, may provide certain assistance with infrastructure necessary to promote or develop new or expanded business enterprises, including airports and port facilities, provided Type A or Type B sales tax revenues do not support the project.[47] This provision also allows for providing assistance for sewer facilities and solid waste facilities. However, only Type B corporations can provide assistance to these facilities because Type A corporations are not allowed to do those types of projects.[48]

Hurricane Ike Disaster Relief. Type A and Type B corporations located wholly or partly within the Hurricane Ike disaster area may provide assistance towards Hurricane Ike disaster area bonds. Type A and Type B corporations authorized to participate in Hurricane Ike disaster area bond projects must be located wholly or partly in one of thirty-four Texas counties. (See footnote, below.) For these eligible corporations, the term "project" is defined to mean the undertaking of costs which are eligible to be paid from the proceeds of qualified Hurricane Ike disaster bonds. The term "project" does not include qualified residential rental projects, or projects the costs of which are payable from qualified mortgage bonds.[49]

Type A Only Projects Which Are Not Required to Create Primary Jobs

Section 504.103 of the Local Government Code specifically allows economic development corporations to undertake two categories of projects without the requirement of creating or retaining primary jobs. The primary purpose of these projects is to provide:

> **Business airports** (general aviation business service airports that are an integral part of an industrial park); and

> **Port-related facilities** (port-related facilities to support waterborne commerce).

Type B Only Projects Which Are Not Required to Create Primary Jobs

Sections 505.152 through 505.154 of the Act specifically permit expenditures of Type B tax proceeds for land, buildings, equipment, expenditures and improvements suitable for the following types of projects:

---

46 *Id.* §§ 501.106, 504.103(c).
47 *Id.* § 501.107.
48 *Id.* § 504.103.
49 *Id.* § 501.452. The 34 counties that are subject to this section are: Angelina, Austin, Brazoria, Chambers, Cherokee, Fort Bend, Galveston, Gregg, Grimes, Hardin, Harris, Harrison, Houston, Jasper, Jefferson, Liberty, Madison, Matagorda, Montgomery, Nacogdoches, Newton, Orange, Polk, Rusk, Sabine, San Augustine, San Jacinto, Shelby, Smith, Trinity, Tyler, Walker, Waller, and Washington.

Professional and amateur sports and athletic facilities. Professional and amateur sports and athletics facilities, including stadiums and ballparks, are permissible Type B projects.[50]

Entertainment, tourist and convention facilities. Entertainment, tourist, and convention facilities, including auditoriums, amphitheaters, concert halls, museums and exhibition facilities are permissible Type B projects.[51]

Public parks and related open space improvements. Public parks, park facilities and events, and open space improvements are permissible Type B projects.[52]

Affordable housing. Projects required or suitable for the development and expansion of "affordable housing" as defined by federal law (42 United States Code Section 12745) are permissible Type B projects.[53]

Water supply facilities. Any water supply facilities, including dams, transmission lines, well field developments, and other water supply alternatives can be permissible Type B projects.[54] Nonetheless, to undertake a water supply facility project, a majority of the qualified voters of the city voting in an election called and held for that purpose must approve the water supply project.[55] The ballot proposition for the election shall be printed to provide for voting for or against the proposition:[56]

> **The use of sales and use tax proceeds for infrastructure relating to** (*insert description of water supply facility*).

Water conservation programs. Water conservation programs, including incentives to install water-saving plumbing fixtures, educational programs, brush control programs, and programs to replace malfunctioning or leaking water lines and other water facilities can be permissible Type B projects.[57] As with water supply facilities, to undertake a water conservation program a majority of the qualified voters of the city voting in an election called and held for that purpose must approve the water conservation program.[58] The ballot proposition for the election shall be printed to provide for voting for or against the proposition:[59]

---

[50] *Id.* § 505.152.
[51] *Id.*
[52] *Id.*
[53] *Id.* § 505.153.
[54] *Id.* § 505.154.
[55] *Id.* § 505.304.
[56] *Id.*
[57] *Id.* § 505.154.
[58] *Id.* § 505.304.
[59] *Id.*

The use of sales and use tax proceeds for infrastructure relating to (*insert description of water conservation program*).

Airport Facilities. Type B corporations may undertake a project which is required or suitable for the development or expansion of airport facilities, including hangars, airport maintenance and repair facilities, air cargo facilities, and related infrastructure located on or adjacent to an airport facility, if the project is undertaken by a corporation created by an eligible city: (i) that enters into a development agreement with an entity in which the entity acquires a leasehold or other possessory interest from the corporation and is authorized to sublease the entity's interest for other projects authorized by this subdivision; and (ii) the governing body of which has authorized the development agreement by adopting a resolution at a meeting called as authorized by law.[60]

Additionally, certain Type B corporations have been given more latitude in deciding what types of projects that they can do without the requirement of creating or retaining primary jobs but they must meet the requisite conditions.

Revenue Requirement. Type B corporations in cities that have not generated more than $50,000 in sales and use tax revenues in the preceding two (2) fiscal years may provide land, buildings, equipment, facilities, and improvements found by the board of directors to be required or suitable for the development, retention, or expansion of business enterprises, provided the city council authorizes the project by adopting a resolution following two (2) separate readings conducted at least one (1) week apart.[61]

Population Requirement. A Type B corporation in a city with a population of 20,000 or less may provide land, building, equipment, facilities, expenditures, targeted infrastructure, and improvements found by the board of directors to promote new or expanded business development provided that, for projects which require an expenditure of more than $10,000, the city council adopts a resolution authorizing the project after giving the resolution at least two (2) separate readings.[62]

Landlocked Communities. For Type B corporations located wholly or partly in a county with a population of two million or more that has within its city limits and extraterritorial jurisdiction fewer than 100 acres that can be used for the development of manufacturing or industrial facilities in accordance with the zoning laws or land use restrictions of the city, the term "project" also includes expenditures found by the board of directors to be required for the promotion of new or expanded business enterprises within the landlocked community.[63]

---

[60] *Id.* § 505.1561.
[61] *Id.* § 505.156.
[62] *Id.* § 505.158.
[63] *Id.* § 505.157.

Undertaking Projects Located Outside of the City

Section 501.159(a) of the Local Government Code provides that an economic development corporation may undertake projects outside of the city limits with permission of the governing body that has jurisdiction over the property. If the project is located completely within the jurisdiction of another municipality, the corporation would need approval of the city council for that municipality.

Uses of Type A and Type B Taxes

Use of a Type A Tax for Infrastructural Improvements
Type A tax proceeds are not intended to fund the general infrastructural needs of a city.[64] For example, Section 504.103 of the Act states that Type A tax proceeds cannot be used to undertake a project the primary purpose of which is to provide transportation facilities, solid waste disposal facilities, sewage facilities, facilities for furnishing water to the general public or air or water pollution control facilities. Section 504.103 further states that Type A tax proceeds may be used for these types of facilities only if the expenditure would "benefit property acquired for a project having another primary purpose."

In 2003, the Texas Legislature amended the Act to allow Type A corporations to expend sales tax proceeds for specific infrastructural improvements necessary to promote or develop new or expanded business enterprises.[65] This provision authorizes and limits expenditures for streets and roads, rail spurs, water and sewer utilities, electric utilities, gas utilities, drainage, site improvements and related improvements, telecommunications and Internet improvements, and beach remediation along the Gulf of Mexico.[66]

Use of Type A Tax for Type B Projects

In 1997, the Texas Legislature amended the Development Corporation Act to allow the voters of an area to approve at an election the use of Type A economic development sales tax funds for a project authorized under Type B.[67] This alternative was authorized to allow cities with a Type A tax to propose Type B projects to the voters without having to repeal or reduce the Type A tax and adopt a Type B tax.

As noted, any use of Type A funds for a Type B project must be approved by the city's voters at an election held on the issue and a public hearing must be conducted before the city holds the election. If the city already has a Type A tax, it only needs to have the voters approve at the election the use of Type A tax proceeds for a particular Type B project or a category of Type B

---

[64] *See* Tex. Att'y Gen. LO-95-072 (1995) (V.T.C.S. article 5190.6, section 4B authorizes the board of directors of a development corporation organized under V.T.C.S. article 5190.6 to determine whether the construction of sanitary sewer lines in an existing residential subdivision would promote or develop new or expanded business enterprises. Although it seems unlikely that the construction of sewer facilities in a residential subdivision would promote or develop new or expanded business enterprises, this office cannot exclude the possibility as a matter of law. The board's determination would be reviewed under an abuse of discretion standard.)

[65] TEX. LOC. GOV'T CODE ANN. § 501.103 (West Supp. 2011).

[66] *Id.*

[67] *Id.* § 504.152.

projects. The city would need to list each project or category of projects on a separate ballot proposition for the voters' approval. Unfortunately, state law does not define what constitutes a separate category of projects. A city should consult with its local legal counsel before it drafts its ballot wording for such an election.

If the city chooses to propose the use of Type A funds for Type B purposes, it must hold a public hearing prior to the election.[68] At the public hearing, the city's residents must be informed of the estimated cost and impact of the proposed project or category of projects. The city must publish notice of the hearing in a newspaper of general circulation in the city at least 30 days before the date set for the hearing. The notice must include the time, date, place and subject of the hearing and must be published on a weekly basis until the date of the hearing.

In an election to approve the use of Type A funds for a Type B purpose, the law requires that a specific Type B project or category of projects be clearly described on the ballot.[69] The ballot proposition must be clear enough for the voters to discern the limits of the specific project or category of projects to be authorized. State law does not indicate what type of limits must be identified. At a minimum, the proposition should clearly identify what types of project are anticipated. Additionally, if Type A funds are to be used to pay maintenance and operating costs (and not just initial construction cost, etc.) of a Type B project, then the ballot proposition must state that fact.

A city may ask the voters to consider the use of Type A funds for a Type B purpose at the same election in which the voters are considering the creation of the Type A tax itself.[70] The city would use one ballot proposition for the adoption of the Type A tax and a separate ballot proposition to approve the use of Type A funds for a Type B purpose. A city may also have the voters consider authorizing the use of Type A funds for several different Type B projects or categories of projects at the same election. As noted earlier, each project or category of projects would need to be placed on a separate ballot proposition for the voters' approval. There does not seem to be any authorization for a city to have the voters consider the use of Type A funds for several different Type B projects or categories of projects within one ballot proposition, unless the city proposes a combined ballot proposition to repeal or reduce the Type A tax and in the same proposition adopt a Type B tax. If an election on a Type B project or category of projects fails to win voter approval, the city must wait at least one year before holding another election on that particular project or category.[71]

Additionally, even when undertaking a properly authorized Type B project, a Type A corporation is governed by all the normal rules applicable to Type A corporations.[72] For instance, if the ballot proposition originally authorizing the Type A tax contained an expiration date for the tax, voter authorization of the use of Type A funds for a Type B purpose would not eliminate the expiration date of the tax.

---

[68]   *Id.* § 504.153.
[69]   *Id.* § 504.152(b).
[70]   *Id.* § 504.152(c).
[71]   *Id.* § 504.154.
[72]   *Id.* § 504.156.

During the 82nd Legislative Session, the Legislature passed a bill that would allow Type A corporations to do Type B projects if:

- The city that created the Type A corporation also has a Type B corporation; and
- The population of the city is 7,500 or less.[73]

The city will have to pass an ordinance allowing the Type A corporation to do Type B projects. These Type A corporations would not have to have an election to do Type B projects. Also, by ordinance, the city may revoke the Type A corporation's ability to do Type B projects under this bill.

Use of Type A Tax and Type B Tax for "Sports Venue" Facilities

Type A and Type B funds may be used to fund "sport venue" projects.[74] Special statutory provisions apply to "sports venue" projects. A project qualifies as a "sports venue" if it is an arena, coliseum, stadium, or other type of area or facility that meets both of the following criteria:[75]

- The primary use or primary planned use is for one or more professional or amateur sports or athletics events; and
- A fee for admission to the sports or athletics events is charged or is planned to be charged, except that a fee need not be charged for occasional civic, charitable or promotional events.

Texas law specifies that any funds authorized by the voters to be spent on a "sports venue and related infrastructure" may be spent on any on-site or off-site improvements that relate to a sports venue and that enhance the use, value, or appeal of the sports venue, including areas adjacent to it. Eligible expenditures would include any costs that are reasonably necessary to construct, improve, renovate, or expand the sports venue. The law specifically lists the following uses as examples of permissible "related infrastructure": stores, restaurants, concessions, on-site hotels, parking facilities, area transportation facilities, roads, water or sewer facilities, parks, and environmental remediation.[76] However, each of these facilities must relate to and enhance the sports venue.

In order for a Type A or Type B corporation to do a "sports venue" project, both the Type A and Type B corporations must follow certain procedures. A city may submit to its voters a ballot

---

[73]   *Id.* § 504.171.
[74]   *Id.* §§ 504.152-.156, 505.201-.206.
[75]   *Id.* §§ 504.151(2), 505.201(2). (Note that the definition of "sports venue" in section 505.201 of the Local Government Code differs from that contained in 504.151 of this Act. Type B corporations have an additional limitation within its definition of "sports venue". Type B corporations cannot fund arena, coliseum, stadium, or other type of area or facility that is or will be owned and operated by a state-supported institution of higher education.)
[76]   *Id.* §§ 504.151(1), 505.201(1).

proposition that would authorize the use of Type A or Type B funds for a specific "sports venue" project or category of projects, including any infrastructure related to that project or category.[77] Such a ballot proposition could contain language enabling the Type A or Type B corporation to use any Type A or Type B funds already collected to support the "sports venue" project. Before an election to authorize the use of the Type A or Type B tax for a sports venue, a public hearing must be conducted.[78] At that hearing, the city's residents must be informed of the cost and impact of the proposed project or category of projects. The city is required to publish notice of the hearing in a newspaper of general circulation in the city at least 30 days before the date set for the hearing. The notice must include the time, date, place, and subject of the hearing and must be published on a weekly basis until the date of the hearing. Accordingly, the city will need to schedule its public hearing early enough so that it can provide at least 30 days notice of the hearing.

In an election to approve the use of Type A or Type B funds for a "sports venue" project, the law requires that a specific "sports venue" project or category of projects be clearly described on the ballot. [79] The description must be clear enough for the voters to discern the limits of the specific project or category of projects to be authorized. State law does not indicate what constitutes a clear description or how to indicate the limits of the specific project. At a minimum, the ballot proposition should clearly indicate the types of projects anticipated. Additionally, if Type A or Type B funds are to be used to pay the maintenance and operating costs (and not just initial construction cost, etc.) of a "sports venue" project, then the ballot proposition must state that fact.[80]

A city may have the voters consider the use of Type A or Type B funds for a "sports venue" project at the same election in which the voters are considering the creation of the Type A or Type B tax itself.[81] A city that pursues such a combined proposition should consult with its local legal counsel and the Comptroller's Office on this issue. State law requires that any "sports venue" election be held on a uniform election date. If a "sports venue" project or category of projects fails to win voter approval, the city must wait at least one year before holding another election on that particular project or category.[82]

Use of Type A and Type B Tax Proceeds for Training Seminars

Certain Type A and Type B economic development corporation officers and city officials are required to complete a training seminar.[83] The officials must complete a seminar once every 24 months.[84] At least one person from each of the following is required to attend a seminar each 24-month period:

77	*Id.* §§ 504.152(a), 505.202(a).
78	*Id.* §§ 504.153, 505.203.
79	*Id.* §§ 504.152(b), 505.202(b).
80	*Id.*
81	*Id.* §§ 504.152(c), 505.202(c).
82	*Id.* §§ 504.154, 505.204.
83	*Id.* § 502.101.
84	*Id.* § 502.101(a).

2013 Economic Development Handbook • *Office of the Attorney General*

19

- the city attorney, the city administrator or city clerk; and

- the executive director or other person who is responsible for the daily administration of the corporation.[85]

The corporation is authorized to use Type A or Type B proceeds to pay for the costs of attending a seminar.[86] The certificates of completion are issued by the person, entity, or organization providing the training seminars on a form approved by the Comptroller's office.[87] The Comptroller's office may impose an administrative penalty in an amount not to exceed $1,000 for failure to attend the seminar.[88]

Specific Procedural Requirements Before a Type B Corporation Can Expend Type B Tax Proceeds

Public Notice Requirement and the 60-Day Right to Petition

A Type B corporation must publish notice of the Type B projects it plans to undertake. This is because the public has a right to submit a petition objecting to a particular Type B project.[89] The petition must be submitted within 60 days of the first published notice of a specific project or type of project and must be signed by more than 10 percent of the registered voters of the city.

If a petition is pursued by the public, the petition can ask that the city hold an election on the issue before that specific project or type of project is undertaken. If the petition is submitted in a timely manner and an election is required, the corporation may not undertake the project until the voters approve the project at an election on the issue. If the voters disapprove the project at the election, the Type B tax proceeds may not be used for that purpose. It is important to note that a petition cannot force an election on a project if the voters have previously approved the specific project or that general category of projects at an earlier election called under the Act.

Public Hearing Requirement for Expending Type B Tax Proceeds

A Type B corporation is required to hold at least one public hearing on any proposed project, including a proposal to expend funds on maintenance and operating expenses of a project.[90] However, a corporation created by an eligible city with a population of less than 20,000 is not required to hold a public hearing if the proposed project is defined by Sections 501.101 through 501.107 of the Act.[91] If a public hearing is required, the hearing must be held before the corporation expends any Type B funds on the project. There is nothing in the Act that prohibits the Type B corporation from holding one public hearing to consider a group of Type B projects. After the projects have been considered at a public hearing and 60 days have passed since the first public notice of the nature of the projects, the development corporation is free to make

---

85   *Id.* § 502.101(a)(1)-(2).
86   *Id.* § 502.101(d).
87   *Id.* § 502.103(a).
88   *Id.* § 502.103(b).
89   *Id.* §§ 505.160, .303.
90   *Id.* § 505.159(a).
91   *Id.* § 505.159(b).

expenditures related to the projects pursuant to the adopted budget, subject to other applicable requirements.

Specific Costs of a Type A and Type B Project That May be Funded

Cities need to know what types of specific expenditures are contemplated within each category available for expenditure of Type A and Type B tax proceeds. For assistance in understanding what is permitted under the Act, cities should review the definition of the term "cost" under Section 501.152 of the Act. Section 501.152 defines what costs may be applied to a Type A or Type B. It states, in pertinent part, that costs for a project may include:

Land and facility improvements: the cost of acquisition, construction, improvement and expansion of land and buildings.

Machinery and supplies: the cost of machinery, equipment, inventory, raw materials and supplies.

Financial transaction costs: the cost of financing charges, interest prior to and during construction, and necessary reserve funds.

Planning costs: the cost of research and development, legal services, development of plans and specifications, surveys, and cost estimates; and other expenses necessary or incident to determining the feasibility and practicability of undertaking the project.

Brownfield Clean-up costs: Should the Texas Governor's office or the Texas Commission on Environmental Quality encourage or request that a Type A or Type B corporation use sales tax proceeds to clean up contaminated property, the corporation may not undertake the project until the use is approved by a majority of the qualified voters of the city voting in an election called and held for that purpose. The ballot proposition is as follows:[92]

> **"The use of sales and use tax proceeds for the cleanup of contaminated property."**

Administrative Expenses of a Type A and Type B Project

Section 501.152 of the Act also states that the cost of a project may include the administrative expenses and other expenses that are incident to placing a project into operation. The law states that these expenses could include "the administrative expenses for the acquisition, construction, improvement, and financing of any project." Additionally, Type A and Type B corporations are permitted to contract with other private corporations to carry out industrial development programs.[93] Also, should a Type A or Type B corporation contract with a broker, agent or other third party for business recruitment, a written contract approved by the board of directors is

---

[92] *Id.* §§ 504.304, 505.305.
[93] *Id.* §§ 504.102, 505.102.

required for any payment of a commission, fee, or other thing of value to the third party.[94] Failure to enter into a written contract could result in a civil penalty not to exceed $10,000.

Maintenance and Operating Expenses of a Type A and Type B Project

It should be noted that there is a difference between "administrative expenses that are necessary to put a project into operation" and the "maintenance and operating expenses" of an ongoing project. Type A and Type B corporations have statutory authority to spend Type A and Type B funds on maintenance and operation expenses for a Type A or Type B project.[95] However, the voters are allowed to petition for an election on the issue of whether to prohibit the Type A or Type B corporation from expending Type A or Type B funds for the maintenance and operation costs of a particular project. Such a petition must be signed by 10 percent of the registered voters of the city. The petition must be presented within 60 days after the city first publishes notice that the tax proceeds are going to be used for maintenance and operations of a specific project. However, an election is not required if the voters has previously approved the use of Type A or Type B proceeds for this purpose at an earlier election under the Act.

Promotional Expenses and Prior Debts

The Act limits Type A and Type B corporations to spending no more than 10 percent of the corporate revenues (Type A and Type B tax proceeds) for promotional purposes.[96] The Act does not define the term "promotional purposes." However, the Texas Attorney General has concluded that a promotional expenditure "must advertise or publicize the city for the purpose of developing new and expanded business enterprises."[97] Further, a corporation is limited to spending not more than 10 percent of its current annual revenues for promotional purposes in any given year. Nonetheless, unexpended revenues specifically set aside for promotional purposes in past years may be expended along with 10 percent of current revenues without violating the cap.[98] Additionally, city council may disapprove a promotional expenditure.[99] If there is some question as to whether a particular expenditure should be considered a promotional expense, the development corporation should consult with its local legal counsel.

A Type A corporation is prohibited from assuming a debt or paying the principal or interest on a debt if the debt existed before the date when the city created the development corporation.[100]

---

[94]   *Id.* § 502.051.

[95]   *Id.* §§ 504.302, 505.303.

[96]   *Id.* §§ 504.105, 505.103. *See* Tex. Att'y Gen. LO-94-037 (Ruling under the former statute, this opinion concluded the Development Corporation of Abilene, which operated under section 4A of the Development Corporation Act, could spend proceeds of the sales and use tax imposed under section 4A for "promotional purposes," subject to the proviso of subsection (b)(1) that no more than 10 percent of corporation revenue could be spent for such purposes, and so long as the expenditures were otherwise consistent with the provisions of the act and state law generally).

[97]   Op. Tex. Att'y Gen. No. GA-0086 (2003) at 2.

[98]   *Id.* at 6.

[99]   *Id.* at 3-5.

[100] TEX. LOC. GOV'T CODE ANN. § 504.104 (West Supp. 2011). *But see* Op. Tex. Att'y Gen. No. DM-299 (1994). (Ruling under the former statute, this opinion indicates that Tex. Rev. Civ. Stat. art. 5190.6, § 4A(q) is not retroactive. A 4A corporation can, therefore, continue to make payments on any obligation that the corporation entered into before the enactment date of 4A(q) (in 1993). This would be true even if the

This limitation does not prevent a development corporation from undertaking or making future expenditures toward a project that is already in operation. It means that the corporation could not reimburse that project for its prior debts. However, the Legislature has not addressed whether a Type B corporation is prohibited from paying principal or interest on a debt if the debt existed before the city created the Type B corporation.

Issuance of Bonds for a Type A or Type B Project

A Type A and Type B corporations may issue bonds, notes and other contractual obligations to fund its projects.[101] The sales tax proceeds received by the corporation may be used to pay the principal and interest on the bonds and any other costs related to the bonds.[102] For example, the Texas Attorney General concluded in Letter Opinion 92-86 that a Section 4A (now Type A) development corporation may finance bonds for the start-up costs of a technical college if the funds are used solely for vocational training purposes. Any bond or debt instrument of the corporation remains an obligation of the corporation and is not an obligation of the city, nor is it backed by the city ad valorem tax rate.[103] The city and the development corporation staff will want to visit with local bond counsel prior to the imposition of any debt obligation or debt instrument. All such bonds would need to receive approval by the Public Finance Division of the Office of the Attorney General.[104]

Creating a Type A or Type B Economic Development Corporation

Creation of a Type A or Type B economic development corporation may be initiated either by the city[105] or by a group of citizens.[106] For citizens to initiate the creation of an economic development corporation, a group of three or more individuals who are qualified voters of the city must file a written application with the city requesting approval of an economic development corporation. The city may not charge a fee for consideration of the application. If the city determines that the corporation should be created, the city must approve the corporation's certificate of formation (formerly known as articles of incorporation)[107] by ordinance or resolution. The ordinance or resolution must indicate what purposes the corporation can further on the city's behalf. The purposes shall be limited to the promotion and development of industrial and manufacturing enterprises to encourage employment and the public welfare. The Type A economic development certificate of formation must state that the corporation is to be governed by Chapter 504 of the Local Government Code.[108] The Type B economic development

---

obligation entered into before the enactment of 4A(q) was one that existed before the creation of the 4A corporation.)

101   TEX. LOC. GOV'T CODE ANN. §§ 501.155, .201, .214 (West Supp. 2011).

102   *Id.* §§ 504.303, 505.104.

103   *Id.* § 501.207.

104   *Id.* § 501.201 (States that a development corporation may issue bonds obtaining the consent of any state department, division or agency, "other than the attorney general under chapter 1202, Government Code.")

105   *Id.* § 504.003(a).

106   *Id.* § 501.051.

107   *Id.* § 501.011.

108   *Id.* § 504.004.

certificate of formation must state that the corporation is to be governed by Chapter 505 of the Local Government Code.[109]

The certificate of formation for all development corporations must contain the items required under Section 501.056 of the Act and must be approved by the municipality's governing body.[110] The city may amend the certificate of formation at its sole discretion at any time.[111]

The certificate of formation must be filed in triplicate with the Secretary of State's Office pursuant to Section 501.057 of the Act. Upon the issuance of the certificate of incorporation, the corporate existence begins. After the issuance of the certificate evidencing the filing of the certificate of formation, the board of directors must hold an organizational meeting to adopt the bylaws of the corporation and to elect officers.[112] The initial bylaws must also be approved by resolution of the governing body of the city.[113] The first meeting of the board of directors of the corporation should be held pursuant to the requirements under Section 501.063 of the Act.

For copies of sample certificates of formation or bylaws, a city may want to contact one of the cities noted in this handbook as having already adopted the Type A or Type B economic development corporation.

A city can create an economic development corporation without having an election to create a sales tax. However if the city wants the economic development corporation to receive sales tax funds, then there has to be an election to adopt a Type A or Type B economic development sales tax.

Initiating an Election to Adopt a Type A or Type B Sales Tax

An election to adopt a Type A or Type B economic development sales tax may be initiated either by:

- city council approval of an ordinance calling for an election on the imposition of the tax[114]; or

- a petition signed by a number of qualified voters that equals at least 20 percent of the voters who voted in the most recent regular city election. If the city council receives such a petition, it is required to pass an ordinance to call an election on the imposition of the tax.[115]

---

[109]   *Id.* § 505.004.
[110]   *Id.* § 501.051(b)(2).
[111]   *Id.* § 501.302.
[112]   *Id.* § 501.063.
[113]   *Id.* § 501.064.
[114]   *Id.* §§ 504.255, 505.256 (Stating that chapter 321 of the Texas Tax Code governs the imposition of a Type A or Type B tax), and TEX. TAX CODE ANN. § 321.401(a) (West 2008) (An election may be called by the adoption of a city ordinance by city council.).
[115]   *See* TEX. LOC. GOV'T CODE ANN. §§ 504.255, 505.256 (West Supp. 2011) (Stating that chapter 321 of the Tax Code governs the imposition of a Type A or Type B tax) and TEX. TAX CODE ANN. § 321.401(c) (West 2008) (Requiring that the city council pass an ordinance calling for a sales tax election if a petition is

Most cities pass the ordinance calling for a Type A or Type B sales tax election on their own motion and do not wait for the election to be initiated by a petition of the voters. If a city orders an election on the sales tax for economic development, it must follow all applicable requirements for elections contained in the Election Code, the Municipal Sales and Use Tax Act (Chapter 321 of the Tax Code), and other Texas statutes relating to elections.[116] Notably, the following requirements must be met:

Potential Election Dates. The election must be held on a uniform election date as provided by Chapter 41 of the Election Code. There are uniform election dates in May and November. The current uniform election dates are:

- the second Saturday in May in an odd-numbered year;
- the second Saturday in May in an even-number year, for an election held by a political subdivision other than a county; or
- the first Tuesday after the first Monday in November.[117]

Time Frame for Ordering the Election. The city should order the election at least 71 days prior to the date of the election, unless the election is the general election for state and county officers.[118] If the election is the general election for state and county officers, then the city should order the election at least 78 days prior to the date of the election.[119] The Tax Code requires only that the city order the election at least 30 days before the date of the election.[120] Nonetheless, it is advisable to provide at least 71 or 78 days' notice, since this is the requirement applicable to most other special elections in Texas and it allows time to comply with other Election Code requirements, such as early voting. In addition, the Election Code provision governing time frames for ordering an election "supersedes a law outside this code to the extent of any conflict."[121]

Notice to be Provided of Election. The city must publish notice of the election at least once in a newspaper of general circulation in the city.[122] The notice must be published not more than 30 days and not less than 10 days before the date of the election. The notice must state the nature and date of the election, the location of each polling place, hours that the polls will be open, and any other election-related information required by

---

[116] *presented). See* TEX. ELEC. CODE ANN. ch. 277 (West 2008 & Supp. 2011) (Requirements for petition signatures).

[116] *See* TEX. LOC. GOV'T CODE ANN. § 504.255, 505.256 (West Supp. 2011) (Stating that chapter 321 of the Tax Code governs elections under chapter 504 and 505 of the Local Government Code) and TEX. TAX CODE ANN. § 321.403 (West 2008) (stating that an election held under chapter 321 of the Tax Code must be held on the next available uniform election date).

[117] TEX. ELEC. CODE ANN. § 41.0052 (West Supp. 2011).

[118] *Id.* § 3.005(c).

[119] *Id.*

[120] TEX. TAX CODE ANN. § 321.403 (West 2008).

[121] TEX. ELEC. CODE ANN. § 3.005(b) (West Supp.2011).

[122] *Id.* § 4.003(a)(1), (c) (West 2010).

law.[123] The notice must also include the wording of all the ballot propositions.[124] The entire notice must generally be provided in both English and Spanish.[125]

Other Procedural Requirements. The city must follow all other applicable procedural requirements under the Election Code for elections. For further information about the requirements contained in the Election Code, contact the Secretary of State's Office, Elections Division, at (800) 252-8683.

Ballot for Economic Development Corporations

Type A Ballot: The Act requires specific wording for a Type A sales tax proposition ballot, as follows:[126]

> **The adoption of a sales and use tax for the promotion and development of new and expanded business enterprises at the rate of (*insert one-eighth, one-fourth, three-eighths, or one-half, as appropriate*) of one percent.**

The actual wording used on the ballot must indicate what rate is proposed for the Type A sales tax. The voters then vote for or against the proposition.

Type B Ballot: Current law does not provide any required wording for the ballot for a Type B sales tax for economic development. Before the Development Act was codified, cities would use great care to include wording that described all of the categories of projects that the city would want to have the Type B corporation to pursue.[127] Cities should be sure to have their legal counsel review any proposed ballot wording prior to its use in an election proposition.

Setting a Limited Time Period for a Type A or Type B Tax

A Type A tax that is approved without a time limit is effective until repealed by election.[128] However, a city may include in the wording of the ballot proposition a limitation on the length of time in years that a Type A tax may be imposed. For example, a city could limit the time period during which a Type A tax is imposed to four years. Once such a limit is approved by the voters, the tax may be extended beyond this time limit or reimposed only if the city has an election at

---

[123]   *Id.* § 4.004(a) (West Supp. 2011).
[124]   *Id.* § 4.004(b).
[125]   *See id.* ch. 272 (West 2010 & Supp. 2011).
[126]   TEX. LOC. GOV'T CODE ANN. § 504.256 (West Supp. 2011).
[127]   *See* Op. Tex. Att'y Gen. No. JC-400 (2001) (The city of Sonora's ballot adopting the 4B sales tax read as follows: "The adoption of an additional one-half of one percent sales and use tax within the City pursuant to the provisions of Article 5190.6, V.A.T.C., with the proceeds thereof to be used and applied in the manner and *to the purposes authorized by Section 4B of the Act, including but not limited* to public facility improvements, commercial facilities, infrastructural improvements, new and expanded business enterprises, and other related improvements, facilities to furnish water to the general public, sewage and solid waste disposal facilities and maintenance and operating costs associated with all of the above projects." JC-400 at 4).
[128]   *TEX. LOC. GOV'T CODE ANN.* § 504.257(d) (West Supp. 2011).

which the voters authorize the extension or reimposition of the tax. If a city decides to include such a time limitation, the required ballot wording is as follows:[129]

> **The adoption of a sales and use tax for the promotion and development of new and expanded business enterprises at the rate of (*insert one-eighth, one-fourth, three-eighths, or one-half, as appropriate*) of one percent to be imposed for (*insert number of years that the tax would be imposed*) years.**

The actual wording used on the ballot must indicate what rate is proposed for the Type A sales tax and the number of years that the tax would be in effect. The voters then vote for or against the proposition.

As noted earlier, there is no required wording for a Type B tax ballot. However, an eligible city may allow the voters to vote on a ballot proposition that limits the length of time that a sales and use tax may be imposed. An eligible city that imposes a tax for a limited time under this subsection may later extend the period of the tax's imposition or reimpose the tax only if the extension or reimposition is authorized by a majority of the qualified voters of the city voting in an election called and held for that purpose in the same manner as an election held under Section 505.2565 of the Act.[130]

Limiting the Types of Projects for a Type A or Type B Tax

On a ballot to adopt the Type A tax or on a ballot to increase or reduce a Type A tax, a city may also limit the use of the tax to a specific project.[131] For example, a city could limit the use of the Type A tax to a project for a specific manufacturing entity or to a specific type of project such as expenditures for an industrial park. If such a limit is approved by the voters, the city may not broaden the purposes for which the Type A tax may be used unless it holds another election. Any desired change would have to go back to the voters for approval at an election on the issue. Once the obligations for the specific project have been satisfied, the corporation is required to notify the Texas Comptroller to cease collecting the Type A tax. To date, no city has limited the use of a Type A tax to a specific project. If a city decides to include such a limitation, the required wording of the ballot is as follows:[132]

> **The adoption of a sales and use tax for the promotion and development of (*insert description of the project*) at the rate of (*insert one-eighth, one-fourth, three-eighths, or one-half, as appropriate*) of one percent.**

The actual wording used on the ballot must indicate what rate is proposed for the Type A sales tax and must include a description of the project. The voters then vote for or against the proposition.

---

129   *Id.* § 504.257(a).
130   *Id,* § 505.2565.
131   *Id.* § 504.260.
132   *Id.* §§ 504.256, .260.

A city may limit the use of the Type B tax to a specific project.[133] However, as noted earlier, there is no required wording for a Type B tax ballot. Accordingly, there is no special wording that must be used to limit the use of the Type B tax to certain projects. If a city wants to limit the use of Type B tax proceeds to certain projects, it may choose to list only the types or categories of projects it desires on the ballot. Also, the Act provides certain authorization to expand the types of projects undertaken if subsequently approved by the eligible voters.[134]

Various Joint Ballot Proposition for a Type A or a Type B Tax

Joint Ballot Proposition for a Type A Tax and a Sales Tax for Property Tax Relief

A city may include the Type A sales tax and the sales tax for property tax relief as separate ballot propositions at the same election. In 1991, the Texas Legislature allowed cities to offer the voters a joint ballot proposition on a sales tax for property tax relief and a Type A sales tax for economic development.[135] In this scenario, the voters would vote for or against one ballot proposition that covers the adoption of both taxes.

Under this joint ballot proposition, the voters are not able to pass the property tax relief sales tax without also passing the Type A sales tax for economic development. Either both taxes pass or both taxes fail. If a city decides to use such a joint proposition, the required wording on the ballot is as follows:[136]

> **The adoption of a sales and use tax within the city for the promotion and development of new and expanded business enterprises at the rate of (*insert one-eighth, one-fourth, three-eighths, or one-half, as appropriate*) of one percent and the adoption of an additional sales and use tax within the city at a rate of (*insert one-eighth, one-fourth, three-eighths, or one-half, as appropriate*) of one percent to be used to reduce the property tax rate.**

The actual wording used on the ballot must indicate what rate is proposed for the Type A sales tax and what rate is proposed for the sales tax for property tax relief. The voters then vote for or against the proposition. If the total local sales tax has reached the legal maximum of two percent, a city may attempt simultaneously to reduce the sales tax for property tax relief and impose the Type A economic development sales tax in one ballot proposition. The city would still use the above-noted ballot wording.[137]

---

[133] *Id.* § 505.2575(a).
[134] *Id.* § 505.2575(b).
[135] *Id.* § 504.261.
[136] *Id.*
[137] Tex. Att'y Gen. LO-93-104 (1993) (For a simultaneous election on the imposition, under section 4A, V.T.C.S. article 5190.6, of a sales and use tax of one-fourth of one percent for economic development and the reduction of its previously adopted additional sales and use tax for the reduction of property taxes under Tax Code section 321.101(b) from a rate of one-half of one percent to one-quarter of one percent, the city should use the proposition language set out in section 4A(p), as follows: The adoption of a sales and use tax within the city for the promotion and development of new and expanded business enterprises at the rate of one-fourth of one percent and the adoption of an additional sales and use tax within the city at the rate of one-fourth of one percent to be used to reduce the property tax rate).

There is nothing that stops a city from using separate ballot items for the passage of a sales tax for property tax relief and a Type A sales tax for economic development. In this case, the voters would vote for or against the adoption of each of the two taxes and the passage of one would not influence the passage of the other. Cities, however, have historically preferred the incentive value of joining the two items onto one ballot proposition. If a city uses separate ballot propositions, it should be noted that it is not possible to make one ballot proposition dependent on the passage of a separate ballot proposition. In other words, the city could choose to offer one proposition proposing a reduction of the sales tax for property tax and a separate proposition for the adoption of a sales tax for economic development. Making the adoption of one of the propositions dependent on the passage of the other can be accomplished only where the Legislature has authorized a joint proposition as described earlier.

Joint Proposition to Reduce or Abolish a Type A Tax and Adopt a Type B Tax

A city may offer a joint ballot proposition that would reduce or abolish an existing Type A tax and at the same time approve the creation of a Type B tax.[138] That is, the city can have the voters approve or reject both items together by one "yes" or "no" vote. However, a city is not required to combine these two issues into one ballot proposition. A city that pursues such a combined proposition should consult with its legal counsel and with the Comptroller's Office on this issue.

A city can still choose to have the voters vote on repealing or reducing a Type A tax and adopting a Type B tax as separate ballot propositions.[139] If the city places the items on separate ballot propositions, it is possible that one, both, or neither of the items would be approved at such an election. A city that chooses to provide these options to the voters would use the ballot wording suggested earlier for each of these items. In no case may a city offer ballot propositions that, if passed, would cause the city to exceed its two percent local sales tax cap.[140]

Joint Proposition of a Type A or Type B Tax and Other Municipal Sales Tax

Cities are allowed to have joint ballot propositions to lower, repeal, raise or adopt various municipal sales taxes.[141] This would include the Type A and Type B tax. If a city wants to lower the Type A or Type B tax and create a street maintenance tax, the city could combine the ballot propositions instead of having separate ballot propositions. If the joint ballot proposition does not pass, then there will be no effect on those sales taxes.

Proposition to Increase or Reduce a Type A or Type B Tax

Type A Sales Tax

A city that has imposed a Type A tax may, on its own, motion call for an election to approve an increase or a reduction of the Type A tax rate.[142] The election would be administered by the same procedure that was used to originally adopt the tax. The Type A tax rate would be reduced or increased if the proposition were approved by a majority of the qualified voters who voted at

---

138   TEX. LOC. GOV'T CODE ANN. § 505.255 (West Supp. 2011).

139   *Id.*

140   *See id.* § 505.256; TEX. TAX CODE ANN. § 321.101(f) (West 2008).

141   *See* TEX. TAX CODE ANN. § 321.409 (West 2008).

142   TEX. LOC. GOV'T CODE ANN. § 504.258 (West Supp. 2011).

an election held on the issue. The rate may be reduced or increased in one or more increments of one-eighth of one percent with a minimum rate of one-eighth of one percent and a maximum rate of one-half of one percent. Also, on petition of at least 10 percent of the registered voters of the city, the city may be compelled to order an election on a proposed increase or decrease of the Type A tax rate.[143]

It should be noted that the Attorney General has concluded in Attorney General Opinion DM-137 (1992) that if there is an election to reduce the Section 4A (now Type A) sales tax or to limit the length of time of its collection, the reduction or limitation may not be applied to any bonds issued prior to the date of the election.

It is not clear what ballot wording would be required for a proposition to increase or reduce a Type A tax rate. Section 504.258 of the Local Government Code states that "the ballot shall be printed in the same manner as the ballot under Section 504.256." Section 504.256 contains the regular wording on the ballot to adopt a Type A sales tax. The ballot wording to adopt the Type A tax is as follows: "The adoption of a sales and use tax for the promotion and development of new and expanded business enterprises at the rate of (insert one-eighth, one-fourth, three-eighths, or one-half, as appropriate) of one percent." A city should consult with its legal counsel, in conjunction with the Local Assistance section of the Comptroller's Office, if it decides to ask the voters to reduce or increase an existing Type A tax. The Economic Development and Analysis Division of the Comptroller's Office can be reached by phone at (800) 531-5441, ext. 3-4679. Prior to the election, the city should also check with the Elections Division of the Secretary of State's Office to determine whether this type of special election would require pre-clearance from the U.S. Department of Justice. The Elections Division can be reached by phone at (800) 252-8683.

Type B Sales Tax
For a Type B corporation, there is no statutory authority that allows a Type B tax to be increased or decreased after its initial adoption.

Proposition to Abolish the Type A or Type B Tax

Type A Sales Tax
On petition of 10 percent or more of the registered voters of the city, the city can be required to order an election on the dissolution of the Type A corporation.[144] If the corporation is dissolved, the Type A tax may not be collected except to pay off any remaining obligations that were executed before the date of the dissolution election. The ballot for the election shall be printed to provide for voting for or against the proposition:[145]

Termination of the (*insert name of the corporation*).

---

[143]   *Id.*
[144]   *Id.* § 504.351(a).
[145]   *Id.* § 504.352.

The election must be held on a uniform election date and the election is subject to all the applicable requirements under law for elections. Prior to the election, the city should check with the Elections Division of the Secretary of State's Office to determine whether this type of election would require pre-clearance from the U.S. Department of Justice. The Elections Division can be reached by phone at (800) 252-8683.

If a majority of the voters voting on the issue approve the dissolution, the corporation continues its operations only long enough to pay off any bonds that were issued before the date of the election and to the extent necessary to dispose of its assets.[146] The Attorney General has concluded that a corporation that is dissolving is required to submit its dissolution plan to city council for its review and approval.[147] However, city council may not use this approval power to prevent the corporation from performing its statutory duty to, "to the extent practicable, . . . dispose of its assets and apply the proceeds to satisfy" the corporation's obligations. The assets are used to pay off any liabilities, and any remaining assets are transferred to the city.[148] The corporation is required to notify the Comptroller's Office to cease collection of the tax once the corporation has satisfied all of its obligations.[149]

Type B Sales Tax Created before September 1, 1999
For a Type B corporation created before September 1, 1999, there is no statutory authority that allows a Type B tax to be abolished after its initial adoption. The city could use its power by resolution under Section 501.401 of the Act to terminate or dissolve the development corporation. If the city takes such an action, the corporation and the tax would continue only for the time period necessary to pay off any outstanding debt.

Type B Sales Tax Created on or after September 1, 1999
For a Type B corporation created on or after September 1, 1999, the Act provides that a city must hold an election on the issue of dissolving the corporation if a proper petition is submitted to the city council.[150] Such a petition must request an election on the dissolution of the Type B corporation and be signed by at least 10 percent of the registered voters of the city. The petition must also meet any other legal requirements that may be applicable, including the general petition requirements found in chapter 277 of the Election Code. The election must be held on the first regular uniform election date that falls more than 61 days after the petition is filed with the city. At the election, the ballot must be printed to read as follows:[151]

Termination of the (*name of corporation*).

If a Type B corporation is dissolved pursuant to an election of this nature, the corporation will continue to operate long enough to pay off all its debts and obligations.

---

146   *Id.* § 504.353.
147   Op. Tex. Att'y Gen. No. JC-0553 (2002) at 6.
148   TEX. LOC. GOV'T CODE ANN. § 504.353(a)(2) (West Supp. 2011).
149   *Id.* § 504.353(c).
150   *Id.* § 505.352 (Provides that the municipality shall hold the election on the next uniform election date as required by Section 3.005 of the Election Code).
151   *Id.* § 505.353.

Once the corporation's debts and obligations are paid off, the corporation is dissolved and its property must be transferred to the city. The city must then notify the Comptroller, who must stop collecting the Type B sales tax by the last day of the first calendar quarter that begins after the city has notified the Comptroller.[152]

Reporting Election Results of a Type A and Type B Tax

The Election Code requires that, no earlier than the eighth day and no later than the eleventh day[153] after the election, the governing body of the city must canvass the ballots and enter the resolution or ordinance declaring the results of the election into the minutes of a meeting. The resolution or ordinance must include the following:[154]

- The date of the election;

- The proposition for which the vote was held;

- The total number of votes cast for and against the proposition; and

- The number of votes by which the proposition was approved.

If the proposed change in the tax rate is approved by a majority of the qualified voters of the city voting at an election on the issue, the city may levy the approved tax. The city secretary must, by certified or registered mail, send the Comptroller a certified copy of the resolution or ordinance and must include a map of the city clearly showing the city's boundaries. After receiving the documents, the Comptroller has 30 days to notify the city secretary that the Comptroller's Office will administer the tax.

If the election fails, the city must wait one full year before bringing the issue to the voters again.[155] However, the Election Code allows the city to hold a subsequent election on the corresponding uniform election date that occurs approximately one year later, even if the date falls several days before a full year has elapsed.[156]

---

[152]   *Id.* § 505.354.

[153]   TEX. ELEC. CODE ANN. § 67.003(a) (West 2010). *But see* TEX. TAX CODE ANN. § 321.405 (West 2008) (Which gives the city 10 days to canvass an election on the proposed adoption of a Type A sales tax. It is not clear whether the Election Code provision or the Tax Code provision is controlling on this issue. Therefore, it is recommended that cities follow the stricter provisions of the Election Code and canvass the election between 8 and 11 days after it has taken place. Also, the Election Code allows the city to canvass the May election results as early as three days after the election, but only if there are no outstanding mail or provisional ballots).

[154]   TEX. TAX CODE ANN. § 321.405 (West 2008).

[155]   *Id.* § 321.406. *But see* TEX. LOC. GOV'T CODE ANN. §§ 504.255, .351, 505.256 (West Supp. 2011).

[156]   TEX. ELEC. CODE ANN. § 41.0041(a) (West 2010).

Effective Date of Type A or Type B Tax

Effective Date of Type A or Type B Sales Tax Election Only

The change in the sales tax rate becomes effective one full calendar quarter after notice of the election has been provided to the Comptroller. The new tax rate applies to purchases on or after the first day of that calendar quarter as provided under Section 321.102(a) of the Tax Code.

> **May Election**: Send notice to the Comptroller no later than the last week in June. On October 1st, the new tax rate will take effect. The city will receive its first payment in December.

> **November Election**: Send notice to the Comptroller no later than the last week in December. On April 1st, the new tax rate will take effect. The city will receive its first payment in June.

Effective Date for Type A Sales Tax and Additional Municipal Sales Tax Election

At the same election, if the city adopts a Type A sales tax and adopts an additional municipal sales taxes, such as a sales tax for property tax relief, the city has two options with regard to the effective date of the tax. The city may opt to have the taxes take effect at the same time (the following October 1st if a full calendar quarter has passed since the election).[157] Or, alternatively, the city may choose to have the Type A tax take effect as soon as one calendar quarter has passed after the election, and have the sales tax for property tax relief take effect the following October 1st (after which a full calendar quarter has passed since the election). In this scenario, the Type A tax would generally take effect before the sales tax for property tax relief.[158] Some cities choose this option to maximize revenues from the tax; other cities choose to make it easier on retailers and allow both taxes to take effect at the same time in October.

Effective Date for Type B Sales Tax and Additional Municipal Sales Tax Election

At the same election, if the city adopts a Type B sales tax and an additional municipal sales tax, such as a sales tax for property tax relief, both taxes will not take effect until the following October 1st (assuming at least a complete calendar quarter has passed since the election).[159] If a complete calendar quarter has not passed since the election, the tax would not take effect until the following October 1st.

Allocation of the Sales Tax Proceeds by the Comptroller

Once the sales tax is effective, the Comptroller remits the sales tax proceeds from the increase in the rate to the municipality with its other local sales tax proceeds. The Municipal Sales and Use

---

[157] TEX. LOC. GOV'T CODE ANN. § 504.255 (West Supp. 2011), TEX. TAX CODE ANN. § 321.102(b) (West 2008) (While the option to have both taxes take effect on October 1 is not expressly set out in state statute, it has been the interpretation of the Comptroller's office that such an option is allowed. Thus, it is currently Comptroller's policy to give cities a choice with regard to the date of implementation for a Type A or Type B sales tax as outlined in this section.)

[158] TEX. TAX CODE ANN. § 321.102(b) (West 2008).

[159] *Id.*, TEX. LOC. GOV'T CODE ANN. § 505.256 (West Supp. 2011).

Tax Act (Chapter 321 of the Tax Code) governs the imposition, computation, administration, abolition, and use of the tax except where it is inconsistent with the statutory provisions within the Development Corporation Act.[160]

The city, upon receiving its local sales tax allotment from the Comptroller, must remit the sales tax for economic development to the economic development corporation responsible for administering the tax.[161] The proceeds of a sales tax for property tax relief would remain with the city.

Directors of a Economic Development Corporation

Board of Directors of a Type A Economic Development Corporation

A Type A corporation is governed by at least a five-member board of directors.[162] The directors are appointed by a majority vote of the city council at an open meeting. The Act does not specify any qualifying criteria for a person who serves as a director on the Type A board. A Type A director is not required to be a city resident or a property owner. The directors serve without compensation but must be reimbursed for actual expenses.[163] The directors are appointed to a term not to exceed six years. Further, should the certificate of formation or the bylaws not address a term of office, then the Type A directors have a six-year term of office.[164] However, the directors serve at the pleasure of the city council and may be removed by the city council at any time without cause.[165]

In JC-349, ruling under the former statute, the Attorney General concluded that a Section 4A director could be appointed to a subsequent term. The opinion noted that neither the Development Corporation Act nor the Texas Non-Profit Corporation Act barred such reappointment. Accordingly, a city council may reappoint a director to a subsequent term, provided there is not a contrary provision in the articles of incorporation, bylaws, city charter, city ordinance or resolution.

Board of Directors of a Type B Economic Development Corporation

A Type B corporation is governed by a seven-member board of directors.[166] The seven directors are appointed by a majority vote of the city council at an open meeting. Unlike Type A corporation boards, the Act does place qualifying criteria for a person who serves as a director on a Type B board. If the Type B corporation is located in a city with a population of 20,000 or more, the Type B director must be a resident of the city.[167] If a Type B corporation is located in a city with a population of less than 20,000, the Type B director must:

---

[160] TEX. LOC. GOV'T CODE ANN. §§ 504.255, 505.256 (West Supp. 2011).
[161] *Id.* §§ 504.301, 505.256.
[162] *Id.* § 504.051(a).
[163] *Id.* § 501.062(d).
[164] Op. Tex. Att'y Gen. No. JC-0349 (2001) at 3.
[165] TEX. LOC. GOV'T CODE ANN. §§ 504.051(b), 501.062(c) (West Supp. 2011) (Referring to the removal of directors).
[166] *Id.* § 505.051(a).
[167] *Id.* § 505.052(a).

1) be a resident of the city;

2) be a resident of the county in which the major part of the area of the city is located; or

3) resides in a place that is within 10 miles of the city's boundaries and is in a county bordering the county in which a major portion of the city is located.[168]

If a city dissolves a Type A corporation and creates a Type B corporation, the Act provides that a person serving as a Type A director at the time that the Type A corporation was dissolved may serve on the newly created Type B board.[169] Since the directors of a Type A corporation are not required to be residents of the city, this change in the law would allow a non-resident to serve as a Type B director in this limited circumstance.

State law limits the number of Type B directors who are also city officers or employees: it states that three of the seven positions must be persons who are not city officials or city employees.[170] The directors serve without compensation but they must be reimbursed for actual expenses.[171] A director serves at the pleasure of the city council for a term of two years; however, the city council may vote to remove a director at any time without having to specify a cause.[172]

General Provisions Regarding Type A and Type B Board of Directors

A majority of the board constitutes a quorum.[173] The board of directors is subject to both the Open Meetings Act and the Public Information Act.[174]. Additionally, the Development Corporation Act requires the board to conduct all of its meetings within the city limits, unless the city is located in a county with a population of less than 30,000.[175] If the city's Type A or Type B corporation is located in a county with a population of less than 30,000, then the board of directors may conduct a board meeting within the county.[176] At one of its first meetings, the board is required to elect a president, a secretary and any other officers that the governing body of the city considers necessary.[177] The corporation's registered agent must be a resident of Texas and the corporation's registered office must be within the boundaries of the city.[178]

If a city collects both a Type A and a Type B sales and use tax, the city must create separate corporations and boards of directors for the Type A and Type B taxes. However, the board members of one corporation may serve on the board of the other corporation. A city may not create more than one corporation to oversee the Type A tax or more than one corporation to oversee the Type B tax.[179]

---

[168]   *Id.* § 505.052(b).
[169]   *Id.* § 505.052(d).
[170]   *Id.* § 505.052(c).
[171]   *Id.* § 501.062(d).
[172]   *Id.* § 501.062(c).
[173]   Id. §§ 504.053, 505.054.
[174]   *Id.* §§ 501.072, 505.054.
[175]   *Id.* §§ 504.054, 505.055.
[176]   *Id.*
[177]   *Id.* §§ 504.052, 505.053.
[178]   *Id.* §§ 504.055, 505.056.
[179]   *Id.* §§ 504.003(b), 505.003(b).

General Powers and Duties of Type A and Type B Development Corporations

Type A and Type B economic development corporations have the following general powers and duties:

Power to Expend Tax Proceeds. The development corporation has the power to expend the proceeds of the economic development sales tax for purposes authorized by the Act. All actions of the development corporation are pursuant to a majority vote of the governing body of the board and subject to oversight by the city.[180] In Texas Attorney General Opinion JC-0488 (2002), ruling under the former statute, the Attorney General noted that the city's spending of sales tax proceeds was "contrary to the Act."[181] Rather, the opinion noted, it was for the corporation to expend the Section 4B (now Type B) tax proceeds for the purposes authorized by the Act subject to city council approval.

Powers of a Nonprofit Corporation. The corporation shall have and exercise all powers and rights of a nonprofit corporation under the Texas Non-Profit Corporation Act (Chapter 22 of the Texas Business Organization Code), except to the extent such powers would be in conflict or inconsistent with the Development Corporation Act.[182]

Legal and Financial Transaction Powers. The corporation shall have the power to sell and lease a project,[183] make secured and unsecured loans,[184] and to sue and be sued.[185] Further, in Texas Attorney General Opinion JC-109 (1999), ruling under the former statute, it was noted that when an economic development corporation sells real property, the corporation is not required to comply with the notice and bidding requirements contained in chapter 272 of the Local Government Code. Nonetheless, the economic development corporation must obtain fair market value when selling real property.[186] If a Type B corporation wants to purchase property for a project wholly or partly with bond proceeds, the Type B corporation is required to obtain an independent appraisal of the property's market value.[187]

Status as Non-stock Corporation. The corporation is a nonprofit, nonmember, non-stock corporation.[188]

Exemption from Federal, State and Local Taxation. In terms of state taxation, Section 501.075 of the Local Government Code provides that economic development corporations are considered public charities within the tax exemption of Article VIII, Section 2, of the Texas Constitution. Whether the corporation is exempt from various

---

[180]   *Id.* § 501.054(b)(2).
[181]   Op. Tex Att'y Gen. No. JC-0488 (2002) at 3.
[182]   TEX. LOC. GOV'T CODE ANN. § 501.054(a) (West Supp. 2011).
[183]   *Id.* §§ 501.153-.154, .159.
[184]   *Id.* § 501.155(a).
[185]   *Id.* § 501.060.
[186]   Op. Tex. Att'y Gen. No. JC-109 (1999) at 2.
[187]   TEX. LOC. GOV'T CODE ANN. § 505.1041 (West Supp. 2011).
[188]   *Id.* § 501.052.

state and local taxes depends on the statutory provisions applicable to that tax. For example, the Comptroller's Office has treated economic development corporations as exempt from state and local sales taxes and the state franchise tax.[189] In order to claim these exemptions, corporations submit a copy of the corporation's certificate of formation to the Exempt Organizations Section of the Comptroller's Office. If a development corporation has qualified for federal tax exempt status prior to applying for state exemptions, a copy of the determination letter from the Internal Revenue Service should be sent to the Comptroller's Office at the time the corporation applies for exemption from the state sales tax and franchise tax. It should be noted that development corporations are exempt from state and local sales and state franchise taxes regardless of their tax exempt status with the Internal Revenue Service. The certificate of formation, and any IRS determination letter, should be submitted with a cover letter containing the development corporation's daytime phone number, charter number and tax identification number. The Comptroller's address is: Office of the Texas Comptroller, Exempt Organizations Section, P.O. Box 13528, Austin, TX 78711-3528.

Projects owned by Type B economic development corporations are exempt from local property taxation under Section 11.11 of the Tax Code, pursuant to Section 505.161 of the Local Government Code. It is currently unclear whether the property owned by Type A economic development corporations is exempt from local property taxation. To determine whether property taxes or other state or local taxes are applicable, a development corporation may wish to visit with its legal counsel and its appraisal district. For more information about tax exemptions, contact the Comptroller's Office Tax Assistance line at (800) 252-5555.

Duty to Comply with Open Meetings Act and Public Information Act. The corporation and its board of directors are subject to the Open Meetings Act and the Public Information Act.[190]

Limited Eminent Domain Power. A Type A corporation may not exercise the power of eminent domain except by action of the city council.[191] However, a Type B corporation may exercise the power of eminent domain only:

1. With approval of the action by the city; and
2. In accordance with and subject to the laws applicable to the city.[192]

Limited Tort Claims Act Protection. The corporation and its directors and employees are not liable for damages arising out of the performance of governmental functions of the corporation.[193] The corporation is considered a governmental entity for purposes of the Texas Tort Claims Act.

---

[189] TEX. TAX CODE ANN. §§ 151.341, 171.074 (West 2008).
[190] TEX. LOC. GOV'T CODE ANN. § 501.072 (West Supp. 2011).
[191] *Id.* § 504.106.
[192] *Id.* § 505.105.
[193] *Id.* §§ 504.107, 505.106.

Limited Power to Own or Operate Project. Generally, the corporation does not have the power to own or operate any project as a business entity other than as a lessor, seller, or lender. However, the corporation does have all the powers necessary to own and operate a project as a business if the project is part of a military installation or military facility that has been closed or realigned, including a military installation or facility closed or realigned under the Defense Base Closure and Realignment Act of 1990 (10 United States Code Section 2687).[194]

Ability of a Home Rule City to Provide an Economic Grant of Money to the Development Corporation. The Act generally prohibits a city from lending its credit or granting any public money or thing of value to an economic development corporation. In other words, a city may not generally provide any funding or services to a development corporation unless the city is fully reimbursed for the value of the expenditure. If a city and an economic development corporation enter into a contract for the provision of city services, such as accounting services, the economic development corporation must provide consideration in exchange for city services.[195]

In 2001, the Texas Legislature created an exception to this general rule.[196] Certain home rule cities are authorized to grant public money to a Type A or Type B corporation under a contract authorized by Section 380.002 of the Local Government Code. The Type A or Type B corporation is required to use the grant of city money for the "development and diversification of the economy of the state, elimination of unemployment or underemployment in the state, and development and expansion of commerce in the state."[197]

Ability of a City to Convey Real Property to an Economic Development Corporation. There are only a few ways a city can convey real property to an economic development corporation. First, if it's the case that the real property was conveyed to the city by gift or as part of a legal settlement and the real property is adjacent to an area designated for development by the Type A or Type B corporation, then Section 253.009 of the Local Government Code would allow the property to be conveyed.[198] Under that provision, the city would have to convey the property to the economic development corporation "for any fair consideration" approved by the city, and the city would have to adopt an ordinance that:

1. describes the property being conveyed;
2. states that the conveyance complies with the requirements of Section 5.022 of the Property Code; and
3. states the consideration paid.

---

[194] *Id.* § 501.160.
[195] Op. Tex. Att'y Gen. No. JC-109 (1999) at 3-5.
[196] TEX. LOC. GOV'T CODE ANN. § 501.007 (West Supp. 2011).
[197] *Id.* § 380.002(b).
[198] *Id.* § 253.009.

A conveyance under this provision does not have to comply with notice and bidding laws, including Chapter 272 of the Local Government Code.

Second, a city with a population of less than 1.9 million can convey real property or an interest in real property to a nonprofit organization under Section 253.011 of the Local Government Code. [199] The term "nonprofit organization" is defined as an organization exempt from federal taxation under Section 501(c)(3) of the Internal Revenue Code of 1986. If an economic development corporation is covered by Section 501(c)(3) of the Internal Revenue Code, then the city can convey real property to an economic development corporation without complying with the notice and bidding requirements of Chapter 272 of the Local Government Code. The city can convey the property to the economic development corporation provided the development corporation agrees to use the property in a manner that primarily promotes a public purpose of the city. Further, should the development corporation at any time fail to use the property in that manner, ownership of the property would automatically revert to the city. The city shall transfer the property by an appropriate instrument of transfer. The instrument must include a provision that: (1) requires the development corporation to use the property in a manner that primarily promotes a public purpose of the city; and (2) indicates that ownership of the property automatically reverts back to the city should the corporation at any time fail to use the property in that manner.

In 2009, the Texas Legislature approved a bill authorizing a city with a population of 20,000 or less to convey real property to an economic development corporation without complying with the notice and bidding requirements of Chapter 272 of the Local Government Code.[200] The city may convey real property to the economic development corporation provided the development corporation agrees to use the property in a manner that primarily promotes a public purpose of the city. Further, should the development corporation at any time fail to use the property in that manner, ownership of the property would automatically revert to the city. The city shall transfer the property by an appropriate instrument of transfer. The instrument must include a provision that : (1) requires the development corporation to use the property in a manner that primarily promotes a public purpose of the city; and (2) indicates that ownership of the property automatically reverts back to the city should the corporation at any time fail to use the property in that manner.

Ability of a City to Provide City Insurance Coverage and Retirement Benefits to Development Corporation Staff/Officers. An economic development corporation may participate in the following types of insurance coverage from the city:[201] health benefits coverage, liability coverage, workers' compensation coverage, and property coverage. These coverages can be obtained under the city's insurance policies, the city's self-funded coverage, or the coverage provided under an Interlocal Agreement with other political subdivisions. Health

---

[199] *Id.* § 253.011 (West 2005).
[200] *Id.* § 253.012 (West Supp. 2011).
[201] *Id.* § 501.067.

benefits coverage may be extended to the economic development corporation's directors and employees and their dependents. Workers' compensation benefits may be extended to the corporation's directors, employees and volunteers. Liability coverage may be extended to protect the corporation and its directors and employees. Also, the law allows economic development corporations to obtain retirement benefits under the city's retirement program and extend those benefits to the corporation's employees. An economic development corporation may not obtain any of these insurance coverages or retirement benefits unless the city consents.

Reverse Auction Procedures for Purchasing. A reverse auction procedure is a method of purchasing where suppliers of services or goods, anonymous to each other, submit bids to provide their services or goods. The bidding is a real-time process usually lasting either one hour or two weeks. The bidding takes place at a previously scheduled time period and at a previously scheduled Internet location.[202] Economic development corporations are authorized to use reverse auction procedures, as defined by Section 2155.062 (d) of the Government Code, for the purchase of goods or services.[203]

Performance Agreements

Economic development corporations cannot simply provide gifts of sales tax proceeds. The Attorney General has noted that expenditures of sales tax proceeds must be made pursuant to a contract or other arrangement sufficient to ensure that the funds are used for the intended and authorized purposes.[204] An economic development corporation is required to enter into a written performance agreement with a business enterprise when the corporation provides funding or makes expenditures on behalf of the business enterprise in furtherance of a permissible economic development project.[205] This performance agreement between the corporation and the business enterprise at a minimum must contain the following:

1. a schedule of additional payroll or jobs to be created or retained;
2. the capital investment to be made by the business enterprise; and
3. the terms under which repayment must be made by the business enterprise to the economic development corporation should the business fail to meet the performance requirements specified in the agreement.[206]

Also, the Texas Legislature requires that both governmental entities and economic development corporations put certain language in any written agreement involving public subsidies to businesses, which would include those given by economic development corporations. The language must specify that the business does not and will not knowingly employ an undocumented worker (which statement must also be in any application for the subsidy). The language also must require repayment of the subsidy at specified rates and terms of interest if the business is convicted of federal immigration violations under 8 U.S. Code Section 1324a(f) not

---

202   Tex. Gov't Code Ann. § 2155.062(d) (West 2008).

203   Tex. Loc. Gov't Code Ann. § 501.074 (West Supp. 2011).

204   Op. Tex. Att'y Gen. No. JC-118 (1999) at 9 ("Expenditures for even project costs must be pursuant to a contractual or other arrangement sufficient to ensure that the funds are used for the purposes authorized."); Tex. Att'y Gen. LO-97-061 at 4-5; LO-94-037 (1994) at 3.

205   Tex. Loc. Gov't Code Ann. § 501.158 (West Supp. 2011).

206   *Id.*

later than the 120th day after receiving notice of the violation from the public entity or economic development corporation. [207]

Requirement for Third-Party Contracts for Business Recruitment

Additionally, Type A and Type B corporations are required to enter into written contracts approved by the board of directors when the corporation uses a third party for certain business recruitment efforts. The written contract requirement does not apply to the payment of an employee of the Type A or Type B corporation.[208] Nonetheless, should the corporation pay a commission, fee, or other thing of value to a broker, agent, or other third party for business recruitment or development, a written contract is required.[209] Failure to enter into a written contract with a third party recruiter could result in a civil penalty up to $10,000.[210] The Texas Legislature has authorized the Attorney General to commence an action to recover the penalty in Travis County district court or in the county district court where the violation occurs.[211]

Incentives to Purchasing Companies

In 2003, the Texas Legislature addressed purchasing companies and their ability to receive an incentive from a Type A or Type B corporation.[212] Type A and Type B corporations may not offer to provide economic incentives to businesses whose business consists primarily of purchasing taxable items using resale certificates and then reselling those same items to a related party. A related party means a person or entity which owns at least 80 percent of the business enterprise to which sales and use taxes would be rebated as part of an economic incentive.[213]

Oversight of a Economic Development Corporation

Section 501.073 of the Act provides that the city shall approve all programs and expenditures of the development corporation and shall annually review any financial statements of the corporation. It further provides that at all times the city will have access to the books and records of the development corporation. Additionally, Section 501.054(b)(2) of the Act states that the powers of the corporation shall be subject at all times to the control of the city's governing body. Also, Section 501.401 of the Act gives the city authority to alter the structure, organization, programs or activities of the development corporation at any time. This authority is limited by constitutional and statutory restrictions on the impairment of existing contracts. Additionally, bond covenants may restrict the restructuring or dissolution of an economic development corporation. Finally, the city council retains a certain degree of control over the corporation by virtue of its power at any time to replace any or all of the members of the board of directors of the development corporation.[214]

---

[207]   TEX. GOV'T CODE ANN § 2264.001 - .101 (West 2008).
[208]   TEX. LOC. GOV'T CODE ANN. § 502.051(a) (West Supp. 2011).
[209]   *Id.*
[210]   *Id.* § 502.051(b).
[211]   *Id.* § 502.051(c).
[212]   *Id.* § 501.161.
[213]   *Id.* § 501.161(a).
[214]   *Id.* § 501.062(c).

Economic Development Corporation Is Not Considered a Political Subdivision

State law typically imposes certain requirements or conditions upon political subdivisions such as cities. A frequent concern is whether state law requirements imposed upon cities also applies to Type A or Type B economic development corporations. Section 501.055(b) of the Local Government Code states that an economic development corporation "is not a political subdivision or political corporation for purposes of the laws of this state", including Section 52, Article III of the Texas Constitution. Accordingly, a statute's reference to the term "political subdivision" does not include a Type A or Type B economic development corporation.

The Attorney General has considered whether certain statutes apply to economic development corporations. The Attorney General has concluded that Chapter 171 of the Local Government Code, governing conflicts of interest, does not apply to an economic development corporation.[215] Likewise, Chapter 272 of the Local Government Code, governing the city sale of real property, is not applicable to economic development corporations.[216] Nor is the prevailing wage law contained in Chapter 2258 of the Government Code applicable to a worker employed by or on behalf of an economic development corporation.[217] Economic development corporations should consult their legal counsel when considering the application of a particular statute.

Annual Reporting Requirement for Economic Development Corporations

Section 502.151 of the Development Corporation Act requires both Type A and Type B economic development corporations to submit an annual, one-page report to the Comptroller's Office. The report must be submitted by February 1st of each year and must be in the form required by the Comptroller.

The report must include the following:

- A statement of the corporation's primary economic development objectives

- A statement of the corporation's total revenues for the preceding fiscal year

- A statement of the corporation's total expenditures for the preceding fiscal year

- A statement of the corporation's total expenditures during the preceding fiscal year in each of the following categories:

    - administration
    - personnel
    - marketing or promotion
    - direct business incentives
    - job training
    - debt service
    - capital costs
    - affordable housing

---

[215] Op. Tex. Att'y Gen. No. JC-338 (2001) at 2.
[216] Op. Tex. Att'y Gen. No. JC-109 (1999).
[217] Op. Tex. Att'y Gen. No. JC-032 (1999).

- payments to taxing units, including school districts
- A list of the corporation's capital assets, including land and buildings (for example, industrial parks, recreation and sports facilities, etc.)
- Any other information required by the Comptroller[218]

If a corporation fails to file the required report or include all the required information, the Comptroller may impose an administrative penalty against the corporation of $200.[219] However, before imposing such a penalty, the Comptroller must provide written notice to the corporation of its error or omission in filing the report. That notice must include information on how to correct the error. Once it has received notice, the corporation has 30 days to correct its reporting error before the Comptroller may impose the $200 penalty. The form may be submitted to the Comptroller's Office by mail or through the Comptroller's Office website at http://www.texasahead.org/lga/econdev.html.

For more information on filing the required form, contact the Comptroller's Office at (800) 531-5441, extension 3-4679.

---

[218] TEX. LOC. GOV'T CODE ANN. § 502.151(a) (West Supp. 2011).
[219] *Id.* § 502.152.

II. Alternative Tax Initiatives for Local Development

City/County Venue Project Tax

Chapters 334 and 335 of the Local Government Code provide cities and counties the authority to finance a wide array of economic development projects called sports and community venue projects ("venue projects"). Cities and counties are authorized to propose at an election both the approval of venue projects and the revenue sources that would fund those projects. Cities and counties may choose to propose a venue project tax if they are interested in diversifying the sources of revenue they have to promote a venue project. The venue project revenue sources that can be adopted include a sales tax, a hotel occupancy tax, a short-term motor vehicle rental tax, an event parking tax, an event admissions tax and a venue facility use tax. Additionally, the venue sales tax can be proposed in certain limited cases even if the city is already at its maximum sales tax rate.

A city or county may undertake a venue project under Chapter 334 of the Local Government Code if it receives voter approval of the venue project and its financing. At this election, the city or county must specifically indicate which of six different taxes or fees it will use to pay for the costs of the project.

Alternatively, two or more cities, two or more counties, or a combination of cities and counties may create a "sports and community venue district" under Chapter 335 of the Local Government Code. Subject to voter approval, such a district may carry out the same type of projects and propose the same financing methods as an individual city or county can under Chapter 334.

Finally, Section 321.508 of the Tax Code allows a city to call an election on the dedication of up to 25 percent of its existing sales tax to pay off debt issued to finance one or more economic development projects located in the city.

Eligibility to Undertake a Venue Project

Chapter 334 of the Local Government Code applies to all cities and counties in Texas[220], with certain special conditions set forth for certain specific political subdivisions.[221] Even cities and counties that already participate in a rapid transit authority or are currently at their limit for the local sales tax can utilize this chapter. In the case of an entity that is at its maximum local sales tax rate, the ballot would have to indicate which sales tax would be reduced to accommodate the newly proposed sales tax to fund the venue project.

Permissible Projects Under Chapter 334

Chapter 334 allows a city or county to undertake a "venue project." The term "venue project" is defined as a "venue and related infrastructure that is planned, acquired, established, developed,

---

[220]   TEX. LOC. GOV'T CODE ANN. § 334.001(2) (West 2005). (Definition of governing body).
[221]   *Id.* § 334.002.

constructed, or renovated under this chapter."[222] The term "venue" is defined as being one of the following:[223]

An arena, coliseum, stadium or other type of area or facility:[224]

- that is used or will be used for professional or amateur sports, or for community and civic and charitable events; and

- where a fee for admission to these events will be charged;

A convention center or a related improvement that is located in the vicinity of the convention center. The term "related improvement" is used rather broadly and includes such things as a convention center, civic center, civic center building, civic center hotel, auditorium, theater, opera house, music hall, exhibition hall, rehearsal hall, park, zoo, museum, aquarium or plaza;

A tourist development area along an inland waterway;

A municipal parks and recreation system, improvements or additions to a parks and recreation system, or an area or facility that is part of a municipal parks and recreation system. However, neither the motor vehicle rental tax nor the local hotel occupancy tax authorized by Chapter 334 may be used as a revenue source to pay for a venue project of this nature;[225]

An economic development project authorized by Section 4A or Section 4B of the Development Corporation Act of 1979, Article 5190.6 of Texas Revised Civil Statutes, as that Act existed on September 1, 1997;[226] or

A watershed protection and preservation project; a recharge, recharge area, or recharge feature protection project; a conservation easement; or an open-space preservation program intended to protect water.

Section 334.001(3) defines the term "related infrastructure" to include any on-site or off-site improvements that relate to and enhance the use, value or appeal of a venue, and any other expenditure that is reasonably necessary to construct, improve, renovate or expand a venue. The statute lists the following examples of improvements that would qualify as related infrastructure:

---

[222] *Id.* § 334.001(5). *See id.* §§ 334.0082, .0083 (West Supp. 2011) (Certain cities and counties are allowed to do additional venue projects).

[223] *Id.* § 334.001(4) (West 2005).

[224] *See id.* § 334.0415. (It should be noted that a city or county would not be able to use the provisions of Chapter 334 to finance a professional sports stadium if the city or county had already contracted with a professional sports team prior to November 1, 1998, for the team to relocate and play in the stadium. This prohibition only applies if the team is already playing under an existing contract in a stadium owned by another Texas city or county. Even in this circumstance, a stadium may be financed under Chapter 334 if the other city or county (where the team is currently playing) consents).

[225] *Id.* §§ 334.1015, .2515.

[226] The Development Act of 1979 was codified on April 1, 2009 and is now located in Chapters 501 through 507 of the Local Government Code. Since there was not a change of this section during the 82nd Legislative Session, the reference to the civil statute will remain.

stores, restaurants, on-site hotels, concessions, parking, transportation facilities, roads, water or sewer facilities, parks or environmental remediation.

A city or county may use Chapter 334 only to construct a project that falls within the definition of the term "venue" or the term "related infrastructure." However, once the venue facility is constructed, state law permits the facility to be used for an event that is not related to one of the above-described venue purposes, such as a community-related event.[227] Also, if an already existing facility would qualify as a venue project under Chapter 334, a city or a county may use the authority granted under Chapter 334 to aid that facility even though it was originally constructed or undertaken under the authority of other law.[228]

Procedure for Authorizing a Venue Project

Step One:

The city or county must obtain approval for the project from the Comptroller's Office.

Before a city or county may have an election to undertake a venue project, it must obtain approval of the project from the Comptroller's Office.[229] The Comptroller reviews the project to determine whether the proposed financing would "have a significant negative fiscal impact on state revenue." To obtain this approval, the city or county must send to the Comptroller a copy of the resolution proposing the venue project.[230] This resolution must indicate each proposed project and each method of financing for the project.[231] Within 14 days of the Comptroller's receipt of the resolution, it must perform the required state fiscal impact analysis and provide the city or county with written notice of its decision.[232] If the Comptroller determines that the resolution would have a significant negative impact on state revenue, the Comptroller must indicate in writing how the local government could change the resolution so that there would not be such a negative impact.[233] If the Comptroller fails to provide the required analysis in less than 30 days, the resolution is considered to be approved by the Comptroller.[234]

If the Comptroller finds that a venue project resolution will have a negative fiscal impact on state revenue, the city or county has 10 days to appeal the Comptroller's decision.[235] The appeal is made to the Comptroller, and the Comptroller has another 10 days to provide a new analysis and written notice to the city or county.[236] If the Comptroller's ruling is still negative, the analysis must again include information on how the local government could change the resolution so that

---

[227]   TEX. LOC. GOV'T CODE ANN. § 334.004 (West 2005).
[228]   *Id.* § 334.003 (West Supp. 2011). (Note that the venue revenues under this section cannot be used for the demolition of the venue nor the subsequent construction of a new venue.)
[229]   *Id.* §§ 334.021(a)(1), .024 (West 2005). *But see* Sections 7, 8 and 9 of Tex. H.B. 92, 75th Leg., R.S. (1997) (Excepting certain cities, counties and venue districts from the requirements of holding an election and obtaining Comptroller approval if their voters had already approved certain sports facilities in an election held before the effective date of this legislation).
[230]   *Id.* § 334.022(a).
[231]   *Id.* § 334.021(b).
[232]   *Id.* § 334.022(b).
[233]   *Id.* § 334.022(c).
[234]   *Id.* § 334.022(d).
[235]   *Id.* § 334.023(a).
[236]   *Id.* § 334.023(b).

there would not be such a negative impact on state revenue.[237] If the Comptroller fails to provide the required analysis within 30 days, the resolution is automatically considered approved.[238] If the Comptroller continues to hold that the venue project would have a negative impact on state revenue, the city or county would be unable to order the required election on the venue project.[239]

Step Two:

Certain cities or counties must also obtain approval from the local transit authority.

If a venue project resolution contains a proposed sales tax, the city or county must determine whether that tax would result in the reduction of a sales tax rate that funds a transit authority created under either Chapter 451 or Chapter 452 of the Transportation Code.[240] This issue would arise only if the area was subject to a transit authority sales tax and if the adoption of a venue project sales tax would place the city or county beyond the two percent cap for the local sales tax. If these circumstances would arise because of the proposed venue project, the city or county must send the transit authority a copy of the venue resolution for approval by the authority. This resolution must designate each venue project and each method of financing that the city or county proposes to use to finance the project.[241] If the proposed financing for the venue project would not cause a reduction in the transit authority sales tax, this approval from the transit authority is not required.

Within 30 days of the transit authority's receipt of the resolution, it must determine whether the reduction in the transit authority's tax rate would have a significant negative impact on its ability to provide services or would impair any existing contracts.[242] The transit authority must also provide the written results of its analysis to the city or county within this 30 day period. If the transit authority's ruling is negative, it must state how the city or county could change the venue project resolution so that there would not be a negative impact on the transit authority's ability to provide transit service or fulfill existing contracts.[243] If the transit authority fails to provide this analysis within the required period, the authority is deemed to have approved the resolution.[244]

If the transit authority finds that a venue project resolution would have a significant negative impact on the authority's ability to provide service or would impair existing contracts, the city or county may appeal the negative ruling within 10 days.[245] The appeal is made to the transit authority, and the authority must provide a new analysis and written notice to the city or county within 10 days of its receipt of the appeal.[246] If the transit authority's ruling is still negative, the analysis must include information on how the local government could change the resolution so that there would not be a negative impact on the authority's ability to provide service or fulfill

---

237 *Id.* § 334.023(c).
238 *Id.* § 334.023(d).
239 *Id.* § 334.024.
240 *Id.* §§ 334.021(a)(2); .0235(a).
241 *Id.* § 334.021(b).
242 *Id.* § 334.0235(b).
243 *Id.* § 334.0235(c).
244 *Id.* § 334.0235(d).
245 *Id.* § 334.0236(a).
246 *Id.* § 334.0236(b).

existing contracts.[247] If the transit authority fails to provide the required analysis within 10 days, the resolution is automatically considered approved.[248] If the transit authority continues to find that the venue project would have a negative impact, the city or county will be unable to hold the required election to approve the proposed venue project.[249]

Step Three:

The city or county must hold an election on the venue project.

Once the city or county has received the required approvals from the Comptroller and, if necessary, from the transit authority, the city or county may order an election on the proposed venue project.[250] The order calling the election must meet all of the following criteria:[251]

- Allow the voters to vote separately on each venue project;

- Designate the venue project(s);

- Designate each method of financing authorized by Chapter 334 that the city or county wants to use to finance the venue project and designate the maximum rate for each method; and

- Allow the voters to vote, in the same proposition or in separate propositions, on each method of financing authorized by Chapter 334 that the city or county wants to use to finance the project and the maximum rate of each method.

In addition to the above requirements for the election order, there is required wording for the ballot proposition. The ballot must be printed to allow voting for or against the following proposition:[252]

> **Authorizing *(insert name of city or county)* to *(insert description of venue project)* and to impose a *(insert the type of tax)* tax at the rate of *(insert the maximum rate of the tax)* for the purpose of financing the venue project.**

If more than one method of financing is to be voted on in one proposition, the ballot must be printed to permit voting for or against the proposition:[253]

> **Authorizing *(insert name of city or county)* to *(insert description of venue project)* and to impose a *(insert each type of tax)* tax at the rate of *(insert the maximum rate of each tax)* for the purpose of financing the venue project.**

---

[247]   *Id.* § 334.0236(c).

[248]   *Id.* § 334.0236(d).

[249]   *Id.* § 334.024.

[250]   *Id. But see* Section 7, 8 and 9 of Tex. H.B. 92, 75th Leg., R.S. (1997) (Excepting certain cities, counties and venue districts from the requirements of holding an election and of obtaining Comptroller approval if their voters had already approved certain sports facilities in an election held before effective date of this legislation).

[251]   *Id.* § 334.024(b).

[252]   *Id.* § 334.024(c).

[253]   *Id.* § 334.024(d).

If the venue project is for improvements or additions to an existing park or recreation facility, then the description of the project in the ballot proposition must identify each park or recreation facility by name or location. [254] If the venue project is for the acquisition or improvement of a new park or recreation facility, then the description of the project in the ballot must specify the general location where the new park, recreational system or facility will be located. If the venue project includes improvements and/or additions to all parks and/or recreation facilities of the city, then the ballot proposition description need not contain the name or location of the facilities.

The Election Code governs the procedure for holding an election under Chapter 334. [255] A city or county will want to check with the Elections Division at the Secretary of State's Office if the city or county has any questions about the requirements of the Election Code. The Elections Division may be reached by phone at (800) 252-8683.

Imposing a Sales Tax Under Chapter 334

General Authority to Impose a Venue Project Sales Tax

A city (by ordinance) or a county (by order) may impose, reduce or repeal a sales tax under the authority of Chapter 334. [256] As indicated earlier, the venue project and the sales tax have to be approved by the voters at an election in order for the city or county to impose this tax. [257] A city or county can adopt a sales tax rate of one-eighth, one-fourth, three-eighths or one-half of one percent and on the ballot must specify which tax rate will be adopted. [258]

Ballot Proposition to Adopt a Venue Project Sales Tax

The adoption of the venue project sales tax may be included in the same ballot proposition that proposes the venue project. The ballot must be printed to allow voting for or against the following proposition: [259]

> **Authorizing *(insert name of city or county)* to *(insert description of venue project)* and to impose a *(insert the type of tax)* tax at the rate of *(insert the maximum rate of the tax)* for the purpose of financing the venue project.**

If more than one method of financing is to be voted on in one proposition, the ballot must be printed to permit voting for or against the proposition:

> **Authorizing *(insert name of city or county)* to *(insert description of venue project)* and to impose a *(insert each type of tax)* tax at the rate of *(insert the maximum rate of each tax)* for the purpose of financing the venue project.**

---

254   *Id.* § 334.024(f).
255   *Id.* § 334.024(e)
256   *Id.* § 334.081(a)-(b).
257   *Id.* § 334.081(c).
258   *Id.* § 334.083.
259   *Id.* § 334.081(c)(2) (Refers to tax being approved at an election held under section 334.024).

Increasing the Venue Project Sales Tax

A sales tax that was adopted under Chapter 334 to benefit a venue project may be increased if the increase is approved at an election.[260] If there is an election to approve an increase in the sales tax to fund a venue project, the ballot wording must permit voting for or against the following proposition:[261]

> **The adoption of a sales and use tax for the purpose of financing *(insert description of venue project)* at the rate of *(insert rate)* of one percent.**

The rate of the sales tax increased under Chapter 334 can be one-eighth, one-fourth, three-eighths, or one-half of one percent.[262] With certain exceptions, other issues concerning administration of a Chapter 334 sales tax by a city are governed by the provisions of Chapter 321 of the Tax Code.[263] If the Chapter 334 sales tax is imposed by a county, Chapter 323 of the Tax Code generally governs the administration of the tax.[264]

Effective Date of Venue Project Sales Tax

A sales tax imposed under Chapter 334 cannot take effect until at least one full quarter after the city or county has sent notice to Comptroller of the election results.[265] After one full quarter has expired, the tax will then take effect on the first day of the next calendar quarter. The Comptroller is responsible for collecting the sales tax and remitting it to the city or county, which must then deposit the money into the venue project fund.[266]

Termination of Venue Project Sales Tax

When all bonds and obligations payable from money in the venue project fund are paid, the venue project sales tax must be abolished.[267] Alternatively, if the full amount of money needed to pay these obligations, excluding guaranteed interest, has been set aside in a trust account dedicated to pay these obligations, the sales tax must be ended. Additionally, a city or county may abolish the Chapter 334 sales tax on its own motion. Regardless of the cause for the termination of the sales tax, the city or county must notify the Comptroller of the tax's abolition no later than 60 days before the date on which the tax is set to expire.

Application of Two Percent Local Sales Tax Cap to Chapter 334 Sales Tax

Generally, state law requires that all local sales taxes, when combined, not exceed a total rate of two percent in any area. However, a city or county is not automatically forbidden from adopting or increasing a sales tax to pursue a Chapter 334 venue project merely because the adoption of the tax would cause the combined local sales taxes in an area to exceed this two percent cap.

---

[260] *Id.* § 334.084(a).
[261] *Id.* § 334.084(c).
[262] *Id.* § 334.084(b).
[263] *Id.* § 334.082(a), (d). *See id.* § 334.082(c) (Sections 321.101(b) and 321.506 of the Tax Code are not applicable to sales taxes authorized under Chapter 334).
[264] *Id.* § 334.082(b), (d). *See id.* § 334.082(c) (Section 323.101(b) of the Tax Code is not applicable to sales taxes authorized under Chapter 334).
[265] *Id.* § 334.087.
[266] *Id.* § 334.088.
[267] *Id.* § 334.089.

Instead, state law allows the adoption of the venue sales tax to cause the local sales tax rate of one of the other taxing authorities in the area to be automatically reduced or require the city or county to withdraw from the other taxing authority.[268] There are four taxing authorities that are affected by the adoption of a venue project sales tax if the adoption would cause the maximum sales tax rate to exceed two percent:[269]

1) a rapid transit authority created under Chapter 451 of the Transportation Code;

2) a regional transportation authority created under Chapter 452 of the Transporation Code;

3) a crime control district created under Chapter 363 of the Local Government Code; or

4) an economic development corporation created under Chapter 504 or 505 of the Local Government Code.

Automatic Reduction of Sales Tax Rate to Adopt a Venue Project Sales Tax

If an area is already at its maximum local sales tax rate of two percent and a proposed venue project election would place the locality beyond the maximum local sales tax rate, the venue project sales tax election is also to be treated as an election to reduce the tax rate of another taxing authority.[270] Only two of the taxing authorities above would have their sales tax rate automatically reduced in this manner: the crime control district and the economic development corporation. If there is only one such authority whose sales tax is affected, the ballot proposition for the adoption of the Chapter 334 sales tax must clearly state that the affected taxing authority's tax rate will be reduced. If more than one such taxing authority's tax rate is affected, the Chapter 334 sales tax election must allow voters to choose which authority's tax will be reduced. The sales tax rate of the chosen taxing authority is then reduced to the highest rate that would allow the locality not to exceed the two percent cap.

If another taxing entity's sales tax rate is reduced automatically at such an election, the taxing entity's sales tax rate is reduced throughout the entity's jurisdiction.[271] A taxing authority does not have the power to reduce its sales tax rate only in one part of its jurisdiction. The rate must be uniform throughout its jurisdiction. However, the taxing authority's sales tax would automatically increase if the Chapter 334 rate is later reduced or later expires, but only if the tax was reduced originally by the adoption of a venue project sales tax.[272]

Voters may adopt or raise any dedicated or special purpose municipal sales tax on a combined ballot proposition that also lowers or repeals any such tax.[273] The language in the ballot must contain the language appropriate for such changes to the tax as required in any stand-alone election. A negative vote on the combined ballot would leave the sales tax situation unchanged. This would not apply to counties wishing to adopt or to raise a venue project sales tax.

---

[268]   *Id.* § 334.085 (West Supp. 2011).
[269]   *Id.* § 334.085(a).
[270]   *Id.* § 334.085(b).
[271]   *Id.* § 334.085(d).
[272]   *Id.* § 334.085(c).
[273]   TEX. TAX CODE ANN. § 321.409 (West 2008).

Required Withdrawal from a Transit Authority To Adopt a Venue Project Sales Tax

If the enactment or increase of a Chapter 334 sales tax would cause the combined local sales tax rate to exceed two percent and the taxing authority whose sales tax would have to be reduced is a transit authority, the city or county imposing the tax must withdraw from the transit authority. As indicated above, there are two types of transit authorities to which this rule applies: a rapid transit authority and a regional transportation authority.[274] The rules are slightly different for each type of transit authority and are discussed separately below:

> **Chapter 451 Rapid Transit Authority**. If the transit authority is organized under Chapter 451 of the Transportation Code, a separate election first must be held on the issue of withdrawing the affected cities from the transit authority.[275] The Chapter 334 sales tax may not be imposed in a city unless the voters of that city have previously approved their city's withdrawal from the transit authority. Once a city has voted to withdraw from the transit authority, the transit authority no longer has any duty to provide services within the city unless required to do so by federal law. In conducting an election to decide whether a city will withdraw from a Chapter 451 transit authority, a city must follow the requirements of Subchapter M in Chapter 451 of the Transportation Code.

> **Chapter 452 Regional Transportation Authority**. If the transportation authority is organized under Chapter 452 of the Texas Transportation Code, an election to approve or increase the Chapter 334 venue sales tax is treated as an election to withdraw from the transportation authority.[276] The ballot language at this election must clearly state that the adoption of the Chapter 334 sales tax will result in automatic withdrawal of the county or city from the transportation authority. Even if the voters choose to withdraw from the transportation authority by approving the Chapter 334 tax, the city or county still may not impose the Chapter 334 sales tax until the county or city's financial obligations to the transportation authority are satisfied in accordance with Subchapter Q of Chapter 452 of the Transportation Code. Also, in conducting an election on whether to withdraw from a Chapter 452 transportation authority, a city or county must follow the requirements of Subchapter Q in Chapter 452 of the Transportation Code.

Additional Taxes and Fees that Voters Can Approve

1. Short-Term Motor Vehicle Rental Tax

Authority to Adopt the Motor Vehicle Rental Tax

With permission of the voters, a city or a county may fund venue projects within its jurisdiction by imposing a tax on the rental of a motor vehicle within the city or county.[277] Any such tax must be approved at an election held in accordance with the rules of Chapter 334. The ballot language for the motor vehicle rental tax must specify the maximum rate of the rental tax that can be adopted.[278] In addition, the rental tax may only be imposed if the city or county issues

---

[274]   TEX. LOC. GOV'T CODE ANN. § 334.085(a)(1)-(2) (West Supp. 2011).
[275]   *Id.* § 334.085(b-1).
[276]   *Id.* § 334.0855 (West 2005).
[277]   *Id.* § 334.102.
[278]   *Id.* § 334.103(b).

bonds or other obligations for the venue project within one year of imposing the rental tax.[279] The tax would apply only to agreements to rent a motor vehicle to another for consideration for a period of not longer than 30 days.[280] It is important to note that the motor vehicle rental tax may not be imposed to fund a venue project that is an area or facility that is part of a municipal parks and recreation system.[281]

Ballot Proposition to Adopt a Motor Vehicle Rental Tax

The adoption of the motor vehicle rental tax may be included in the same ballot proposition that proposes the venue project. The ballot must be printed to allow voting for or against the following proposition:[282]

> **Authorizing** *(insert name of city or county)* **to** *(insert description of venue project)* **and to impose a** *(insert the type of tax)* **tax at the rate of** *(insert the maximum rate of the tax)* **for the purpose of financing the venue project.**

If more than one method of financing is to be voted on in one proposition, the ballot must be printed to permit voting for or against the proposition:

> **Authorizing** *(insert name of city or county)* **to** *(insert description of venue project)* **and to impose a** *(insert each type of tax)* **tax at the rate of** *(insert the maximum rate of each tax)* **for the purpose of financing the venue project.**

Effective Date and Ending Date of the Motor Vehicle Rental Tax

After approval by the voters, the motor vehicle rental tax becomes effective on the date prescribed by the ordinance or order imposing the tax.[283] The tax is on the gross receipts from the rental of a motor vehicle.[284] Its rate may be set only in increments of one-eighth of one percent, and in most cases may not exceed five percent.[285] All revenue from the tax must be deposited in the venue project fund.[286] Additionally, the city or county cannot continue to impose a motor vehicle rental tax once the bonds or other obligations for the project have been paid in full.[287]

Ability to Decrease, Abolish or Increase the Motor Vehicle Rental Tax

Once in place, the motor vehicle rental tax may be decreased or abolished, by ordinance or order, on the city or county's own motion.[288] However, the tax may be increased only if the increase is

---

279   *Id.* § 334.112(b).
280   *See id.* § 334.101(a)(2) (Defining the term "rental" to mean an agreement by an owner of a vehicle authorizing exclusive use of that vehicle by another for consideration *for 30 days or less* [emphasis added]).
281   *Id.* § 334.1015.
282   *Id.* § 334.102(c)(2). (Referring to the tax being approved at an election under section 334.024.)
283   *Id.* § 334.112.
284   *Id.* § 334.109.
285   *Id.* § 334.103(a). *See also id.* § 334.103(c). (Providing that a county with a population of 2 million or more that is adjacent to a county with a population of more than 1 million may by order impose the rate to a maximum of 6%).
286   *Id.* § 334.115.
287   *Id.* § 334.112(b).
288   *Id.* § 334.102(b).

approved at an election on the issue and the resulting tax rate will not in most cases exceed five percent.[289] At an election to increase the motor vehicle rental tax, the ballot must be worded to allow voting for or against the following proposition:[290]

> **The increase of the motor vehicle rental tax for the purpose of financing** (*insert description of venue project*) **to a maximum rate of** (*insert new maximum rate*) **percent.**

Collection and Enforcement of the Motor Vehicle Rental Tax

The Comptroller's Office is not involved in the collection of the motor vehicle rental tax. Instead, the tax is collected by the owner of the motor vehicle rental agency and remitted to the city or county.[291] The order or ordinance imposing the tax should specify how the rental tax is to be reported and remitted to the city or county.[292] Additionally, the order or ordinance may also prescribe penalties for the failure to keep the required records, report when required, or pay the tax when due. Finally, the city or county attorney is empowered to bring a lawsuit to collect the rental tax.

All the gross receipts of an entity that rents motor vehicles are presumed to be subject to the motor vehicle rental tax, except for those receipts for which the entity can provide an exemption certificate.[293] In addition to any local record-keeping requirements, state law requires motor vehicle rental agencies to keep records reflecting the gross receipts from motor vehicle rentals and the tax paid on each rental.[294] These records must be kept for at least four years. Failure to keep such records is a misdemeanor offense.[295]

State law also requires that persons buying a motor vehicle rental business withhold an amount sufficient to cover any delinquent motor vehicle rental taxes that are due to the city or county out of the purchase price.[296] The buyer must withhold this amount until the seller provides a proper receipt from the city or county showing that the tax has been paid or that no tax is due. If the buyer does not withhold the required amount, the buyer becomes liable for any delinquent rental taxes owed by the purchased motor vehicle rental business.[297] The buyer of a motor vehicle rental business may request that the city or county provide a receipt showing that no motor vehicle rental tax is due from the business to be purchased or, if tax is due, what amount of tax is owed.[298] The city or county is then required to issue the statement not later than the 60th day

---

[289]   *Id.* § 334.104(a). *See also id.* § 334.1041 (Allowing a county with a population of 2 million or more that is adjacent to a county with a population of more than 1 million may by order increase the rate to a maximum of 6% if the increase is approved by the voters).

[290]   *Id.* §§ 334.104(b), .1041(c).

[291]   *Id.* §§ 334.105(a), .113(a). *See Id.* § 334.108. (State law requires that each bill or other receipt for a taxed rental contain the following language in a conspicuous location: "____ (insert name of taxing county or city) requires that an additional tax of ____ percent (insert tax rate) be imposed on each motor vehicle rental for the purpose of financing ____ (describe venue project).").

[292]   *Id.* § 334.113.

[293]   *Id.* § 334.109.

[294]   *Id.* § 334.110.

[295]   *Id.* § 334.111.

[296]   *Id.* § 334.114(a).

[297]   *Id.* § 334.114(b).

[298]   *Id.* § 334.114(c).

after receipt of the request. If the city or county fails to issue the statement within this period, the purchaser is released from the obligation to withhold the amount due from the purchase price.[299]

Cities and counties are required to allow a person who is required to collect and remit the motor vehicle rental tax to retain one percent of the amount collected as reimbursement for the costs of collecting the tax.[300] Nonetheless, a person required to collect and remit the motor vehicle rental tax is not entitled to the one percent reimbursement if the person fails to remit the tax to the city or county within 15 days of the end of the collection period.[301] The date postmarked by the United States Postal Service is considered to be the date of receipt by the city or county.

Exemptions from the Motor Vehicle Rental Tax

Certain entities (primarily public entities) are exempt from a motor vehicle rental tax imposed under Chapter 334.[302] The city or county should consult Subchapter E in Chapter 152 of the Tax Code to discern which entities are exempt from the rental tax.

Additionally, certain types of vehicles do not fall within the definition of "motor vehicle" under Chapter 334 and cannot be taxed.[303] For instance, the rental of trailers, road-building machines, trucks with a rating of more than one-half ton, trains, farm machines or bicycles is not taxable.

2. Admissions Tax on Tickets Sold at a Venue Project

If a city or county has issued bonds for a venue project, the city or county may impose a tax on each admission ticket sold for an event at the venue project.[304] The admissions tax must have been approved at an election held in accordance with the rules of Chapter 334, and the ballot language must specify the maximum rate of the tax being adopted.[305] The admission tax rate may not exceed 10 percent of the price of an admission ticket.[306]

Ballot Proposition to Adopt an Admissions Tax

The adoption of the admissions tax may be included in the same ballot proposition that proposes the venue project. The ballot must be printed to allow voting for or against the following proposition:[307]

> **Authorizing *(insert name of city or county)* to *(insert description of venue project)* and to impose a *(insert the type of tax)* tax at the rate of *(insert the maximum rate of the tax)* for the purpose of financing the venue project.**

---

299   *Id.* § 334.114(d).

300   *Id.* § 334.1135(a).

301   *Id.* § 334.1135(b).

302   *Id.* § 334.107.

303   *Id.* § 334.101(a)(1). (Definition of motor vehicle.)

304   *Id.* § 334.151(a). *But see* TEX. CONST. art. VIII, § 1 (f); *Hoefling v. City of San Antonio*, 20 S.W. 85, 88 (Tex. 1892); *City of Houston v. Harris County Outdoor Advertising Association*, 879 S.W.2d 322, 326-327 (Tex. App. -- Houston [14th Dist.] 1994, pet. denied); *State v. Rope*, 419 S.W.2d 890, 897 (Tex. Civ. App. -- Austin 1967, writ ref'd n.r.e.).

305   TEX. LOC. GOV'T CODE ANN. §§ 334.151(c), .152(c) (West 2005).

306   *Id.* § 334.152(b).

307   *Id.* § 334.151(c)(2). (Referring to the tax being approved at an election under section 334.024).

If more than one method of financing is to be voted on in one proposition, the ballot must be printed to permit voting for or against the proposition:

> **Authorizing** *(insert name of city or county)* **to** *(insert description of venue project)* **and to impose a** *(insert each type of tax)* **tax at the rate of** *(insert the maximum rate of each tax)* **for the purpose of financing the venue project.**

Effective Date and Ending Date of Admissions Tax

After approval by the voters, the venue project admissions tax becomes effective on the date prescribed by the ordinance or order imposing the tax.[308] The admissions tax is imposed only on tickets sold as admission to an event held at the venue project, and all revenue from the tax must be deposited into the venue project fund.[309] Once the venue project's bonds or other obligations are paid in full, the city or county can no longer impose an admissions tax.[310]

Decrease, Abolition or Increase of the Admissions Tax

Once in place, the admissions tax may be decreased or abolished on the city or county's own action.[311] The tax can be increased only if the increase is approved at an election and the resulting tax rate will not exceed 10 percent of the price of an admission ticket.[312] At an election to increase the admissions tax, the ballot must be worded to allow voting for or against the following proposition:

> **The increase of the admissions tax for the purpose of financing** *(insert description of venue project)* **to a maximum rate of** *(insert new percentage rate)* **percent of the price of each ticket sold as admission to an event held at an approved venue.**

Collection and Enforcement of the Admissions Tax

The Comptroller's Office is not involved in the collection of the admissions tax. Instead, the tax is collected by the owner or lessee of the venue project and remitted to the city or county.[313] The order or ordinance imposing the admissions tax should specify how the tax is to be reported and remitted to the city or county.[314] Additionally, the order or ordinance may prescribe penalties for the failure to keep the required records, report when required, or pay the tax when due.[315] Finally, the city or county attorney is empowered to bring a lawsuit to collect the admissions tax.

A county or city may allow the lessee or owner of the venue project to retain a percentage of the admission taxes collected as reimbursement for the costs of collecting the tax.[316] The ordinance

---

[308] *Id.* § 334.155(a).
[309] *Id.* §§ 334.152(a), .157.
[310] *Id.* § 334.155(b).
[311] *Id.* § 334.152(d).
[312] *Id.* § 334.153.
[313] *Id.* §§ 334.154(a), .156(a).
[314] *Id.* § 334.156(a).
[315] *Id.* § 334.156(b).
[316] *Id.* § 334.156(c).

or order may also provide that the venue project owner or lessee may retain this reimbursement only if the owner or lessee meets the local requirements for paying the tax and filing the reports.

3. Tax on Event Parking at a Venue Project

A city or a county may impose a tax for each motor vehicle that parks in a parking facility of a venue project.[317] As with other taxes imposed under Chapter 334, the parking tax must have been approved at an election and the ballot language must specify the maximum rate of the tax being adopted.[318] Also, the city or county is authorized to impose the parking tax only if bonds or other obligations have been issued under Chapter 334 for the venue project.[319]

The tax rate may be designated as a percentage of the price charged for event parking by the owner or lessee of the venue project or as a flat amount on each parked motor vehicle.[320] However, the tax may not exceed $3.00 per vehicle for a venue event.[321] This tax applies to parking that occurs during a period beginning three hours before and ending three hours after an event at a venue project, unless the approved venue project consists of three or more separate but adjacent venue facilities.[322] If the approved venue does consists of three or more separate but adjacent venue facilities, then the tax can apply during any hours.

Ballot Proposition to Adopt an Event Parking Tax

The adoption of the event parking tax may be included in the same ballot proposition that proposes the venue project. The ballot must be printed to allow voting for or against the following proposition:[323]

> **Authorizing *(insert name of city or county)* to *(insert description of venue project)* and to impose a *(insert the type of tax)* tax at the rate of *(insert the maximum rate of the tax)* for the purpose of financing the venue project.**

If more than one method of financing is to be voted on in one proposition, the ballot must be printed to permit voting for or against the proposition:

> **Authorizing *(insert name of city or county)* to *(insert description of venue project)* and to impose a *(insert each type of tax)* tax at the rate of *(insert the maximum rate of each tax)* for the purpose of financing the venue project.**

Effective Date and Ending Date for Event Parking Tax

After approval by the voters, the parking tax becomes effective on the date prescribed by the ordinance or order imposing the tax.[324] The tax may continue only until the venue project's

---

317   *Id.* § 334.201(a) (West Supp. 2011).
318   *Id.* §§ 334.201(c), .202(c).
319   *Id.* § 334.205(b) (West 2005).
320   *Id.* § 334.202(a) (West Supp. 2011).
321   *Id.* § 334.202(b). *See also id.* § 334.202(b-1) (Allows a city with a population of more than 700,000 within a county with a population of more than one million adjacent to a county with a population of more than two million to impose a parking tax rate not to exceed $5 for each motor vehicle).
322   *Id.* § 334.201(b), (b-1).
323   *Id.* § 334.201(c) (Referring to the tax being approved at an election under section 334.024).

bonds or other obligations have been fully paid.[325] As with the other taxes, all revenue from the parking tax must be deposited in the venue project fund.[326]

Decrease, Abolition or Increase of the Event Parking Tax

The parking tax may be decreased or abolished, by ordinance or order, on the city or county's own motion.[327] The tax may be increased only if the increase is approved at an election and the resulting tax rate will not exceed $3.00.[328] At an election to increase the parking tax, the ballot must be worded to allow voting for or against the following proposition:

> **The increase of the parking tax for the purpose of financing (*insert description of venue project*) to a maximum rate of (*insert new rate*).**

Collection and Enforcement of the Event Parking Tax

The Comptroller's Office is not involved in the collection of the event parking tax. Instead, the tax is collected by the owner or lessee of the venue project and remitted to the city or county.[329] The order or ordinance imposing the parking tax should specify how the tax is to be reported and remitted to the city or county.[330] Additionally, the order or ordinance may prescribe penalties for the failure to keep the required records, report when required, or pay the tax when due. Finally, the city or county attorney is empowered to bring a lawsuit to collect the parking tax.

By order or ordinance, a county or city may allow the lessee or owner of the venue project to retain a percentage of the parking taxes collected as reimbursement for the costs of collecting the tax.[331] The ordinance or order may also provide that the venue project owner or lessee may retain this reimbursement only if the owner or lessee meets the local requirements for paying the tax and filing reports.

4. Imposing an Additional Hotel Occupancy Tax

Another way to fund a venue project within its boundaries is for a city (by ordinance) or a county (by order) to impose an additional hotel occupancy tax of up to two percent on the use of a hotel room.[332] This additional hotel occupancy tax must be approved at an election and the ballot language must specify the maximum rate of the tax being adopted.[333] The additional hotel occupancy tax may be imposed only if the city or county issues bonds or other obligations for a

---

[324]   *Id.* § 334.205 (West 2005).

[325]   *Id.* § 334.205.

[326]   *Id.* § 334.207.

[327]   *Id.* § 334.202(d) (West Supp. 2011).

[328]   *Id.* § 334.203. *See also id.* § 334.2031 (Allows a city with a population of more than 700,000 within a county with a population of more than one million adjacent to a county with a population of more than two million ability to increase a parking tax rate not to exceed $5 for each motor vehicle).

[329]   *Id.* §§ 334.204, .206(a) (West 2005).

[330]   *Id.* § 334.206(a)-(b).

[331]   *Id.* § 334.206(c).

[332]   *Id.* § 334.254(a). *See also id.* § 334.254(c) (Dallas County is authorized to impose an additional hotel occupancy tax of up to three percent of the price paid for a room in a hotel).

[333]   *Id.* §§ 334.252(b)(2), .254(b).

venue project within one year of imposing the tax.[334] If an additional hotel occupancy tax is approved, the voters can decide to use ad valorem (property) tax revenue for a venue project.[335]

However, the additional local hotel occupancy tax may not be imposed to fund a venue project that is an area or facility that is part of a municipal parks and recreation system or that is a certain Type A or Type B economic development project.[336] Nor may the hotel occupancy tax be imposed to finance a watershed protection and preservation project, recharge protection project, conservation easement or open space preservation program.[337] See the section below on General Powers and Duties for further explanation.

Application of the Additional Hotel Occupancy Tax

If approved by the voters, the Chapter 334 hotel occupancy tax is in addition to any local hotel occupancy tax that the city or county may impose under Chapter 351 or 352 of the Tax Code.[338] The rate of a hotel occupancy tax imposed under Chapter 334 of the Local Government Code may be set at any percentage that was approved by the voters, but generally may not exceed two percent of the price of a hotel room.[339] Chapter 334 does not prohibit the adoption of this additional tax even if the city or county is already at its statutory maximum for the local hotel occupancy tax under Chapter 351 or Chapter 352 of the Tax Code. The additional hotel occupancy tax may be charged only for a room that: [340]

1. meets the definition of "hotel" under Section 156.001 of the Tax Code;

2. costs at least $2.00 per night; and

3. is ordinarily used for sleeping.

Certain types of accommodations do not fall within the definition of the term "hotel" for purposes of the Chapter 334 hotel occupancy tax. For instance, hospitals, sanitariums, nursing homes, and dormitories or other non-hotel housing facilities owned by institutions of higher education may not charge the tax.[341] Also, the Comptroller's Office has interpreted the statute to exclude recreational vehicles (RVs) and RV rental spaces from taxation.[342]

---

[334] *Id.* § 334.257(b).

[335] *Id.* § 334.0241.

[336] *Id.* § 334.2515. *See also id.* 334.2516 (West Supp. 2011) (Authorizing additional hotel occupancy tax revenue being used by the city of Grand Prairie for a convention center facility or related infrastructure to be constructed on certain park property acquired by purchase or lease).

[337] *Id.* § 334.2517 (West 2005).

[338] *Id.* § 334.253(c).

[339] *Id.* § 334.254(a). *See also id.* § 334.254(c) (Authorized Dallas County to impose a three percent rate with voter approval).

[340] *Id.* §§ 334.251, .252(a).

[341] *Id.* § 334.251 (Referring to the definition of hotel according to section 156.001 of the Tax Code).

[342] However, RV's may become taxable if they become fixed in place and lose their mobile nature.

Ballot Proposition to Adopt an Additional Hotel Occupancy Tax

The adoption of the additional hotel occupancy tax may be included in the same ballot proposition that proposes the venue project. The ballot must be printed to allow voting for or against the following proposition:[343]

> **Authorizing** *(insert name of city or county)* **to** *(insert description of venue project)* **and to impose a** *(insert the type of tax)* **tax at the rate of** *(insert the maximum rate of the tax)* **for the purpose of financing the venue project.**

If more than one method of financing is to be voted on in one proposition, the ballot must be printed to permit voting for or against the proposition:

> **Authorizing** *(insert name of city or county)* **to** *(insert description of venue project)* **and to impose a** *(insert each type of tax)* **tax at the rate of** *(insert the maximum rate of each tax)* **for the purpose of financing the venue project.**

Effective Date and Ending Date of the Additional Hotel Occupancy Tax

Once approved, the hotel occupancy tax becomes effective on the date prescribed by the ordinance or order imposing the tax.[344] A city or county is not authorized to impose or continue a venue project hotel occupancy tax if the bonds or obligations for the venue project have been paid in full or if no such obligations were issued.[345] All revenue from the tax must be deposited into the venue project fund.[346]

Decreasing, Abolishing or Increasing the Additional Hotel Occupancy Tax

Unlike the other taxes discussed above, Chapter 334 does not provide any authority for a city or county to decrease or abolish the additional hotel occupancy tax. However, Chapter 334 expressly states that the additional hotel occupancy tax may only be increased if the increase is approved at an election on the issue and the resulting additional tax rate will not exceed two percent.[347] At an election to increase the hotel occupancy tax, the ballot must be worded to allow voting for or against the following proposition:

> **The increase of the hotel occupancy tax for the purpose of financing** *(insert description of venue project)* **to a maximum rate of** *(insert new rate)* **percent.**

Collection of the Additional Hotel Occupancy Tax

The Comptroller's Office is not involved in the collection of any local hotel occupancy tax. Instead, the tax is collected by the local hotels and remitted to the city or county.[348] The order or ordinance imposing the hotel occupancy tax should specify how the tax is to be reported and

---

[343] TEX. LOC. GOV'T CODE ANN. § 334.252(b)(2) (West 2005) (Referring to the tax being approved at an election under section 334.024).

[344] *Id.* § 334.257(a).

[345] *Id.* § 334.257(b).

[346] *Id.* § 334.258.

[347] *Id.* § 334.255.

[348] *See id.* § 334.253 (making parts of Chapters 351 and 352 of the Tax Code applicable to a hotel occupancy tax imposed under Chapter 334 of the Local Government Code).

remitted to the city or county. Section 334.253 of the Local Government Code makes certain provisions of the Tax Code applicable to the imposition, computation, administration, collection and remittance of the Chapter 334 hotel tax. These tax statutes provide for specific penalties which may be assessed against hotel operators who file late or false tax returns.[349] For instance, a city ordinance may include a provision that makes it a criminal misdemeanor offense to fail to collect the tax, fail to file a return, file a false return, or fail to timely make the remittances.[350] Municipal courts may assess a fine not to exceed $500 for any such offense.[351] Under the applicable sections of the Tax Code, counties do not have the authority to criminalize the failure to comply with local hotel occupancy tax requirements. However, cities and counties are given the authority to take the following actions against a hotel operator who fails to report or collect the local hotel occupancy tax:[352]

- require the forfeiture of any revenue the city allowed the hotel operator to retain for its cost of collecting the tax (only a city can do this, not a county);

- bring a civil suit against the hotel operator for noncompliance;

- ask the district court to enjoin operation of the hotel until the report is filed and/or the tax is paid; and

- any other remedies provided under Texas law.

The most noteworthy of these remedies is the ability to request that the district court close down the hotel if the hotel occupancy taxes are not turned over. Often, a city or county has gained compliance simply by informing the hotel operator of the possibility of such a closure.

The hotel occupancy tax ordinance or order may also require that persons buying a hotel retain out of the purchase price an amount sufficient to cover any delinquent hotel occupancy taxes that are due to the city or county.[353] If the buyer does not remit to the city or county such amount or show proof that the hotel is current in remitting its hotel occupancy taxes, the buyer becomes liable for any delinquent hotel occupancy taxes due on the purchased hotel. The buyer of a hotel may request that the city or county provide a receipt showing that no hotel occupancy tax is due on the property to be purchased. The city or county is then required to issue the statement not later than the 60th day after the request. If the city or county fails to issue the statement within the deadline, the purchaser is released from the obligation to withhold the amount due from the purchase price.

Cities or counties may allow hotel operators to retain up to one percent of the amount of hotel occupancy taxes collected as reimbursement for the costs of collecting the tax.[354] Cities and counties are not themselves permitted to retain any of the collected tax to cover costs of imposing or collecting the tax. Cities, but not counties, may also require that such reimbursement

---

[349]   *Id.* § 334.253. (Refers to sections 351.004 and 352.004 of the Tax Code.)
[350]   *Id.* (Refers to section 351.004.)
[351]   *Id.* § 54.001(b) (West 2008).
[352]   *Id.* § 334.253 (West 2005). (Refers to sections 351.004, 351.005 and 352.004 of the Tax Code.).
[353]   *Id.* (Refers to sections 351.0041 and 352.0041 of the Tax Code).
[354]   *Id.* (Refers to sections 351.005 and 352.005 of the Tax Code).

will automatically be forfeited by a hotel that fails to pay tax or file a report as required by the city.[355]

Hotel owners should note that each bill or receipt for a hotel charge that is subject to the Chapter 334 hotel occupancy tax must contain a statement listing the applicable hotel occupancy tax rate collected by the hotel from the customer.[356] This statement must list the State of Texas and the State's rate (6%), as well as all other taxing authorities and the hotel occupancy rate they impose.

Exemptions from the Chapter 334 Hotel Occupancy Tax

Certain entities are exempt from the hotel occupancy tax imposed under Chapter 334 of the Local Government Code.[357] Texas statutes allow an exemption from the hotel occupancy tax for persons who have contracted to use a hotel room for more than 30 consecutive days.[358] Additionally, the hotel occupancy tax does not apply to certain federal and other high-level officials traveling on federal or state business.[359] Rather than paying the hotel tax, federal employees, foreign diplomatic personnel and certain high-level state employees simply present a tax exemption certificate to the hotel.[360]

Officers or employees of a state agency, institution, board or commission who are traveling on official business must pay the hotel occupancy tax but are entitled to a refund from the involved governmental taxing entities.[361] The state and local governments refund the hotel occupancy tax to the exempt employee through a separate process. For information on how the state handles refunds of the state hotel occupancy tax, contact the Comptroller's Office at (800) 531-5441, extension 6-5913 or (512) 466-5913. A city or county may want to request a copy of the Comptroller's refund application form for the state hotel occupancy tax and adapt that form for handling refunds of the municipal or county hotel occupancy tax.

City and county officers and employees are not exempt from the state or local hotel occupancy tax even if the officers or employees are traveling on official business. Further, cities may not authorize additional exemptions from the hotel occupancy tax. For example, with regard to a hotel tax imposed under Chapter 351 of the Tax Code, the Attorney General ruled in JM-865 (1988) that cities could not grant an exception to the tax for religious, charitable or educational organizations without new constitutional or statutory authority to do so.

5. Facility Use Tax on Members of a Major League Team

If bonds have been issued under Chapter 334 of the Local Government Code by a county or city for a venue project within the city or county, the city or the county may impose a tax per game

---

[355] *Id.* (Refers to section 351.005 of the Tax Code).
[356] *Id.* § 334.256(a).
[357] *Id.* § 334.253 (Refers to sections 351.002(c), 351.006, 352.002(c) and 352.007 of the Tax Code).
[358] *Id.* (Refers to sections 351.002(c) and 352.002(c) of the Tax Code).
[359] *Id.* (Refers to sections 351.006 and 352.007 of the Tax Code). *See LaQuinta Inns, Inc. v. Sharp*, No. 95-15739 (53rd Dist. Ct., Travis County, Tex. April 30, 1996).
[360] *See* 34 TEX. ADMIN. CODE § 3.161 (West 2012).
[361] TEX. LOC. GOV'T CODE ANN. § 334.253 (West 2005) (Refers to sections 351.006 and 352.007 of the Tax Code).

against each member of a major league team playing in the venue project.[362] The facility use tax must have been approved at an election held in accordance with the rules of Chapter 334, and the ballot language must specify the maximum rate of the tax being adopted.[363]

Ballot Proposition to Adopt a Facility Use Tax

The adoption of the facility use tax may be included in the same ballot proposition that proposes the venue project. The ballot must be printed to allow voting for or against the following proposition:[364]

> **Authorizing *(insert name of city or county)* to *(insert description of venue project)* and to impose a *(insert the type of tax)* tax at the rate of *(insert the maximum rate of the tax)* for the purpose of financing the venue project.**

If more than one method of financing is to be voted on in one proposition, the ballot must be printed to permit voting for or against the following proposition:

> **Authorizing *(insert name of city or county)* to *(insert description of venue project)* and to impose a *(insert each type of tax)* tax at the rate of *(insert the maximum rate of each tax)* for the purpose of financing the venue project.**

Effective Date and Ending Date of the Facility Use Tax

After approval by the voters, the facility use tax becomes effective on the date prescribed by the ordinance or order imposing the tax.[365] The tax rate may be set at any uniform monetary amount but may not exceed $5,000 per game per member of a professional sports team playing in the venue project.[366] The facility use tax may be imposed only on games actually held in the venue project. The city or county is not authorized to collect such a facility use tax if the venue project bonds have been paid in full or if no such bonds are issued.[367] All revenue from the tax must be deposited in the venue project fund.[368]

Decrease, Abolition, or Increase of Facility Use Tax

Once in place, the facility use tax may be decreased or abolished, by ordinance or order, on the city or county's own motion.[369] The tax may be increased only if the increase is approved at an election and the resulting tax rate would not exceed $5,000 per member per game.[370] At an

---

[362]   *Id.* §§ 334.302, .306. *See* TEX. CONST. art. VIII, Section 1 (f); *Hoefling v. City of San Antonio*, 20 S.W. 85, 88 (Tex. 1892); *City of Houston v. Harris County Outdoor Advertising Association*, 879 S.W.2d 322, 326-327 (Tex. App. -- Houston [14th Dist.] 1994, pet. denied); *State v. Rope*, 419 S.W.2d 890, 897 (Tex. Civ. App. -- Austin 1967, writ ref'd n.r.e.).

[363]   TEX. LOC. GOV'T CODE ANN. §§ 334.302, .303 (West 2005).

[364]   *Id.* § 334.302(c)(2) (Referring to the tax being approved at an election under section 334.024).

[365]   *Id.* § 334.306(a).

[366]   *Id.* § 334.303(a)-(b).

[367]   *Id.* § 334.306(b).

[368]   *Id.* § 334.308.

[369]   *Id.* § 334.303(d).

[370]   *Id.* § 334.304(a).

election to increase the facility use tax, the ballot must be worded to allow voting for or against the following proposition:[371]

> **The increase of the facility use tax for the purpose of financing (*insert description of venue project*) to a maximum rate of (*insert new rate*) a game.**

Collection and Enforcement of the Facility Use Tax

The Comptroller's Office is not involved in the collection of the facility use tax. Instead, the tax is collected by the owner or lessee of the venue project and remitted to the city or county.[372] The order or ordinance imposing the facility use tax should specify how the tax is to be reported and remitted to the city or county.[373] Additionally, the order or ordinance may prescribe penalties for the failure to keep the required records, to report when required, or to pay the tax when due.[374] Finally, the city or county attorney is empowered to bring a lawsuit to collect the facility use tax.

By order or ordinance, a county or city may allow the lessee or owner of the venue project to retain a percentage of the facility use taxes collected as reimbursement for the costs of collecting the tax.[375] The ordinance or order may also provide that the venue project owner or lessee may retain this reimbursement only if the owner or lessee meets the local requirements for paying the tax and filing reports.

It is important to note that the facility use tax may be collected only from members of a "major league team" as defined by Section 334.301 of the Local Government Code. That section defines this term to include a team that is a member of the National Football League, the National Basketball Association or the National Hockey League. The term also includes a major league baseball team or any other professional team.

6. Livestock Facility Use Tax in Certain Cities and Counties

If bonds have been issued under Chapter 334 of the Local Government Code by a certain county or city for a venue project within the city or county, the city or the county may impose a livestock facilities tax for the use or occupancy by livestock of a stall or pen[376] at a designated facility.[377] The livestock facility use tax must have been approved at an election held in accordance with the rules of Chapter 334, and the ballot language must specify the maximum rate of the tax being adopted.[378]

---

[371]   *Id.* § 334.304(b).
[372]   *Id.* §§ 334.305(a), .307(a).
[373]   *Id.* § 334.307(a).
[374]   *Id.* § 334.307(b).
[375]   *Id.* § 334.307(c).
[376]   *Id.* § 334.401(3) (Definition of "stall or pen").
[377]   *Id.* §§ 334.401(1) (Definition of "designated facility"); .402 (This subchapter applies to (1) a county in which the majority of the population of two or more cities with a population of 300,000 or more are located or (2) a city for which the majority of the population is located in a county described in (1)); .403.
[378]   *Id.* §§ 334.403.

Ballot Proposition to Adopt a Livestock Facility Use Tax

The adoption of the livestock facility use tax may be included in the same ballot proposition that proposes the venue project. The ballot must be printed to allow voting for or against the following proposition:[379]

> **Authorizing *(insert name of city or county)* to *(insert description of venue project)* and to impose a *(insert the type of tax)* tax at the rate of *(insert the maximum rate of the tax)* for the purpose of financing the venue project.**

If more than one method of financing is to be voted on in one proposition, the ballot must be printed to permit voting for or against the following proposition:

> **Authorizing *(insert name of city or county)* to *(insert description of venue project)* and to impose a *(insert each type of tax)* tax at the rate of *(insert the maximum rate of each tax)* for the purpose of financing the venue project.**

Effective Date and Ending Date of the Livestock Facility Use Tax

After approval by the voters, the livestock facility use tax becomes effective on the date prescribed by the ordinance or order imposing the tax.[380] The tax rate may be set at any uniform monetary amount but may not exceed $20 for each stall or pen used or occupied at a designated facility for each event[381] in the venue project.[382] The livestock facility use tax may be imposed only at a designated facility that is an approved the venue project.[383] The city or county is not authorized to collect such a livestock facility use tax if the venue project bonds have been paid in full or if no such bonds are issued.[384] All revenue from the tax must be deposited in the venue project fund.[385]

Decrease, Abolition, or Increase of Livestock Facility Use Tax

Once in place, the livestock facility use tax may be decreased or abolished, by ordinance or order, on the city or county's own motion.[386] The city or county can impose different tax rates based on the duration of an event.[387] However, the rate must be uniform for each event of similar duration and the rate may not exceed the maximum rate adopted by the voters.[388]

The tax may be increased only if the increase is approved at an election and the resulting tax rate would not exceed $20 for each event.[389] At an election to increase the livestock facility use tax, the ballot must be worded to allow voting for or against the following proposition:[390]

---

[379]   *Id.* § 334.403(c)(2) (Referring to the tax being approved at an election under section 334.024).

[380]   *Id.* § 334.408.

[381]   *Id.* § 334.401(2) (Definition of "event").

[382]   *Id.* § 334.404(a)-(b).

[383]   *Id.* § 334.403(b).

[384]   *Id.* § 334.403(c)(1).

[385]   *Id.* § 334.410.

[386]   *Id.* § 334.404(e).

[387]   *Id.* § 334.404(d).

[388]   *Id.*

[389]   *Id.* § 334.405(a).

[390]   *Id.* § 334.405(b).

The increase of the facility use tax for the purpose of financing (*insert description of the designated facility*) to a maximum rate of (*insert new maximum ratenot to exceed $20*) per event.

Collection, Enforcement and Exemption of the Livestock Facility Use Tax

The Comptroller's Office is not involved in the collection of the livestock facility use tax. Instead, the tax is collected by the owner or lessee of a designated facility and remitted to the city or county.[391] The order or ordinance imposing the livestock facility use tax should specify how the tax is to be reported and remitted to the city or county.[392] Additionally, the order or ordinance may prescribe penalties for the failure to keep the required records, to report when required, or to pay the tax when due.[393] Finally, the city or county attorney is empowered to bring a lawsuit to collect the livestock facility use tax.

By order or ordinance, a county or city may allow the lessee or owner of a designated facility to retain a percentage of the livestock facility use taxes collected as reimbursement for the costs of collecting the tax.[394] Also, the ordinance or order may provide that the owner or lessee of a designated facility may retain this reimbursement only if the owner or lessee meets the local requirements for paying the tax and filing reports.

It is important to note that the livestock facility use tax is a debt owed to the owner or lessee of the designated facility by the user or sublessee of the designated facility.[395] This tax is not considered an occupation tax imposed on the owner or lessee of the designated facility, the user or the sublessee of the designated facility or the owner of the livestock. Also, the city or county by ordinance or order may exempt county junior livestock shows from paying the livestock facility use tax.[396]

7. Special Motor Vehicle Tax Authorized in Certain Cities

A city with a population of more than 500,000 that is located in a county bordering Mexico has special authority to impose a tax on the rental of motor vehicles.[397] Unlike the previously discussed motor vehicle rental tax, this tax may be used only to pay for the costs associated with an annual post-season college bowl game held in the city.[398] Otherwise, this tax is governed by the same provisions that govern the previously discussed motor vehicle rental tax, including the requirement that the tax be approved at an election.[399] At present, this provision applies only to the city of El Paso.

---

[391] *Id.* § 334.409(a).
[392] *Id.* § 334.409(b).
[393] *Id.* § 334.409(c).
[394] *Id.* § 334.409(d).
[395] *Id.* § 334.407.
[396] *Id.* § 334.406.
[397] *Id.* §§ 334.352, .353.
[398] *Id.* §§ 334.351, .354.
[399] *Id.* § 334.353(b)-(c).

General Powers and Duties of the City or County Undertaking a Venue Project

Once a venue project has been approved by the voters, the city or county has the following general powers and duties with regard to that project:[400]

Delegation of Management of Project. A city or county may contract with a public or private entity, including a sports team, to develop the venue project or to perform any other action that the city or county could do under Chapter 334.[401] If such a contract is with a school district, junior college or institution of higher education (as defined in the Education Code), the contract may provide for joint ownership and operation or for joint use of the venue project.[402] However, the city or county may not contract with another entity to have that entity conduct a city or county election under Chapter 334.[403]

Property Tax Exemption for Venue Project Property. A venue project is exempt from taxation under Section 11.11 of the Tax Code while the city or county owns the project.[404] However, each year the operators of a venue project must pay to a school district an amount equal to the taxes that would have been paid on the unimproved real property if the real property was removed from the school district's property tax rolls.[405] This requirement does not apply if the venue project operator is a political subdivision of the state.

Exemption from Competitive Bidding. Competitive bidding laws do not apply to an approved venue project.[406]

Limitation on Use of Property Taxes. A city or county generally may not use property taxes to construct, operate, maintain or renovate a venue project.[407] However, the voters of a city or county that imposes an additional hotel occupancy tax described above may approve the use of a specific percentage or a fixed amount of the revenue derived from property taxes for that entity.[408] At such an election, the ballot must be worded to allow voting for or against the following proposition:[409]

> **Authorizing *(insert name of municipality or county)* to use an amount not to exceed *(insert percentage of property tax revenue or dollar amount to be used)* of the revenue derived from the *(insert "county" or "municipal")* property tax, in addition to the hotel occupancy tax and any other applicable taxes, for the purpose of financing the *(describe the venue project)*.**

---

400   *Generally id.* § 334.041.
401   *Id.* § 334.041(c).
402   *Id.* § 334.041(d).
403   *Id.* § 334.041(c)(2).
404   *Id.* § 334.044(c).
405   *Id.* § 334.044(d).
406   *Id.* § 334.041(e).
407   *Id.* § 334.041(f).
408   *Id.* §§ 334.0241, .041(f)(2).
409   *Id.* § 334.0241(b).

Ability to Dispose of Property. A city or county may acquire or dispose of an interest in property, including a venue project, under the terms and conditions that seem advisable to the city or county.[410]

Application of Public Information Act. Any records of a city or county that relate to an approved venue project or its financing are subject to the Public Information Act.[411]

Harris County Exception. In a county with a population of over 2.8 million, no tax on real or personal property may be used for any venue authorized by an election on November 5, 1996, and constructed after that date.[412]

Sale of Park. Voters need not approve sale or lease of a public square or municipal park related to an approved venue project.[413]

Establishing the Venue Project Fund

A city or county must establish, by resolution, a "venue project fund."[414] The fund must have a separate account for each of the various revenue sources for the venue project. The city or county must then deposit the following monies into the fund:[415]

1) the proceeds of any tax imposed by the city or county under authority of Chapter 334 of the Local Government Code;

2) all revenue from the sale of bonds or other obligations under Chapter 334; and

3) any other money required by law to be deposited into the fund.

A city or county is not required to deposit money into the venue project fund unless it falls into one of the above three categories. However, if a city or county wishes to do so, it may also deposit the following monies into the fund:[416]

1) money received from innovative funding concepts such as the sale or lease of luxury boxes or the sale of licenses for personal seats;

2) any other revenue received by the city or county from the venue project (e.g., stadium rental payments and revenue from parking and concessions);

3) if not otherwise dedicated, revenue from bonuses, royalties, and other payments from ownership of oil, gas, and other mineral rights;

4) if not otherwise dedicated, revenues from any fees, payments, or charges imposed by a joint operating board involving the entity or a nonprofit corporation acting on behalf of the entity; and

---

[410] *Id.* § 334.041(b).
[411] *Id.* § 334.0425.
[412] *Id.* § 334.006.
[413] *Id.* § 334.045.
[414] *Id.* § 334.042(a) (West Supp. 2011).
[415] *Id.* § 334.042(b).
[416] *Id.* § 334.042(c).

5) any revenue the entity determines is appropriately used on behalf of the venue project fund.

Any money deposited into the venue project fund is considered the property of the city or county that deposited it.[417] Once funds are deposited into the venue project fund, the money may be used only for the following purposes:[418]

1) paying or reimbursing the costs of planning, acquiring, developing, establishing, constructing or renovating a venue project in the city or the county;

2) paying costs related to bonds and other obligations issued by the city or county for the project; or

3) paying the costs of operating or maintaining the venue projects.

Authority to Issue Bonds

Once a venue project is approved by the voters, the city or county may issue bonds and other obligations to pay for the costs of the project.[419] These bonds or other obligations must be payable from and secured by the revenues in the venue project fund and must mature within 30 years of the date on which they are issued. Additionally, any such obligations must be approved by the Public Finance Division of the Attorney General's Office. Bonds or other obligations issued under Chapter 334 are not a debt of the city or county. Such obligations do not create a claim against city or county tax revenue or property other than against the revenue sources that are specifically pledged and the venue project for which the bonds are issued.

Uses of Venue Revenues for a Related Venue Project

A city or a county already imposing taxes to fund a venue project may call an election to approve the use of revenue from those taxes (excluding hotel occupancy taxes) to finance a "related" venue project.[420] This allows the use of revenue to support the improvement and maintenance of a facility not originally funded by the venue tax or specified in the original election, but still related to the facility first funded by these taxes. The city or county may not change the rate of the tax or the method of financing that was already authorized. The language in the ballot must read:

> **Authorizing** *(insert name of municipality or county)* **to use an amount not to exceed** *(insert percentage of tax revenue or dollar amount of revenue to be used for each type of tax)* **of the revenue derived from the** *(insert each type of tax)* **tax, to finance the** *(describe the related venue project and its relation to the previously approved venue project).*

Chapter 335 Sports and Community Venue Districts

Chapter 335 of the Local Government Code authorizes cities and counties to join together as a group to undertake community and sports venue projects. Under this chapter, any city or county

---

417   *Id.* § 334.042(e).
418   *Id.* § 334.042(d).
419   *Id.* § 334.043 (West 2005).
420   *Id.* § 334.0242 (West Supp. 2011).

may join with any other city and/or county to form a "venue district."[421] There is no limit to the number of cities and/or counties that may join to form a single venue district. Once formed, the district is vested with all the powers that an individual city or county would have under Chapter 334.[422] The formation of such venue districts may be of particular use for communities that are too small to individually handle or fund a venue project.

Permissible Projects Under Chapter 335

If approved in an election held according to Chapter 335, a venue district may undertake a "venue project".[423] A venue project is defined as a "venue and related infrastructure that is planned, acquired, established, developed, constructed or renovated under this chapter."[424] The term "venue" is defined as being one of the following:[425]

An arena, coliseum, stadium or other type of area or facility:[426]

- that is used or will be used for professional or amateur sports, or for community civic and charitable events; and

- where a fee for admission to these events will be charged;

A convention center or related improvement that is located in the vicinity of the convention center. The term "related improvement" is used rather broadly and includes such things as a convention center, civic center, civic center building, civic center hotel, auditorium, theater, opera house, music hall, exhibition hall, rehearsal hall, park, zoo, museum, aquarium or plaza;

A tourist development area along an inland waterway;

A municipal parks and recreation system, improvements or additions to a park and recreation system, or an area or facility that is part of a municipal parks and recreation system. However, neither the motor vehicle rental tax nor the local hotel occupancy tax authorized by Chapter 335 may be used as a revenue source to pay for a venue project of this nature;[427]

---

[421]   *Id.* § 335.021 (West 2005).
[422]   *Id.* § 335.071(e).
[423]   *Id.* § 335.051.
[424]   *Id.* § 335.001(6) (Refers to the definition of venue project as defined in section 334.001(1) of the Local Government Code).
[425]   *Id.* § 335.001(5) (Refers to the definition of venue as defined in section 334.001(4) of the Local Government Code).
[426]   *See Id.* § 335.0715 (It should be noted that a district would not be able to use the provisions of Chapter 335 to finance a professional sports stadium if the district, city or county had already contracted with a professional sports team prior to November 1, 1998, for the team to relocate and play in the stadium. This prohibition only applies if the team is already playing under an existing contract in a stadium owned by another Texas city or county. Even in this circumstance, a stadium may be financed under Chapter 335 if the other city or county (where the team is currently playing) consents).
[427]   *Id.* § 335.071(e) (Venue district may impose any tax authorized by Chapter 334 and must impose the tax in the same manner as a city or county would under that chapter). *See id.* §§ 334.1015, 334.2515.

An economic development project authorized by Section 4A or Section 4B of the Development Corporation Act of 1979, Article 5190.6 of Texas Revised Civil Statutes, as that Act existed on September 1, 1997;[428] or

A watershed protection and preservation project; a recharge, recharge area, or recharge feature protection project; a conservation easement; or an open-space preservation program intended to protect water.

Section 335.001(4) defines the term "related infrastructure" to include any on-site or off-site improvements that relate to and enhance the use, value or appeal of a venue, and any other expenditure that is reasonably necessary to construct, improve, renovate or expand a venue.[429] The statute lists the following examples of improvements that would qualify as related infrastructure: stores, restaurants, on-site hotels, concessions, parking, transportation facilities, roads, water and sewer facilities, parks or environmental remediation.

A district may use Chapter 335 only to construct a project that falls within the definition of the term "venue" or within the definition of the term "related infrastructure". However, once the venue facility is constructed, state law permits the facility to be used for an event that is not related to one of the above-described venue purposes, such as a community-related event.[430] Also, if an existing facility would qualify as a venue project under Chapter 335, a district may use the authority granted under Chapter 335 to aid that facility even though it was originally constructed or undertaken under the authority of other law.[431]

Creating a Venue District

Two or more counties, two or more cities, or any combination of cities and counties may create a venue district.[432] In order to do this, each of the cities and/or counties that wish to join in the creation of the district must adopt a concurrent order.[433] The concurrent orders must meet all of the following criteria:[434]

- contain identical provisions;

- define the boundaries of the venue district to be coextensive with the combined boundaries of each of the cities and/or counties creating the district;

- designate the number of directors and the manner of appointment of the directors. Also, designate the manner in which the chair of the board will be appointed.

---

[428] The Development Act of 1979 was codified on April 1, 2009 and is now located in Chapter 501 through 507 of the Local Government Code. Since there was not a change of section 334.001(4)(E) of the Local Government Code in the 82nd Legislative Session, the reference to the civil statute will remain.

[429] TEX. LOC. GOV'T CODE ANN. § 335.001(4) (West 2005) (Refers to the definition of related infrastructure as defined in section 334.001(3) of the Local Government Code).

[430] *Id.* § 335.003.

[431] *Id.* § 335.002 (West Supp. 2011).

[432] *Id.* § 335.021 (West 2005).

[433] *Id.* § 335.022.

[434] *Id.*

There must be at least four directors on the board.[435] The directors are appointed by the county judges (if only counties are forming the district), the mayors (if only cities are forming the district), or the county judges and mayors (if both cities and counties are forming the district) as specified in the concurrent order.[436]

Directors of a Venue District

To be eligible for service on the board of directors of a venue district, the person must be a resident of the appointing political subdivision.[437] If an officer, employee or member of a city or county governing body serves as a director, that person may not have any personal interest in a contract executed by the district.

Directors of a venue district board serve staggered two-year terms, and their successors are appointed in the same manner as the original appointees (according to the concurrent orders).[438] A director may be removed by the appointing mayor or county judge at any time without cause. Directors are not entitled to any compensation other than reimbursement for actual expenses.[439] Additionally, certain directors are required to file certain financial statements required of state officers under chapter 572 of the Government Code.[440] The financial statements must be filed with the board of directors and with the Texas Ethics Commission. A director commits a Class B misdemeanor if the director fails to file the financial statement. Also, directors and employees of certain venue district must follow additional requirements concerning codes of conducts.[441]

The presiding officer of a venue district board of directors is designated as provided by the concurrent order.[442] Also, the directors must designate a secretary from among the board's members and any other officers the board considers necessary. The board of directors is subject to the Texas Open Meetings Act[443] and all board meetings must be conducted within the boundaries of the venue district.[444]

---

[435]   *Id.* § 335.031(a). *See id* § 335.035 (West Supp. 2011) (There are additional requirements for a board of a district located in whole or part in a county with a population of 3.3 million or more).

[436]   *Id.* § 335.031(b) (West 2005).

[437]   *Id.* § 335.031(d).

[438]   *Id.* § 335.031(c).

[439]   *Id.* § 335.032.

[440]   *Id.* § 335.1085. *See id.* § 335.102 (West Supp. 2011) (Makes Subchapter F of Chapter 335 of the Local Government Code only applicable to venue districts located in a county with a population of 3.3 million or more).

[441]   *See id.* §§ 335.101 - .110 (West 2005 & Supp. 2011) (Makes Subchapter F of Chapter 335 of the Local Government Code only applicable to venue districts located in a county with a population of 3.3 million or more).

[442]   *Id.* § 335.034. *See id* § 335.035 (West Supp. 2011) (There are additional requirements for a board of a district located in whole or part in a county with a population of 3.3 million or more).

[443]   *Id.* § 335.023(b) (West 2005).

[444]   *Id.* § 335.033.

Procedure for Authorizing a Venue Project

Step One:

The venue district must obtain approval for the project from the Comptroller's Office.

Before a venue district may have an election to undertake a venue project, it must obtain approval of the project from the Comptroller's Office.[445] The Comptroller reviews the project to determine whether the proposed financing would "have a significant negative fiscal impact on state revenue." To obtain this approval, the district must send to the Comptroller a copy of the resolution proposing the venue project.[446] This resolution must indicate each proposed project and each method of financing for the project.[447] Within less than 15 days of the Comptroller's receipt of the resolution, it must perform the required state fiscal impact analysis and provide the district with written notice of its decision.[448] If the Comptroller determines that the resolution would have a significant negative impact on state revenue, the Comptroller must indicate in writing how the district could change the resolution so that there would not be such a negative impact.[449] If the Comptroller fails to provide the required analysis in less than 30 days, the resolution is considered to be approved by the Comptroller.[450]

If the Comptroller finds that a venue project resolution will have a negative fiscal impact on state revenue, the district has 10 days to appeal the Comptroller's ruling.[451] The appeal is made to the Comptroller, and the Comptroller has another 10 days to provide a new analysis and written notice to the city or county.[452] If the Comptroller's ruling is still negative, the analysis must again include information on how the district could change the resolution so that there would not be a negative impact on state revenue.[453] If the Comptroller fails to provide the required analysis within 30 days, the resolution is automatically considered approved.[454] If the Comptroller continues to hold that the venue project would have a negative impact on state revenue, the venue district will not be able to hold the required election on the approval of the venue project.[455]

Step Two:

Certain venue districts must also obtain approval from the local transit authority.

If a venue project resolution contains a proposed sales tax, the venue district must determine whether that tax would result in the reduction of a sales tax rate that funds a transit authority

---

[445]   *Id.* §§ 335.051, .054. *But see* Sections 7, 8 and 9 of Texas House Bill 92, 75th Legislature, Regular Session (1997) (Excepting certain cities, counties and venue districts from the requirements of holding an election and of obtaining Comptroller approval if their voters had already approved certain sports facilities in an election held before the effective date of the legislation).

[446]   TEX. LOC. GOV'T CODE ANN. § 335.052 (West 2005).

[447]   *Id.* § 335.051(b).

[448]   *Id.* § 335.052(b).

[449]   *Id.* § 335.052(c).

[450]   *Id.* § 335.052(d).

[451]   *Id.* § 335.053(a).

[452]   *Id.* § 335.053(b)

[453]   *Id.* § 335.053(c).

[454]   *Id.* § 335.053(d).

[455]   *Id.* § 335.054.

created under either Chapter 451 or Chapter 452 of the Transportation Code.[456] This issue would arise only if the area was subject to a transit authority sales tax and if the adoption of a venue project sales tax would place the district beyond the two percent cap for the local sales tax. If these circumstances would arise because of the proposed venue project, the district must send the transit authority a copy of the venue resolution for approval by the authority. The resolution must designate each venue project and each method of financing that the district proposes to use to finance the project.[457] If the proposed financing for the venue project would not cause a reduction in the transit authority sales tax, approval from the transit authority is not required.

Within 30 days of the transit authority's receipt of the resolution, it must determine whether the reduction in the transit authority's tax rate would have a significant negative impact on its ability to provide services or would impair any existing contracts.[458] The transit authority must also provide the written results of its analysis to the district within this period. If the transit authority's ruling is negative, it must state how the district could change the venue project resolution so that there would not be a negative impact on the transit authority's ability to provide transit service or fulfill existing contracts.[459] If the transit authority fails to provide this analysis within the required period, the authority is deemed to have approved the resolution.[460]

If the transit authority finds that a venue project resolution would have a significant negative impact on the authority's ability to provide service or would impair existing contracts, the district may appeal the negative ruling within 10 days.[461] The appeal is made to the transit authority, and the authority must provide a new analysis and written notice to the district within 10 days of its receipt of the appeal.[462] If the transit authority's ruling is still negative, the analysis must include information on how the district could change the resolution so that there would not be a negative impact on the authority's ability to provide service or fulfill existing contracts.[463] If the transit authority fails to provide the required analysis within 10 days, the resolution is automatically considered approved.[464] If the transit authority continues to find that the venue project would have a negative impact, the district will be unable to hold the required election for the approval of the venue project.[465]

Step Three:

The venue district must hold an election on the venue project.

Once the district has received the required approvals from the Comptroller and, if necessary, from the transit authority, the venue district may order an election on the proposed venue project.[466] The order calling the election must meet all of the following criteria:[467]

---

[456]   *Id.* §§ 335.051(a)(2), .0535(a).
[457]   *Id.* § 335.051(b).
[458]   *Id.* § 335.0535(b).
[459]   *Id.* § 335.0535(c).
[460]   *Id.* § 335.0535(d).
[461]   *Id.* § 335.0536(a).
[462]   *Id.* § 335.0536(b).
[463]   *Id.* § 335.0536(c).
[464]   *Id.* § 335.0536(d).
[465]   *Id.* § 335.054.
[466]   *Id. But see* Sections 7, 8 and 9 of Tex. H. B. 92, 75th Leg., R.S. (1997) (Excepting certain cities, counties and venue districts from the requirements of holding an election and of obtaining Comptroller approval if their

- Allow the voters to vote separately on each venue project;

- Designate the venue project(s);

- Designate each method of financing authorized by Chapter 335 that the district wants to use to finance the venue project and designate the maximum rate for each method; and

- Allow the voters to vote, in the same proposition or in separate propositions, on each method of financing authorized by Chapter 335 that the district wants to use to finance the project and the maximum rate of each method.

In addition to the above requirements for the election order, there is required wording for the ballot proposition. The ballot must be printed to allow voting for or against the following proposition:[468]

> **Authorizing (*insert name of the venue district*) to (*insert description of venue project*) and to impose a (*insert the type of tax*) tax at the rate of (*insert the maximum rate of the tax*) for the purpose of financing the venue project.**

If more than one method of financing is to be voted on in one proposition, the ballot must be printed to permit voting for or against the proposition:[469]

> **Authorizing (*insert name of the venue district*) to (*insert description of venue project*) and to impose a (*insert each type of tax*) tax at the rate of (*insert the maximum rate of each tax*) for the purpose of financing the venue project.**

If the venue project is for improvements or additions to an existing park or recreation facility, the description of the project in the ballot proposition must identify each park or recreation facility by name or location. If the venue project is for the acquisition or improvement of a new park or recreation facility, the description of the project in the ballot must specify the general location where the new park, recreational system or facility will be located.

The Election Code governs the procedure for holding an election under Chapter 335.[470] A venue district will want to check with the Elections Division at the Secretary of State's Office if the district has any questions about the requirements of the Election Code. The Elections Division may be reached by phone at (800) 252-8683. Also, an individual may not print, broadcast, or publish, or cause to be printed, broadcast or published, campaign material that contain false and misleading information concerning the authorization of a venue project.[471] The Ethics Commission will investigate any complaints and impose penalties in accordance with Chapter 571 of the Government Code.

---

voters had already approved certain sports facilities in an election held before effective date of this legislation).

[467]   TEX. LOC. GOV'T CODE ANN. § 335.054(b) (West 2005).

[468]   *Id.* § 335.054(c).

[469]   *Id.* § 335.054(d).

[470]   *Id.* § 335.054(f) (West 2005).

[471]   *Id.* § 335.055.

General Powers and Duties of a Venue District

Once a venue project has been approved by the voters, the venue district has the following general powers and duties with regard to that project:[472]

- **Imposition of Taxes and Fees.** Subject to the approval of the district voters, a venue district may impose any tax that a city or county can impose under Chapter 334 of the Local Government Code. The district must follow all the rules set forth for such taxes in Chapter 334.[473]

  Under Chapter 334 of the Local Government Code, there are slightly different regulations governing the imposition of an additional hotel occupancy tax by a city and the imposition of such a tax by a county.[474] The conservative course would be to follow the rules set out for a county since these rules are slightly more restrictive than those applicable to cities.

  Similarly, under Chapter 334, there are different regulations governing the imposition of a city sales tax for a venue project and the imposition of a county sales tax for a venue project, and it is currently unclear which rules a venue district should follow.[475] A venue district wishing to impose either a sales tax or a hotel occupancy tax should discuss this issue with legal counsel.

- **Eminent Domain.** Subject to the requirements of Chapter 21 of the Property Code, a venue district has the power of eminent domain. Additionally, there are special provisions for a venue district involved in the appeal of an eminent domain proceeding.[476]

- **Employment of Staff and Adoption of Rules.** The district may employ the necessary personnel and adopt rules to govern the operation of the district and its employees and property.[477]

- **Inability to Adopt a Property Tax.** A venue district may not levy an ad valorem (property) tax.[478]

- **Acceptance of Donations.** The district may accept donations.[479]

- **Application of the Public Information Act.** The district is subject to the Public Information Act.[480]

- **Application of the Open Meetings Act.** The district is subject to the Open Meetings Act.[481]

---

[472]   *Generally id.* § 335.071.

[473]   *Id.* § 335.071(e).

[474]   *See id.* § 334.253.

[475]   *See id.* § 334.082.

[476]   *Id.* § 335.071(h). S*ee also id.* § 335.0711 (West Supp. 2011) (Limits the power to own or acquire real property by eminent domain for districts located in a county with a population of 3.3 million or more).

[477]   *Id.* § 335.071(a)(4)-(5) (West 2005).

[478]   *Id.* § 335.071(f).

[479]   *Id.* § 335.071(a)(2).

[480]   *Id.* §§ 335.023(c), .0725 (Specifying that the Public Information Act applies to district records related to an approved venue project and the revenue used to finance the project).

[481]   *Id.* § 335.023(b).

- **Status as Political Subdivision.** A venue district is considered to be a political subdivision of the state and of the cities and counties that created it.[482]

- **Delegation of Project Management.** A venue district may contract with a public or private entity, including a sports team, to develop the venue project or to perform any other action that the district could do under Chapter 335.[483] If such a contract is with a school district, junior college or institution of higher education (as defined in the Education Code), the contract may provide for joint ownership and operation or for joint use of the venue project.[484] However, the district may not contract with another entity to have that entity conduct a district election under Chapter 335.[485]

- **Property Tax Exemption for Venue District Property.** A venue project is exempt from taxation under Section 11.11 of the Tax Code while the venue district owns the project.[486] However, each year the operators of a venue project must pay to a school district an amount equal to the taxes that would have been paid on the unimproved real property if the real property was removed from the school district's property tax rolls.[487] This requirement does not apply if the venue project operator is a political subdivision of the state.

- **Exemption from Competitive Bidding.** Competitive bidding laws do not apply to an approved venue project.[488]

- **Ability to Dispose of Property.** A venue district may acquire or dispose of an interest in property, including a venue project, under the terms and conditions that seem advisable to the district board.[489]

- **Sue and be Sued.** A venue district, through its board, may sue and be sued in any state court in the name of the district.[490]

- **Exemption from Construction Contracting Law.** Chapter 2267 of the Government Code does not apply to an approved venue project.[491]

Establishing the Venue Project Fund

A venue district must establish, by resolution, a "venue project fund."[492] The fund must have a separate account for each of the various revenue sources for the venue project. The district must then deposit the following monies into the fund:[493]

1) the proceeds of any tax imposed by the district under authority of Chapter 335;

2) all revenue from the sale of bonds or other obligations under Chapter 335;

---

[482]   *Id.* § 335.023(a).
[483]   *Id.* § 335.071(b).
[484]   *Id.* § 335.071(c).
[485]   *Id.* § 335.071(b)(2).
[486]   *Id.* § 335.074(c).
[487]   *Id.* § 335.074(d).
[488]   *Id.* § 335.071(d).
[489]   *Id.* § 335.071(a)(3).
[490]   *Id.* § 335.005.
[491]   *Id.* § 335.077 (West Supp. 2011).
[492]   *Id.* § 335.072 (West 2005).
[493]   *Id.* § 335.072(b).

3) money received under section 335.075 of the Local Government Code from a political subdivision that created the district; and

4) any other money required by law to be deposited into the fund.

A district is not required to deposit money into the venue project fund unless it falls into one of the above four categories. However, if a district wishes to do so, it may also deposit the following monies into the fund:[494]

1) money received from innovative funding concepts such as the sale or lease of luxury boxes or the sale of licenses for personal seats; and

2) any other revenue received by the district from the venue project (e.g., stadium rental payments and revenue from parking and concessions).

Any money deposited into the venue project fund is considered the property of the district that deposited it.[495]

Once funds are deposited into the venue project fund, the money may be used only for the following purposes:[496]

1) paying or reimbursing the costs of planning, acquiring, developing, establishing, constructing, or renovating a venue project in the venue district;

2) paying costs related to bonds and other obligations issued by the district for the project; or

3) paying the costs of operating or maintaining the venue projects.

Authority to Issue Bonds

Once a venue project is approved by the voters, the venue district may issue bonds and other obligations to pay for the costs of the project.[497] These bonds or other obligations must be payable from and secured by the revenues in the venue project fund and must mature within 30 years of the date on which they are issued. Additionally, any such obligations must be approved by the Public Finance Division of the Attorney General's Office. Bonds or other obligations issued under Chapter 335 are not a debt of the venue district. Such obligations do not create a claim against district tax revenue or property other than against the revenue sources that are specifically pledged and the venue project for which the bonds are issued.

It is important to note that a venue district has the authority to issue short-term obligations and enter into credit agreements under Chapter 1371 of the Government Code. For purposes of that statute, a district is considered to be a "public utility" and an approved venue project is an "eligible project."

---

[494]   *Id.* § 335.072(c).

[495]   *Id.* § 335.072(e).

[496]   *Id.* § 335.072(d).

[497]   *Id.* § 335.073 (Note that if a district is created in Harris County and the City of Houston, then any bonds or other obligations issued by the district are subject to prior approval by Harris County and the City of Houston).

Contributions from Other Political Subdivisions

If a political subdivision receives sales tax revenue from businesses operating in a venue project sponsored by a venue district, the political subdivision may voluntarily contribute part or all of those sales tax revenues to the venue district.[498] To contribute sales tax revenue to the district, the governing body of the political subdivision must find that the venue project which generated the sales tax will add to the economic, cultural or recreational development or well-being of the political subdivision's residents. Additionally, if the sales tax revenue is contributed to assist the district in securing debt that was issued to fund a venue project, then such contributions must stop as soon as the debt is paid off. As with tax money raised by the venue district, sales tax contributions from other political subdivisions must be deposited into the venue project fund. However, such contributions from a political subdivision are not considered to be methods of financing of the district and thus appear not to need voters' approval.[499]

Pledge of Existing City Sales Tax Revenue for Venue Projects

A city may pledge up to 25 percent of its existing sales tax to pay off debt issued for one or more venue projects located in the city.[500] Section 321.508 of the Tax Code is separate from and in addition to any authority a city may have under Chapters 334 or 335 of the Local Government Code. The term "venue project" has the same definition as it does in Chapter 334 of the Local Government Code.[501]

The only types of sales tax that may be pledged for a venue project are the general city sales tax ("municipal sales and use tax") and the sales tax for property tax relief ("additional municipal sales and use tax").[502] A city may pledge its sales tax only if it is approved by the voters at an election held on this issue. The ballot at this election must be printed to allow voting for or against the following proposition:[503]

> **Authorizing the City of (*insert name of city*) to pledge not more than (*insert percentage of sales tax to be pledged*) percent of the revenue received from the (*insert "municipal sales and use tax," "additional municipal sales and use tax," or both*) previously adopted in the city to the payment of obligations issued to pay all or part of the costs of (*insert description of each venue project*).**

If the voters approve the pledge of the sales tax, the city may issue bonds and other forms of debt that are payable from and secured by the pledged sales tax revenue.[504] The money from this debt may be used only to pay for the costs of the venue projects described in the ballot proposition.

---

[498] *Id.* § 335.075.

[499] *Id.* § 335.075(d) (States that such contributions are not to be considered a "method of financing" for purposes of Subchapter D of Chapter 335. That subchapter (Section 335.051) requires that the voters approve all the Chapter 335 "methods of financing" used by a venue district).

[500] TEX. TAX CODE ANN. § 321.508 (West 2008).

[501] *Id.* § 321.508(g) (Referring to the definition of sport and community venue project as defined by section 334.001(1) of the Local Government Code).

[502] *Id.* § 321.508(a).

[503] *Id.* § 321.508(b).

[504] *Id.* § 321.508(c).

This pledge of the sales tax continues only until the debt is paid off.[505] The city may direct the Comptroller to deposit the pledged money into a trust or account as required by the terms of the debt.[506]

Dissolution of Certain Venue Districts

Venue districts wholly located in a county with a population of less than 15,000 may be dissolved by the governing body of each political subdivision that created the district.[507] Each of the governing bodies would adopt a concurrent order dissolving the venue district. Once the district is dissolved, the assets and liabilities of the venue district would be transferred to the county in which the district was located. After the county has paid all the districts liabilities, the county shall use the remaining assets for an approved venue project of the county.

---

[505] *Id.* § 321.508(d).

[506] *Id.* § 321.508(e).

[507] TEX. LOCAL GOV'T CODE ANN. §§ 335.151 - .153 (West Supp. 2011).

III. Local Property Tax Incentives

Property Tax Abatement

Local governments often use tax abatements to attract new industry and commercial enterprises and to encourage the retention and development of existing businesses. More than 1000 tax abatement agreements have been executed by Texas local governments since the early 1980s. These agreements are credited with producing many new or retained jobs.[508] In 2009, the Texas Legislature re-authorized local governments to continue using property tax abatements until September 1, 2019.[509] The statutes governing tax abatement are located in chapter 312 of the Tax Code.

Incorporated cities, counties and special districts are allowed to enter into tax abatement agreements. However, school districts may not enter into tax abatement agreements under Chapter 312 of the Tax Code.[510] Instead, a school district's ability to limit appraised values on certain property is found in the Texas Economic Development Act, chapter 313 of the Tax Code.[511]

Whether a city or a county may initiate a tax abatement agreement depends upon the location of the property that would be subject to the tax abatement.[512] If the property subject to abatement is located within the city limits, the city would be the lead party in the tax abatement. If the property to be abated is located within the extraterritorial jurisdiction (ETJ) of the city, either the city or the county may serve as the lead party. If the property is located outside the city's boundaries and outside the city's ETJ, the county must serve as the lead party for tax abatement.

Tax abatement involves six steps for any participating taxing unit:

Step One:

Each taxing unit that wants to consider tax abatement proposals must adopt a resolution indicating its intent to participate in tax abatement.[513]

The resolution can be a mere statement indicating the local government's "intent" to consider providing tax abatements. The resolution does not bind the government to grant approval of any proposed agreements. The resolution must be adopted at an open meeting by a simple majority vote of the taxing unit's governing body. If the entity is a home rule city, it is possible that the city's charter may require more than a simple majority for approval for the abatement.

---

[508] *See* 2010 Biennial Reports of Reinvestment Zone for Tax Abatement Registry, Tax Abatement Agreement Registry & Tax Increment Financing Zone Registry, published by Texas Comptroller of Public Accounts.

[509] TEX. TAX CODE ANN. § 312.006 (West Supp. 2011).

[510] *Id.* § 312.002(f) (West 2008).

[511] *Id.* ch. 313 (West 2008 & Supp. 2011).

[512] *See id.* §§ 312.204, .206, .401 (West 2008).

[513] *Id.* § 312.002(a).

Step Two:

Each taxing unit must adopt tax abatement guidelines and criteria.[514]

The guidelines and criteria are a set of conditions that any tax abatement proposal must meet in order to be eligible for tax abatement by the involved taxing unit. Some taxing units adopt very general guidelines and criteria in order to have flexibility in the types of proposals they may consider. Other local governments prefer to include very specific criteria that must be met in order to limit the number of requests for tax abatement.

The guidelines and criteria are effective for a period of two years.[515] They must provide for the availability of tax abatement to both new facilities and structures and for the expansion or modernization of existing facilities and structures.[516] The guidelines and criteria may be amended or repealed only by a favorable vote of three-fourths of the members of the governing body.[517] However, it is important to note that these guidelines do not limit a governing body's discretion to choose whether or not to enter into any particular abatement agreement, and they do not give any person a legal right to require the governing body to consider or grant a specific application for tax abatement.[518] Further, the guidelines and criteria adopted by a county may include a requirement of a tax abatement application fee not to exceed $1000.[519]

Each taxing unit may have a different set of guidelines and criteria that it adopts. However, local governments such as the city, county and other districts frequently will adopt similar (and sometimes identical) guidelines and criteria to make participation in tax abatement more convenient for businesses. The Comptroller's Office acts as the state registry for all tax abatement documents.[520]

Step Three:

After holding a public hearing and providing notice, the taxing unit that is the lead party in the tax abatement must designate an area as a "reinvestment zone."[521]

Incorporated cities or towns may designate reinvestment zones only within the city limits or within the city's ETJ.[522] The designation of the reinvestment zone by a city must be made by ordinance.[523] A county may designate a reinvestment zone only within an area

---

514   *Id.*
515   *Id.* § 312.002(c).
516   *Id.* § 312.002(a).
517   *Id.* § 312.002(c).
518   *Id.* § 312.002(d)(1), (3).
519   *Id.* § 312.002(e).
520   *Id.* § 312.005(a). *See* 2010 Biennial Reports of Reinvestment Zone for Tax Abatement Registry, Tax Abatement Agreement Registry & Tax Increment Financing Zone Registry, published by Texas Comptroller of Public Accounts.
521   TEX. TAX CODE ANN. § 312.201 (West 2008).
522   *Id.* § 312.201(a).
523   *Id.*

outside the taxing jurisdiction of an incorporated city or town, and must make such a designation by order.[524] Special districts and appraisal districts are not authorized to designate reinvestment zones.[525] Only one taxing unit (city or county) needs to designate a reinvestment zone.

School districts may designate reinvestment zones only when the area is entirely within the territory of the school district for purposes of Subchapter B or C of Chapter 313 of the Tax Code.[526] This authority supersedes any tax abatement restrictions placed on school districts by other sections of Chapter 312 of the Tax Code. Since a school district may designate a reinvestment zone only for the purposes of Chapter 313 of the Tax Code, a city or county may not use a school district-designated reinvestment zone to offer a tax abatement to a property owner. However, a school district may use a reinvestment zone designated by a city or county.[527]

The designation of the reinvestment zone must be preceded by a public hearing. Seven days' written notice of the hearing must be given to the presiding officer of each of the other taxing units that has taxing jurisdiction over real property within the zone.[528] Notice of the hearing must also be published at least seven days before the hearing in a newspaper of general circulation in the city.[529] There is no statutorily required wording that must be used for either of the above notices.

At the public hearing on the reinvestment zone, the governing body that is designating the reinvestment zone (city, county or school district) must make several findings. First, the governing body must find that the improvements sought are feasible and practical and would be a benefit to the zone after the expiration of the tax abatement agreement.[530] Additionally, the governing body must find that the zone meets one of the applicable criteria for reinvestment zones.[531] The criterion usually cited is that the designation of the zone is reasonably likely to contribute to the retention or expansion of primary employment or to attract major investment to the zone. The above findings should be approved by the governing body at an open meeting and should be noted in the minutes for that meeting.

If a zone includes several properties, each property owner has a right to ask for the same terms in any tax abatement agreement that is executed. The taxing unit is not obligated to grant a tax abatement to the property owner. However, if a tax abatement is provided, it must be on, at least, the same terms (number of years and percentage of abatement) as the

---

[524]   *Id.* § 312.401(a).
[525]   *Id.* § 312.002(g).
[526]   *Id.* § 312.0025.
[527]   *See id.* § 313.021(2)(A)(i) (West Supp. 2011).
[528]   *Id.* §§ 312.201(d)(2) (West 2008), .401(b).
[529]   *Id.* §§ 312.201(d)(1), .401(b).
[530]   *Id.* § 312.201(d).
[531]   *Id.* § 312.202.

other agreements within that zone.[532] Some taxing units make the boundaries of the zone contiguous with the property that is subject to the tax abatement. By limiting the zone to the involved property, the taxing unit is not obligated to use the same terms or percentage of tax abatement for other properties that are located outside of the zone. A larger reinvestment zone is often adopted by a taxing unit that wants to target a particular area of the city or of the county for development. In 2009, the average commercial or industrial reinvestment zone was about 131 acres in size while the average residential zone was less than half an acre.[533] It is important to note, though, that a city is not limited to declaring only one reinvestment zone.

A reinvestment zone may be almost any shape or size. However, the Attorney General has concluded that such a zone must be contiguous and must include some portion of the earth's surface. For instance, a tax abatement reinvestment zone cannot be confined to one floor of a multistory building.[534] Also, whatever shape and size a reinvestment zone does finally take, once the zone is officially designated there is no authority to modify its boundaries.

Any interested person is entitled to speak and present evidence for or against the designation of a reinvestment zone at the public hearing.[535] If the zone designation is approved, the designation lasts for five years and may be renewed for successive periods of up to five years.[536] The term of a tax abatement agreement may continue for up to 10 years, even if the reinvestment zone is not renewed after the initial five-year term.[537]

It should be noted that designation of an area as an enterprise zone under the Texas Enterprise Zone Act (Government Code Chapter 2303) would also constitute designation of the area as a reinvestment zone.[538] Reinvestment zones that are enterprise zones are effective for the duration of the enterprise zone (seven years). Participants would still need to execute the tax abatement agreement according to the rest of the administrative requirements contained in chapter 312 of the Tax Code (outlined below).

---

[532] *Id.* § 312.204(b).

[533] *See* 2010 Biennial Reports of Reinvestment Zone for Tax Abatement Registry, Tax Abatement Agreement Registry & Tax Increment Financing Zone Registry, published by Texas Comptroller of Public Accounts.

[534] Op. Tex. Att'y Gen. No. DM-456 (1997) (A county is not authorized to amend a Tax Code chapter 312 tax abatement agreement by deleting land from an existing reinvestment zone. A county reinvestment zone under chapter 312 must be contiguous and may not consist of only a portion of a building. The Texas Legislature intended to leave the substance of criteria for tax abatement agreements to the discretion of each county commissioners court, subject to very general constraints and certain specific limitations imposed by chapter 312).

[535] TEX. TAX CODE ANN. §§ 312.201(d), .401(b) (West 2008).

[536] *Id.* §§ 312.203, .401(c).

[537] *Id.* §§ 312.203, .204(a), .401(c) (West 2008), .402(a-2) (West Supp. 2011).

[538] *Id.* §§ 312.2011 (West 2008), .4011.

Step Four:

At least seven days before the lead taxing unit grants a tax abatement, it must deliver written notice of its intent to enter into the agreement to the presiding officer of each of the other taxing units in which the property is located. The notice must include a copy of the proposed tax abatement agreement.[539]

A tax abatement agreement may exempt from taxation all or part of the increase in the value of the real property for each year covered by the agreement.[540] The agreement may be for a period not to exceed 10 years.[541] There is a trend toward tax abatements with shorter time periods. While the median time frame for tax abatement agreements has historically been seven years, many new tax abatement agreements are for terms of three to five years.

A new provision authorized by the Texas Legislature in 2009 allows a taxing unit and a property owner to defer the beginning of the abatement period until a date in the future other than the January following the execution of the agreement. The duration of the abatement period still may not exceed 10 years.[542]

The tax abatement must be conditioned on the property owner making specific improvements or repairs to the property,[543] and only the increase in the value of the property may be exempted. The real property's current value may not be exempted. The current value of real property is the taxable value of the real property and of any fixed improvements as of January 1 of the year in which the tax abatement agreement is executed. For example, consider a business that has a property site valued at $500,000 as of January 1 of the year of the tax abatement agreement. If the business agrees to significantly enlarge the facility, resulting in its valuation increasing to $800,000, the taxing units may abate from taxation up to $300,000 of the property value (the portion of the value that exceeds the base value of $500,000).

Property within the zone that is owned or leased by a member of the governing body of the city or by a member of a zoning or planning board or commission of the city is not eligible for tax abatement.[544] However, if the property owner's property is subject to a tax abatement agreement when the owner becomes a member of the governing body or

---

[539]   *Id.* § 312.2041.

[540]   *Id.* §§ 312.204(a) (West 2008), .402(a), (a-1), (a-2) (West Supp. 2011).

[541]   *Id.* §§ 312.204(a) (West 2008), .402(a-2) (West Supp. 2011). *See also* Op. Tex. Att'y Gen. No. JC-133 (1999).

[542]   TEX. TAX CODE ANN. § 312.007(b) (West Supp. 2011).

[543]   *Id.* §§ 312.204(a) (West 2008), .402(a-2) (West Supp. 2011). *See also* Op. Tex. Att'y Gen. No. JC-106 (1999) (The movement of a structure from one location on a piece of property in a reinvestment zone to another location on the property may constitute a "specific improvement or repair" to the property for purposes of a tax abatement agreement under Property Redevelopment and Tax Abatement Act, chapter 312 of the Tax Code, if it improves or repairs the property in the ordinary sense and if the improvement or repair is consistent with the purpose of the reinvestment zone designation).

[544]   TEX. TAX CODE ANN. § 312.204(d) (West 2008). *See also* Op. Tex. Att'y Gen. No. GA-0600 (2008).

zoning or planning commission, the property owner would not lose the benefit of the tax abatement agreement due to the person's new membership on the governing body, board or commission.[545] Similarly under Section 312.402(d) of the Tax Code, property owned or leased by a member of the commissioners court may not be subject to a tax abatement agreement by a county. But again, should the property owner become a member of the county commissioners court, the member would not lose the benefit of a tax abatement agreement already in effect due to the person's new membership on the commissioners court.[546] The tax abatement laws do not address similar conflicts with other taxing entities. However, regardless of what taxing unit is involved, a Attorney General opinion indicates that the Tax Code does not preclude a governing body from entering into a tax abatement agreement with a corporation merely because a member of the governing body owns a very small percentage of shares in that corporation.[547] If a governing body is considering granting a tax abatement to a corporation in which one of the governing body's members has a financial interest, the governing body will want to consult with legal counsel regarding the possible application of these and other laws.

The tax abatement agreement may also abate all or part of the value of tangible personal property (including inventory or supplies)[548] that is brought onto the site after the execution of the tax abatement agreement. A taxing unit may not abate the value of personal property that was already located on the real property at any time before the period covered by the tax abatement agreement.[549] The abatement for personal property cannot be for a term that exceeds 10 years. Under a recent Attorney General opinion, a prior tax abatement agreement concerning specific property does not preclude a municipality from agreeing to abate taxes on different business personal property at the same location.[550]

Certain information provided by a property owner regarding a request for tax abatement is considered confidential for a limited time period.[551] The confidentiality of the information continues until the tax abatement agreement is executed. This confidentiality may be, and often is, waived by the mutual consent of both the taxing unit and the property owner.

---

[545]   TEX. TAX CODE ANN. § 312.204(d) (West 2008).
[546]   *Id.* § 312.402(d) (West Supp. 2011).
[547]   Tex. Att'y Gen. LO-98-001 (Tax Code section 312.402(d) does not preclude a commissioners court from entering into a tax abatement agreement with a corporation merely because a commissioners court member owns a very small percentage of shares in the corporation or the corporation's parent or because a commissioners court member invests in the corporation by way of a mutual fund).
[548]   TEX. TAX CODE ANN. §§ 312.204(a) (West 2008), .402(a) (West Supp. 2011).
[549]   *Id.* §§ 312.204(a) (West 2008), .402(a-2) (West Supp. 2011).
[550]   Op. Tex. Att'y Gen. No. GA-304 (2005).
[551]   TEX. TAX CODE ANN. § 312.003 (West 2008).

Step Five:

To adopt the tax abatement agreement, the taxing unit must approve the agreement by a majority vote of its governing body at its regularly scheduled meeting. [552]

It is important to note that the approval of the agreement by the taxing unit must occur at a "regularly scheduled meeting." The statute does not define the term "regularly scheduled meeting." It may be advisable to schedule the adoption of an agreement only at a regular meeting of the governmental body (not specially called or emergency meetings.)

At the meeting to consider approval of the tax abatement agreement, the governing body of the taxing unit must make a finding that the terms of the agreement and the property subject to the agreement meet the applicable guidelines and criteria. [553] Upon approval of the agreement by the governing body, the agreement is executed in the same manner as other contracts entered into by the applicable taxing unit. [554]

Section 312.205(a) of the Tax Code sets out certain mandatory provisions for a tax abatement agreement. A tax abatement agreement must:

- list the kind, number and location of all proposed improvements to the property;

- provide access to and authorize inspection of the property by the taxing unit to ensure compliance with the agreement;

- limit the use of the property consistent with the taxing unit's development goals;

- provide for recapturing property tax revenues that are lost if the owner fails to make the improvements as provided by the agreement;

- include each term that was agreed upon with the property owner;

- require the owner to annually certify compliance with the terms of the agreement to each taxing unit; and

- allow the taxing unit to cancel or modify the agreement at any time if the property owner fails to comply with the terms of the agreement. [555]

Section 312.205(b) of the Tax Code contains a list of optional provisions that may be included in the abatement agreement including a tax revenue recapture provision. The lead entity executing the agreement may want to incorporate any desired provisions from this list and include any other provisions that may be beneficial.

---

[552]   *Id.* § 312.207.
[553]   *Id.* § 312.002(b).
[554]   *Id.* § 312.207(b).
[555]   *See id.* § 312.205 (Section 312.402(a-2) governs county tax abatement agreements).

Step Six:

***The other taxing units may enter into an abatement agreement or choose not to provide an abatement. There is no penalty for choosing not to abate.*[556]**

As mentioned earlier, if the property subject to abatement is located within the city limits, the city must be the lead party in the tax abatement. If the property to be abated is located within the ETJ of the city, either the city or the county may serve as the lead party. If the property is located outside the city's boundaries and outside the city's ETJ, the county must serve as the lead party for tax abatement.

Should a city execute a tax abatement agreement pertaining to property located within the city, the remaining taxing units may execute a written tax abatement agreement. There is no deadline for the remaining taxing units to execute their tax abatement agreement.[557] Each taxing unit may adopt a tax abatement agreement with terms that differ from the agreement adopted by the city.[558]

A county may be the first taxing entity to grant a tax abatement only if the property was located outside of the taxing jurisdiction of an incorporated city or town.[559] If the county is the first to adopt the abatement, the other eligible taxing units may either grant a tax abatement agreement or choose not to participate in the tax abatement.[560] Again, there is no deadline for the other taxing units to execute their abatement agreement. Further, the other taxing units have the option of granting a tax abatement with terms that differ from the abatement granted by the county.[561]

If a property subject to abatement is located within the ETJ of the city, once the city or the county designates the reinvestment zone, any taxing unit may initiate a tax abatement agreement.[562] If the city adopts a tax abatement agreement in its ETJ, the agreement takes effect upon the later annexation of the property by the city.[563] If a city designates a reinvestment zone that includes property within the ETJ of the city, but does not execute an abatement agreement, the governing bodies of the other taxing units (the county and certain special districts) may initiate a tax abatement agreement.[564] The terms of the agreement do not have to be identical to the terms of a municipal agreement.[565] Further, a taxing unit may execute an agreement even if the city does not execute an agreement for the property. However, if the governing body of another eligible taxing unit has previously executed as agreement to exempt all or part of the value of the property and

---

[556]   *Id.* §§ 312.206(a) (West 2008), .402(b) (West Supp. 2011).
[557]   *Id.* § 312.206(a) (West 2008).
[558]   *Id.* ("...The agreement is not required to contain terms identical to those contained in the agreement with the municipality...").
[559]   *Id.* § 312.401(a).
[560]   *Id.* §§ 312.206(a) (West 2008), .402(b) (West Supp. 2011).
[561]   *Id.*
[562]   *Id.* § 312.206(c) (West 2008).
[563]   *Id.* § 312.204(c).
[564]   *Id.* § 312.206(c).
[565]   *Id.*

that agreement is still in effect, the terms of the subsequent agreement relating to the share of the property that is to be exempt in each year that the existing agreement remains in effect must be identical to those of the existing agreement.

A county commissioners court may, but is not required to, enter into a tax abatement agreement on behalf of a district that by statute has its tax rate set or levied by the county.[566] Before the county may enter into an agreement on behalf of such a district, the county itself must have entered into a tax abatement agreement for the same property. However, the agreement on behalf of the district need not contain the same terms as the agreement entered into by the county.

The chief appraiser of each appraisal district that appraises property for a taxing unit that has designated a reinvestment zone or has executed a tax abatement agreement must deliver to the Comptroller's Office a report describing the zone, its size, types of property located on it, its duration, the guidelines and criteria, terms of any abatement agreements, and any other information required by the Comptroller.[567] Also, to be sent to the Comptroller is a copy of the resolution or order designating the reinvestment zone and a copy of the executed tax abatement. These reports must be submitted by June 30 of the year following the designation of a zone or the execution of a tax abatement agreement. To facilitate the required reporting process, the Comptroller's Office has standard reporting forms that can be used to remit this information. You can locate and download a copy of the specific form at http://www.texasahead.org/tax_programs/proptax_abatement/forms.php. Phone inquiries can be made to the Economic Development & Analysis Division at (800)531-5441, ext. 3-4679..

The taxing units will also want to advise any property owner who is given an abatement to be timely in filing an exemption application for the tax abatement each year with the appraisal district. An application must be filed by April 30 for each tax year that the abatement is in effect.[568] A copy of this form may be found at http://www.window.state.tx.us/taxinfo/taxforms/50-116.pdf.

School Districts

A school district may not enter into a tax abatement agreement under chapter 312 of the Tax Code.[569] A school district's ability to limit appraised property values is governed by the Texas Economic Development Act found in chapter 313 of the Tax Code.[570]

---

[566]   *Id.* § 312.004(a).
[567]   *Id.* § 312.005(a)(1)-(3).
[568]   *Id.* § 11.43 (West Supp. 2011).
[569]   *Id.* § 312.002(f) (West 2008).
[570]   *Id.* ch. 313 (West 2008 & Supp. 2011).

Owners & Lessees of Real Property and Tax Abatement Agreements

Certain eligible taxing units may enter into a tax abatement agreement with the owner of taxable real property, the owner of a leasehold interest on tax exempt real property, or lessees of taxable real property. [571]

Cities, Owners of Real Property, Owners of Leasehold Interest in Real Property and Lessees of Real Property

Cities are eligible to enter into a tax abatement agreement with the owner of taxable real property that is located in a reinvestment zone, but that is not in an improvement project that is financed by tax increment bonds. [572] The tax exemption can include a portion of:

- the real property's value,

- the tangible personal property's value that is located on the real property, or

- both. [573]

The tax abatement agreement cannot exceed 10 years and the owner of the property must make specific improvements or repairs to the property.

Also, cities are eligible to enter into a tax abatement agreement with the owner of a leasehold interest in tax-exempt real property that is located in a reinvestment zone, but that is not in an improvement project financed by tax increment bonds. [574] The tax exemption includes a portion of the value of property subject to ad valorem (property) taxes, including leasehold interest, improvements, or tangible personal property located on the real property. As above, the tax abatement cannot exceed 10 years and the owner of the leasehold interest must make specific improvements or repairs to the real property.

Cities are not eligible to enter into a tax abatement agreement with lessees of taxable real property.

Counties, Owners of Real Property, Owners of Leasehold Interest in Real Property and Lessees of Real Property

Counties, like cities, are eligible to enter into a tax agreement with the owner of taxable real property that is located in a reinvestment zone. [575] The tax exemption can include a portion of:

- the real property's value,

---

[571] *Id.* §§ 312.204(a) (West 2008), .402 (a), (a-1), (a-3) (West Supp. 2011). *See also* Op. Tex. Att'y Gen. No. GA-0600 (2008).
[572] TEX. TAX CODE ANN. § 312.204(a) (West 2008).
[573] *Id.*
[574] *Id.*
[575] *Id.* § 312.402(a) (West Supp. 2011).

- the tangible personal property's value that is located on the real property, or
- both.[576]

The tax abatement agreement cannot exceed 10 years and the owner of the property must make specific improvements or repairs to the property.[577]

Also, counties are eligible to enter into a tax abatement agreement with the owner of a leasehold interest in tax-exempt real property that is located in a reinvestment zone.[578] The tax exemption includes a portion of the value of property subject to ad valorem (property) taxes, including leasehold interest, improvements, or tangible personal property located on the real property.[579] As above, the tax abatement cannot exceed 10 years and the owner of the leasehold interest must make specific improvements or repairs to the real property.

Counties, unlike cities, are eligible to enter into a tax abatement agreement with the lessee of taxable real property located in a reinvestment zone.[580] The tax exemption can include:

- all or a portion of the value of the fixtures, improvements, or other real property owned by the lessee and located on the property that is subject to the lease,
- all or portion of the value of tangible personal property owned by the lessee and located on the real property that is the subject of the lease, or
- all or a portion of the value of both the fixtures, improvements, or other real property and the tangible personal property owned by the lessee and located on the property that is subject to the lease.[581]

Again, the tax abatement cannot exceed 10 years and the lessee of taxable real property must make specific improvements or repairs to the real property.[582]

Tangible Personal Property Located on Real Property

Both cities and counties are eligible to enter into a tax abatement agreement concerning tangible personal property located on real property. Cities can enter a tax abatement concerning tangible personal property located on taxable or tax-exempt real property.[583] Also, counties can enter a tax abatement with the owner of tangible personal property located on real property in a reinvestment zone, the owner of tangible personal property

---

[576] *Id.*

[577] *Id.* § 312.402(a-2) (This section states that the execution, duration and other terms of an agreement entered into under this section are governed by the provisions of sections 312.204, 312.205, and 312.211).

[578] *Id.* § 312.402(a-1).

[579] *Id.* § 312.402(a-2).

[580] *Id.* § 312.402(a-3).

[581] *Id.*

[582] *Id.* § 312.402(a-2).

[583] *Id.* § 312.204(a) (West 2008).

or an improvement located on tax-exempt real property.[584] Cities and counties need to follow all the same procedures for giving a tax abatement agreement for tangible personal property that they would with a tax abatement agreement for real property. Additionally, agreements made prior to September 1, 2001 with lessees to exempt a portion of tangible personal property located on real property are validated as of the date the agreements were entered into.[585]

Special Tax Abatement Provisions to Encourage Voluntary Cleanup

Section 312.211 of the Tax Code allows a special type of tax abatement when a property owner voluntarily agrees to clean up contaminated property. In order to qualify for this special treatment, a property must meet all of the following criteria:[586]

- The real property must be located in a reinvestment zone;

- The real property cannot be an improvement project financed by tax increment bonds; and

- The real property must be subject to a voluntary cleanup agreement under Section 361.606 of the Health and Safety Code.

This tax abatement agreement may also include tangible personal property located on the real property described above.[587]

There are several important differences between the traditional tax abatement and Section 312.211 voluntary cleanup tax abatement. Unlike regular tax abatement, the city or county may abate more than just the increase in value that takes place after the abatement agreement is signed. If a voluntary cleanup property meets the above criteria, a city or county may agree to abate up to 100% of the total value of the property during the first year of the agreement. During the second year of the agreement, a city or county may agree to abate up to 75% of the property's total value. Up to 50% of the property's total value may be abated in the third year and up to 25% in the fourth year.[588] In other words, the tax abatement may include abatement of not only the increase in value, but also a percentage of the original value of the property.

Also in contrast to regular tax abatement, an agreement under this section may not last longer than four years.[589] Finally, a city or county must establish guidelines for a Section 312.211 tax abatement that are separate from the city's guidelines for a traditional tax abatement. Unlike the guidelines that a city or county must establish for regular tax abatements, the guidelines for a Section 312.211 tax abatement are not required to make tax abatement available for both new facilities and for the expansion or modernization of

---

[584]   *Id.* §§ 312.402(a), (a-1) (West Supp 2011).

[585]   Tex. H.B. 1448, § 4, 77th Leg., R.S. (2001).

[586]   TEX. TAX CODE ANN. § 312.211(a) (West 2008).

[587]   *Id.* § 312.211(a)(2).

[588]   *Id.* §§ 312.211(b) (West 2008), .402(a-2) (West Supp. 2011). *See* TEX. HEALTH & SAFETY CODE ANN. § 361.609 (West 2010) (For requirements for a certificate of completion).

[589]   TEX. TAX CODE ANN. § 312.211(b) (West 2008).

existing facilities.[590] Rather, the guidelines for a Section 312.211 tax abatement must base the granting of a tax abatement on successful cleanup of the property involved.

In order for an agreement under Section 312.211 to take effect, the property owner must first receive a certificate of completion for the property under Section 361.609 of the Health and Safety Code.[591] The city or county may cancel or modify an agreement under Section 312.211 if the use of the land changes from what was specified in the certificate of completion and the city or county determines that the new use may result in an increased risk to human health or to the environment.[592] If a city or county enters into an abatement agreement under Section 312.211, the city or county may not simultaneously enter into a regular tax abatement agreement for the same property.[593] And school districts may not enter into a tax abatement agreement under Section 312.211.[594]

Before the property owner may receive a voluntary cleanup tax abatement, he or she must submit a copy of the certificate of completion to the chief appraiser of the appraisal district where the property is located.[595] The certificate should be submitted to the chief appraiser with an application for an exemption under Section 11.28 of the Tax Code. The abatement agreement takes effect on January 1st of the next tax year after the certificate is received by the chief appraiser. Once the proper certificate is submitted, the property owner will not need to submit it again each year.[596] Of course, the appraisal district can approve a tax exemption for a tax abatement only if the local governments have already approved the abatement by vote of their governing bodies.

In all other respects, a tax abatement under Section 312.211 of the Tax Code functions like any other tax abatement. For instance, all the normal public hearing and notice requirements apply to a reinvestment zone and to a tax abatement established under this section.[597] Other taxing units, with the exception of school districts, may join in the Section 312.211 abatement subject to the same procedural rules as apply to a regular abatement.[598] Also, the terms of such an abatement are subject to the same general rules as are the terms of a regular tax abatement.[599] Those terms must include a recapture provision, list the proposed improvements to the property, and provide access to the property so that city employees, among others, may ensure compliance.[600] Counties may initiate a Section 312.211 abatement in the same areas where they may initiate a regular tax abatement.[601]

---

[590]   *Id.* § 312.002(a).

[591]   *Id.* § 312.211(b).

[592]   *Id.* §§ 312.211(f) (West 2008), .401(a-2) (West Supp. 2011).

[593]   *Id.* §§ 312.211(g) (West 2008), .401(a-2) (West Supp. 2011).

[594]   *Id.* § 312.211(h) (West 2008). *See also id.* § 312.002(f).

[595]   *Id.* § 312.211(c).

[596]   *Id.* § 312.211(d).

[597]   *Id.* § 312.201.

[598]   *Id.* § 312.206(a).

[599]   *Id.* § 312.211(g).

[600]   *Id.* § 312.205(a).

[601]   *Id.* § 312.402 (West Supp. 2011).

Tax Increment Financing

Tax increment financing is a tool that local governments can use to publicly finance needed structural improvements and enhanced infrastructure within a defined area. These improvements usually are undertaken to promote the viability of existing businesses and to attract new commercial enterprises to the area. The statutes governing tax increment financing are located in Chapter 311 of the Tax Code.

The cost of improvements to the area is repaid by the contribution of future tax revenues by each taxing unit that levies taxes against the property. Specifically, each taxing unit can choose to dedicate all, a portion, or none of the tax revenue that is attributable to the increase in property values due to the improvements within the reinvestment zone. The additional incremental tax revenue that is received from the affected properties is referred to as the tax increment. Each taxing unit determines what percentage of its tax increment, if any, it will commit to repayment of the cost of financing the public improvements. In addition, the governing body of a city may determine, in an ordinance designating an area as a reinvestment zone or in an ordinance adopted subsequent to the designation of a zone, the portion or amount of tax increment generated from municipal sales and use taxes attributable to the zone, above the sales tax base, to be deposited into the tax increment fund.[602]

Tax increment financing may be initiated only by a city or county.[603] Once a city or county has begun the process of establishing a tax increment financing reinvestment zone, other taxing units are allowed to consider participating in the tax increment financing agreement.[604]

Cities and counties may ~~to~~ exercise any power that is necessary to carry out tax increment financing.[605] They may acquire real property through purchase or condemnation, or other means, enter into necessary agreements, and construct or enhance public works facilities and other public improvements.[606] In addition, cities and counties may sell real property on the terms and conditions and in the manner they consider advisable to implement the project plan.[607] The power for cities and counties to acquire and sell real property prevails over any law or municipal charter to the contrary.[608] The use of tax increment financing for improvements to educational facilities in a city is prohibited unless those facilities are located in a reinvestment zone created on or before September 1, 1999.[609] However, the cost of school buildings, other educational buildings, other educational facilities, or other

---

[602] TEX. TAX CODE ANN. § 311.0123(b) (West 2008).
[603] *Id.* § 311.003 (West Supp. 2011). *But see* TEX. CONST. art VIII § 1-g(b).
[604] TEX. TAX CODE ANN. § 311.013(f) (West Supp. 2011).
[605] *Id.* § 311.008(b).
[606] *Id.* § 311.008(b)(2).
[607] *Id.*
[608] *Id.* § 311.008(c).
[609] *Id.* § 311.008(b)(4)(C).

buildings owned by or on behalf of a school district, community college districts, or other political subdivisions of the state are part of the definition of project costs.[610]

Initiating the Process

As mentioned above, tax increment financing may be initiated only by a city or county. An area may be considered for tax increment financing only if it meets at least one of the following criteria:[611]

- The area's present condition must substantially impair the city or county's growth, retard the provision of housing, or constitute an economic or social liability to the public health, safety, morals or welfare. Further, this condition must exist because of the presence of one or more of the following conditions:

  - a substantial number of substandard or deteriorating structures,

  - inadequate sidewalks or street layout,

  - faulty lot layouts,

  - unsanitary or unsafe conditions,

  - deterioration of site or other improvements,

  - a tax or special assessment delinquency that exceeds the fair market value of the land,

  - defective or unusual conditions of title,

  - conditions that endanger life or property by fire or other cause, or,

  - if the city has a population of 100,000 or more, structures (which are not single-family residences) in which less than 10 percent of the square footage has been used for commercial, industrial, or residential purposes during the preceding 12 years;

- The area is predominantly open or undeveloped and, because of obsolete platting, deteriorating structures or other factors, it substantially impairs the growth of the city or county;

---

[610] *Id.* § 311.002(1)(K). *Compare* § 311.008(b)(4)(C), "A municipality or count may exercise any power necessary and convenient to carry out [Chapter 311 of the Tax Code], including the power to[,] consistent with the project plan for the zone[,] in a reinvestment zone created on or before September 1, 1999, *acquire, construct, or reconstruct education facilities*[.]" *to* § 311.002(1)(K) which defined "project cost" to include "the costs of school buildings, other educational buildings, other educational facilities, or other buildings owned by or on behalf of a school district, community college district, or political subdivision of this state[.] (emphasis added).

[611] *Id.* § 311.005(a). *See* Op. Tex. Att'y Gen. No. GA-0514 (2007) (A city may not designate an area as a reinvestment zone under Tax Code section 311.005(a)(5) unless the area is "unproductive, underdeveloped, or blighted" within the meaning of article VIII, section 1-g(b) of the Texas Constitution, even if the area's plan of tax increment financing does not include issuance of bonds or notes.)

- The area is in or adjacent to a "Federally assisted new community" as defined under Tax Code Section 311.005(b); or

- The area is described in a petition requesting that the area be designated as a reinvestment zone. The petition must be submitted by the owners of property constituting at least 50 percent of the appraised property value within the proposed zone.

In addition, if the proposed project plan for a potential zone includes the use of land in the zone in connection with the operation of an existing or proposed regional commuter or mass transit rail system, or for a structure or facility that is necessary, useful, or beneficial to such a regional rail system, the governing body of a city may designate an area as a reinvestment zone.[612]

Within developed areas of the city or county, the criterion usually cited to justify a reinvestment zone is that the area's present condition substantially impairs the local government's growth because of a substantial number of substandard or deteriorating structures. If the area is not developed, the city or county often cites the criterion that the area is predominantly open, or undeveloped, and that it substantially impairs the growth of the city or county because of obsolete platting, deteriorating structures or other factors.

A decision by a local government that an area meets the first or second criteria to become a reinvestment zone will be given much deference by a reviewing court should that decision be challenged by a private lawsuit. Unless the decision is arbitrary or capricious, willful and unreasoning, taken without consideration and in disregard of the facts and circumstances, it will be upheld.[613]

A reinvestment zone for tax increment financing may not be created if:[614]

- More than 30% of the property in the proposed reinvestment zone (excluding publicly-owned property) is used for residential purposes,[615] or

- The total appraised value of taxable real property in the proposed reinvestment zone and in the existing reinvestment zones exceed either:

  - For cities with a population of 100, 000 or more: 25% of the total appraised value of taxable real property within the city and its industrial districts,[616] or

  - For cities with a population of less than 100,000: 50% of the total appraised value of taxable real property within the city and its industrial districts.[617]

---

[612] TEX. TAX CODE ANN. § 311.005(a-1) (West 2008).

[613] *See Hardwicke v. City of Lubbock*, 150 S.W.3d 708, 716-17 (Tex. App.-Amarillo 2004, no pet.)

[614] TEX. TAX CODE ANN. § 311.006 (West Supp. 2011).

[615] *Id.* § 311.006(a)(1). See also *id.* § 311.006(e) (Does not apply if the district is created pursuant to a petition of the landowners).

[616] *Id.* § 311.006(a)(2)(A).

[617] *Id.* § 311.006(a)(2)(B).

The boundaries of an existing reinvestment zone for tax increment financing may be reduced or enlarged by ordinance or resolution of the governing body that created the zone.[618] There are limitations if a city makes any changes to an existing reinvestment zones boundaries. A city may not change the boundaries to include property in excess of the restrictions listed above.[619]

If the boundaries of a tax increment reinvestment zone are enlarged, a school district is not required to pay into the tax increment fund any of the district's tax increment produced from property located in the added area.[620] However, the school district may voluntarily enter into an agreement with the city or county that created the zone to contribute all or part of the district's tax increment from such an area. The school district may enter into such an agreement at any time before or after the reinvestment zone is created or enlarged. The agreement may include conditions for payment of the tax increment into the fund and must specify the portion of the tax increment to be paid into the fund and the years for which the tax increment is to be paid into the fund.

The other taxing units are also not required to pay into the tax increment fund any of its tax increment produced if the boundaries of a tax increment reinvestment zone are enlarged.[621] Like the school districts, the other taxing units voluntarily enter into an agreement with the city or county that created the zone to contribute all or part of the district's tax increment from the enlarged area. The other taxing units may enter into such an agreement at any time before or after the reinvestment zone is enlarged. The agreement may include conditions for payment of the tax increment into the fund and must specify the portion of the tax increment to be paid into the fund and the years for which the tax increment is to be paid into the fund. Also, the agreement may specify the projects to which the taxing unit's tax increment will be dedicated.

Also, the city or county that designated a reinvestment zone by ordinance or resolution or by order or resolution, respectively, may extend the term of all or a portion of the reinvestment zone after notice and hearing in the manner provided for the designation of the zone. A taxing unit other than the city or county that designated the zone is not required to participate in the zone or portion of the zone for the extended term unless the taxing unit enters into a written agreement to do so.[622]

Procedure for Designating a Reinvestment Zone

If an area qualifies for tax increment financing, the process involves 8 steps. The 8 steps are as follows:

---

618   *Id.* § 311.007.
619   *Id.* § 311.006(b).
620   *Id.* § 311.013(k).
621   *Id.* § 311.013(f).
622   *Id.* § 311.007(c).

Step One:

The governing body must prepare a preliminary reinvestment zone financing plan.[623]

The Tax Code does not specify what the preliminary financing plan must contain. However, it may be prudent to include each of the items that are required for the final reinvestment zone financing plan discussed in Step Five of this section.[624] One of the items required in the reinvestment zone financing plan is a detailed list of the estimated project costs of the zone, including administrative expenses. "Project costs" are the expenditures made or estimated to be made and monetary obligations incurred or estimated to be incurred by the reinvestment zone that are listed in the project plan as the cost of public works, public improvements, programs, or other projects benefiting the zone, including other cost incidental to those expenditures and obligations.[625] "Project Cost" includes:

- Capital cost, including the actual cost of:
    - the acquisition and construction of public works, public improvements new buildings, structures, and fixtures;
    - the acquisition, demolition, alteration, remodeling, repair or reconstruction of existing buildings, structures, and fixtures;
    - the remediation of conditions that contaminate public or private land or building;
    - the preservation of the façade of a public or private building;
    - the demolition of public or private buildings;
    - the acquisition of land and equipment and the clearing and grading of land;
- Financing cost;
- Real property assembly cost;
- Professional service cost;
- Imputed administrative cost;
- Relocation cost;
- Organizational cost;
- Interest before and during construction and for one year after completion of construction, whether or not capitalized;
- Cost of operating the reinvestment zone and project facilities;
- Amount of any contributions made by the city or county from general revenue for the implementation of the project plan;

---

[623]   *Id.* § 311.003(b).
[624]   *See Id.* § 311.011(c).
[625]   *Id.* § 311.002(1).

- Cost of school building, other educational buildings, other educational facilities, or other buildings owned by or on behalf of a school district, community college district, or other political subdivision of this state; and

- Payments made at the discretion of the governing body of the city or county that the governing body finds necessary or convenient to the creation of the zone or to the implementation of the project plans for the zone.[626]

Project costs may also include the cost of economic development programs authorized by section 311.010(h) of the Tax Code.

While in the process of creating the preliminary financing plan, the city or county should also be preparing a proposed project plan.[627] The proposed project plan should also include the necessary terms as discussed in Section Five. Through the process of creating the reinvestment zone, the city or county will have to describe their tentative plan for the development of the zone. As part of the proposed project plan, the city or the county can acquire, construct, reconstruct or install public works, facilities, or sites or other public improvements, including utilities, streets, street lights, water and sewer facilities, pedestrian malls and walkways, parks, flood and drainage facilities or parking as long as it is consistent with the project plan for the zone.[628]

Step Two:

The governing body must publish notice of a public hearing at least 7 days before the hearing on the creation of the reinvestment zone.[629]

Not later than the 7th day before the date of the hearing, notice of the hearing must be published in a newspaper having general circulation in the city or county on the creation of the reinvestment zone.

Step Three:

The governing body must hold a public hearing on the creation of the reinvestment zone.[630]

Before adopting an ordinance or order providing for a reinvestment zone, the city or county must hold a public hearing on the creation of the zone and its benefits to the city or county and to property in the proposed zone. At the hearing an interested person may speak for or against the creation of the zone, its boundaries, or the concept of tax increment financing.[631] Owners of property that is located within a proposed zone must be given a reasonable opportunity to object to the inclusion of their property within the proposed zone.[632]

---

626   *Id.* § 311.002(1)(A)-(L).
627   *See Id.* § 311.008(b)(1).
628   *Id.* § 311.008(b)(4)(B).
629   *Id.* § 311.003(c).
630   *Id.*
631   *Id.*
632   *Id.* § 311.003(d).

Step Four:

After the public hearing, the governing body of the city or county may, by ordinance or order, designate a contiguous area as a reinvestment zone for tax increment financing purposes and create the board of directors for the reinvestment zone. [633]

Cities can also designate a noncontiguous geographic area within the city limits, in the extraterritorial jurisdiction of the city or in both as a reinvestment zone. The ordinance or order must be adopted by a simple majority vote of the governing body at an open meeting. Home rule cities may have a higher voting contingent required by the city charter. The adopted ordinance or order should include a finding that development of the area would not occur in the foreseeable future solely through private investment. Also, the ordinance or order must contain a number of other provisions concerning the reinvestment zone. These provisions include: [634]

- a description of the boundaries of the zone with sufficient detail to identify the territory within the zone.;

- a designation of the board of directors for the zone and an indication of the number of directors of the board; [635]

- a provision that the zone will take effect immediately on passage of the ordinance;

- an indication of the date for termination of the zone;

- a name for the zone as provided under Section 311.004(a)(5) of the Tax Code;

- a provision establishing a tax increment fund for the zone;

- findings that the improvements within the zone will significantly enhance the value of the taxable property within the zone and will be of general benefit to the city or county, and that the area meets the criteria for designation of a reinvestment zone under Section 311.005 of the Tax Code. This finding does not have to identify the specific parcels of real property. [636]

If designating a reinvestment zone pursuant to a petition of the property owners, the city or county must specify in its ordinance that the reinvestment zone is designated pursuant to Section 311.005(a)(4) of the Tax Code. [637]

It should be noted that designation of an area as an enterprise zone under the Texas Enterprise Zone Act (Government Code Chapter 2303) would also constitute designation

---

[633]   *Id.* § 311.003(a).
[634]   *Id.* § 311.004(a) (West 2008).
[635]   *See id.* §§ 311.009 (West Supp. 2011), .0091 (Addresses cities with a population of 1.1 million or more that are located wholly or partially in a county with a population of less than 1.8 million).
[636]   *Id.* § 311.004(b) (West 2008).
[637]   *Id.* § 311.004(c).

of the area as a reinvestment zone for tax increment financing purposes.[638] Such a designation would eliminate further public hearing requirements other than those provided under the Texas Enterprise Zone Act. Participants would still need to execute the tax increment "project" and "financing" plan according to the requirements contained in Chapter 311 of the Tax Code (outlined in Step Seven).

Also, property within the zone that is owned or leased by a member of the governing body of the city or by a member of a zoning or planning board or commission of the city is not eligible for tax increment financing.[639] However, if the property owner's property is subject to a tax increment financing agreement when the owner becomes a member of the governing body or of the zoning or planning commission, the property owner would not lose the benefit of the tax increment financing agreement due to the person's new membership on the governing body, board or commission.[640]

Board of Directors

The size, composition and qualifications of the board of directors depend on whether the reinvestment zone was initiated by the city or county or by petition of the property owners.

Zones Initiated by Governing Body

If the zone was created by the governing body on its own initiative, the board of directors consists of at least five and not more than 15 members, unless more than 15 members are required under Section 311.009 of the Tax Code. The board is composed of one appointee from each taxing unit that levies taxes on real property in the zone if the taxing unit has approved the payment of all or part of the tax increment produced by the unit into the tax increment fund for the zone. A taxing unit may waive its right to appoint a member. The governing body of the city or county that designated the zone may appoint not more than ten directors to the board; except that if there are fewer than five directors appointed by taxing units other than the city or county, the governing body of the city or county may appoint more than ten members as long as the total membership of the board does not exceed 15 members.[641] The board members appointed by the governing board that created the zone must be:

- at least 18 years of age, and
- be a resident of:
    - the county in which the zone is located,
    - a county adjacent to the county in which the zone is located, or
    - own real property in the zone, whether or not the individual resides in the county in which the zone is located or a county adjacent to that county.[642]

---

638   *Id.* § 311.0031. (Please note that Chapter 2303 of the Government Code sets out the qualifications to be designated an enterprise zone, but does not set out procedures for designation).

639   *Id.* § 312.204(d).

640   *Id.*

641   *Id.* § 311.009(a) (West Supp. 2011).

642   *Id.* § 311.009(e)(1).

Zones Initiated by Petition of Property Owners

If the reinvestment zone was created pursuant to a petition of the property owners, the board of directors must consist of nine members.[643] Each taxing unit, other than the city or county that designated the zone, that levies taxes on real property in the zone may appoint one member of the board if the taxing unit has approved the payment of all or part of the tax increment produced by the unit into the tax increment fund for the zone. The local state senator and representative in whose districts the zone is located are each members of the board, or they may appoint a substitute to serve for them. If the zone is located in more than one senate district or house district, then the senator or representative in whose district a larger portion of the zone is located is the member of the zone's board.

If fewer than seven taxing units, other than the city or county that designated the zone, are eligible to appoint members of the board of directors of the zone, the city or county may appoint a number of members of the board such that the board comprises nine members. If at least seven taxing units, other than the city or county that designated the zone, are eligible to appoint members of the board of directors of the zone, the city or county may appoint one member.[644]

To be eligible for appointment to the board by the governing body of the city or county that designated the zone, an individual must be at least 18 years of age, and own real property in the zone or be an employee or agent of a person who owns real property in the zone.[645]

Board Membership

Each year, the governing board of the city or county creating the zone appoints one member of the board to serve as chairman.[646] The chairman serves for a term of one year that begins on January 1st of the following year. The board of directors may also elect a vice-chair to preside in the absence or vacancy of the chairman. The board may elect other officers as it considers appropriate. A vacancy on the board is filled by appointment of the governing body of the taxing unit that appointed the director.[647]

State law specifies that a member of the board of directors of a tax increment financing reinvestment zone is not considered a public official.[648] Because of this provision, the Attorney General has held that a city council member is not prohibited from simultaneously serving as a member of the board of directors of a tax increment

---

[643]   *Id.* § 311.009(b).
[644]   *Id.*
[645]   *Id.* § 311.009(e)(2).
[646]   *Id.* § 311.009(f).
[647]   *Id.* § 311.009(d).
[648]   *Id.* § 311.009(g)(1).

reinvestment zone created by his or her municipality.[649] In addition, state law clarifies that such a director may be appointed to serve on the board of directors of a local government corporation created under the Texas Transportation Corporation Act (Transportation Code Chapter 431, Subchapter D).[650]

Step Five:

After the city or county has adopted the ordinance or order creating the zone, the board of directors of the zone must prepare both a "project plan" and a "reinvestment zone financing plan."[651]

The project plan must include:[652]

- a description and map showing existing uses and condition of real property within the zone and proposed uses of that property;

- proposed changes to zoning ordinances, the master plan of the city, building codes or other municipal ordinances or subdivision rules and regulations of the county;

- a list of estimated non-project costs; and

- a statement of the method for relocating persons who will be displaced, if any, as a result of implementation of the plan.

If a zone is created pursuant to petition in a county that has a population in excess of 3.3 million, there are certain special requirements of the project plan involving residential housing that must be observed.[653]

The reinvestment zone financing plan must contain the following nine items:[654]

1) a detailed list of the estimated project costs of the zone, including administrative expenses;

2) a statement listing the proposed kind, number and location of all public works or public improvements to be financed by the zone;

3) a finding that the plan is economically feasible and an economic feasibility study;

4) the estimated amount of bonded indebtedness to be incurred;

5) the estimated time when related costs or monetary obligations are to be incurred;

---

[649] Op. Tex. Att'y Gen. No. GA-0169 (2004).
[650] TEX. TAX CODE ANN. § 311.009(g)(2) (West Supp. 2011).
[651] *Id.* § 311.011.
[652] *Id.* § 311.011(b).
[653] *Id.* § 311.011(f).
[654] *Id.* § 311.011(c).

6) a description of the methods for financing all estimated project costs and the expected sources of revenue to finance or pay project costs, including the percentage of tax increment to be derived from the property taxes of each taxing unit anticipated to contribute tax increment to the zone that levies taxes on real property within the zone;

7) the current total appraised value of taxable real property in the zone;

8) the estimated captured appraised value of the zone during each year of its existence; and

9) the duration of the zone.

The financing plan may provide that the city or county will issue tax increment bonds or notes, the proceeds of which are used to pay project costs for the reinvestment zone.[655] Any such bonds or notes are payable solely from the tax increment fund and must mature on or before the date by which the final payments of the tax increment into the tax increment fund are due.[656] Tax increment bonds are issued by ordinance of the city or order of the county without any additional approval required, other than that of the Public Finance Section of the Attorney General's Office. The characteristics and treatment of these obligations is covered in detail in Section 311.015 of the Tax Code.

After both the project plan and the financing plan are approved by the board of directors of the zone, the plans must also be approved by ordinance or order of the governing body that designated the zone.[657] The ordinance or order must be adopted at an open meeting by a simple majority vote of the governing body, unless the city is a home rule city and a higher voting contingent is required by the city charter. The ordinance or order must find that the plans are feasible.[658]

At any time after the zone is adopted, the board of directors may adopt an amendment to the project plan.[659] The amendment takes effect on approval of the change by ordinance by the city or order by the county that created the zone and in certain cases may require an additional public hearing. A school district that participates in a zone is not required to increase the percentage or amount of the tax increment to be contributed by the school district because of an amendment to the project plan or reinvestment zone financing plan for the zone unless the governing body of the school district by official action approves the amendment.[660]

---

[655] *Id.* § 311.015 (It should be noted that this section of the Tax Code does not include a county as having the ability to issue tax increment bonds or notes. However, section 311.008 does give counties "any power necessary and convenient to carry out" Chapter 311, including entering into agreements with bondholders).

[656] *Id.* § 311.015(l).

[657] *Id.* § 311.011(d).

[658] *Id.*

[659] *Id.* § 311.011(e).

[660] *Id.* § 311.011(g).

Finally, once a city or county designates a tax increment financing reinvestment zone or approves a project plan or financing plan, the city or county must deliver to the Comptroller's Office a report containing: a general description of each reinvestment zone, a copy of each project plan or financing plan adopted, and "any other information required by the comptroller" that helps in the administration of the central registry and tax refund for economic development (Tax Code, Chapter 111, subchapter F).[661] The report must be submitted by April 1st of the year following the year the zone is designated or plan is approved.

Step Six:

After the project plan and the reinvestment zone financing plan are approved by the board of directors and by the city or county's governing body, the other taxing units with property within the zone must collect the percentage of their increased tax revenues that will be dedicated to the tax increment fund.[662]

The tax increment fund[663] is made up of the contributions by the respective taxing units of a portion of their increased tax revenues that are collected each year under the plan.[664] The taxing units can determine the amount of their tax increment for a year either by:

- the amount of property tax levied and *assessed* by the unit for that year on the captured appraised value of real property that is taxable and located in the reinvestment zone; or

- the amount of property taxes levied and *collected* by the unit for that year on the captured appraised value of real property taxable and located in the reinvestment zone.

In practice, taxing units have generally committed in early negotiations with the city or county as to what portion of the tax increment they will contribute to the tax increment fund for the zone.

---

661   *Id.* § 311.019(b) (West 2008) (Note: This section still refers to Subchapter F, Chapter 111 of the Tax Code. Subchapter F was repealed by S.B. 1, Art. 3 during the 82nd Legislative Session, First Called Session. However, the repeal of Subchapter F by S.B. 1, Art. 3 does not affect an eligible person's right to claim a refund of state sales and use and state franchise taxes that was established under Section 111.301 of the Tax Code in relation to taxes paid before the effective date of Art. 3 (October 1, 2011) in a calendar year for which the person paid ad valorem taxes to a school district as provided by Section 111.301, Tax Code, before the effective date of Art. 3 (October 1, 2011). An eligible person's right to claim a refund of state sales and use and state franchise taxes that was established under Section 111.301 of the Tax Code in relation to taxes paid before the effective date of Art. 3 (October 1, 2011) in a calendar year for which the person paid ad valorem taxes to a school district as provided by Section 111.301 of the Tax Code before the effective date of Art. 3 (October 1, 2011) is governed by the law in effect on the date the right to claim the refund was established, and the former law is continued in effect for that purpose. Therefore, the reference to Subchapter F will remain.).

662   *Id.* § 311.013 (West Supp. 2011).

663   *See id.* § 311.014 (West 2008). (Describes the tax increment fund's composition).

664   *Id.* § 311.012(a) (West Supp. 2011).

For example, consider a city that as part of its tax increment project plan has agreed to put in improved sidewalks throughout the zone at a cost of $20,000. If the property values in the district are projected to increase by 2% after the sidewalk improvements, each of the affected taxing units may choose to dedicate all, a portion of, or none of the property taxes that are due to the 2% increase in property values within the zone. The decision as to what percentage of the increased tax revenues to contribute to the tax increment fund is entirely discretionary with the governing bodies of each of the taxing units.[665] The city itself has the flexibility to determine its portion of the tax increment produced by the city that must be paid into the tax increment fund.[666] However, if the city does not make a determination of its portion of the tax increment produced by the city that must be paid into the tax increment fund, then the city is required to pay into the fund the entire tax increment produced.

Any agreement to contribute must indicate the portion of the tax increment to be paid into the fund and the years for which the tax increment will be paid. In addition to any other terms to which the parties may agree, the agreement may specify the projects to which a participating taxing unit's tax increment will be dedicated and that the taxing unit's participation may be computed with respect to a base year later than the original base year of the zone.[667] The agreement may also include other conditions for payment of the tax increment. Only property taxes attributable to real property within the zone are eligible for contribution to the tax increment fund.[668] Property taxes on personal property are not eligible for contribution into the tax increment plan.

Cities are allowed to deposit the amount of sales tax attributable to reinvestment zone into the tax increment fund, in an increment above the sales tax base[669] attributable to the zone in the year the zone was created.[670] Cities may choose not to contribute sales tax increment into a tax increment fund. Before the issuance of a bond, note, or other obligation that pledges the payments of sales tax increment into the tax increment fund, the governing body of the city may enter into an agreement to authorize and direct the Comptroller to:

1. Withhold from any payment to which the city may be entitled the amount of the payment into the tax increment fund;
2. Deposit that amount into the tax increment fund; and
3. Continue withholding and making additional payments into the tax increment fund until an amount sufficient to satisfy the amount due has been met.[671]

---

[665]   *Id.* § 311.013(f).
[666]   *Id.* § 311.013(l). *See also id.* § 311.013(m) (For special rules for such reduction in the tax increment in certain populous counties).
[667]   *Id.* §311.013(f).
[668]   *See id.* § 311.012 ("[T]ax increment," "captured appraised value," and "tax increment base" all defined with reference to the taxable real property within the reinvestment zone).
[669]   *Id.* § 311.0123(a) (West 2008).
[670]   *Id.* § 311.0123(b).
[671]   *Id.* § 311.0123(c)(1)-(3).

Also, a local government corporation created under Chapter 431 of the Transportation Code, that has contracted with a reinvestment zone and the city may be a party to an agreement with the Comptroller's office as referenced above. This agreement may provide for payments to be made to a paying agent of the local government corporation.[672] The sales tax to be deposited into the tax increment fund may be disbursed from the fund only to:

1. Satisfy claims of holders of tax increment bonds, notes, or other obligations issued or incurred for the reinvestment zone;
2. Pay project costs for the zone; and
3. Make payments in accordance with an agreement dedicating revenue from the tax increment fund made pursuant to Section 311.10(b) of the Tax Code.[673]

Unless otherwise specified by an agreement between the taxing unit and the city or county that created the zone, payment of the taxing unit's increment to the fund must be made by the 90th day after the later of: (1) the delinquency date for the unit's property taxes; or (2) the date the city or county that created the zone submits to the taxing unit an invoice specifying the tax increment produced by the taxing unit and the amount the taxing unit is required to pay into the tax increment fund for the zone.[674] A delinquent payment incurs a penalty of 5% of the amount delinquent and accrues interest at an annual rate of 10%.[675] It is important to note, however, that a taxing unit is not required to pay into the tax increment fund the portion of a tax increment that is attributable to delinquent taxes until those taxes are actually collected.[676]

In lieu of permitting a portion of its tax increment to be paid into the tax increment fund, a taxing unit, including a city, may elect to offer the owners of taxable real property in the zone an exemption from ad valorem taxation for any increase in the property value as provided under the Property Redevelopment and Tax Abatement Act (Tax Code, Chapter 312).[677] Alternatively, a taxing unit, other than a school district, may offer a tax abatement to the property owners in the zone and enter into an agreement to contribute a tax increment into the fund.[678] In either case, any agreement to abate taxes on real property within a tax increment reinvestment zone must be approved both by the board of directors of the zone and by the governing body of each taxing unit that agrees to deposit any of its tax increment into the tax increment fund.[679]

In any contract entered into by the tax increment zone's board of directors with regard to bonds or other obligations, the board may promise not to approve any such tax abatement

---

[672]   *Id.* § 311.0123(d).
[673]   *Id.* § 311.0123(e).
[674]   *Id.* § 311.013(c) (West Supp. 2011).
[675]   *Id.* § 311.013(c-1).
[676]   *Id.* § 311.013(i).
[677]   *Id.* § 311.013(g).
[678]   *Id.* § 311.0125 (West 2008).
[679]   *Id.* §§ 311.013(g) (West Supp. 2011); .0125(b) (West 2008).

agreement.[680] If a taxing unit enters into a tax abatement agreement within a tax increment reinvestment zone, the taxes that are abated will not be considered in calculating the tax increment of the abating taxing unit or that taxing unit's deposit into the tax increment fund.[681]

The Governor's Office of Texas Economic Development and Tourism may recommend that a taxing unit enter into a tax abatement agreement. The board of directors of the zone and the taxing unit's governing body must consider any recommendations made by the Office of Texas Economic Development and Tourism.[682]

Step Seven:

Once the reinvestment zone is established, the board of directors must make recommendations to the governing body of the city or county on the implementation of the tax increment financing.[683]

Once the city, by ordinance, or the county, by order, has created the reinvestment zone, the board of directors may exercise any power granted to them by the Tax Increment Financing Act.[684] By ordinance, resolution or order, the city or county may authorize the board of directors of the reinvestment zone to exercise any of the city or county's powers with respect to the administration, management or operation of the zone or the implementation of the project plan for the zone.[685] However, the city or county may not authorize the board of directors to issue bonds, impose taxes or fees, exercise the power of eminent domain, or give final approval to the project plan. The board of directors may exercise any of the powers granted to the city or county under Section 311.008 of the Tax Code, except that the city or county must approve any acquisition or sale of real property.[686] Also, the city or county, by ordinance, resolution or order, may choose to restrict any power granted to the board of directors by Chapter 311 of the Tax Code.[687]

The board of directors and the city or county can contract with a local government corporation created under the Texas Transportation Corporation Act (Transportation Code Chapter 431, Subchapter D) or a political subdivision to manage the reinvestment zone and/or implement the project or financing plan.[688] The board, the local government corporation or political subdivision administering the zone can contract with the city to pay for city services in the zone out of the portion of the tax increment fund produced by the city, regardless of whether the service or their cost is identified in the project or financing plan.[689]

---

[680]   *Id.* § 311.0125(c) (West 2008).
[681]   *Id.* § 311.0125(d).
[682]   *Id.* § 311.0125(e).
[683]   *Id.* § 311.010(a) (West Supp. 2011).
[684]   *Id.* § 311.010(e).
[685]   *Id.* § 311.010(a).
[686]   *Id.* § 311.010(d)(2), .008(b)(2).
[687]   *Id.* § 311.010(d)(1).
[688]   *Id.* § 311.010(f).
[689]   *Id.* § 311.010(i).

Either the board of directors, city or county may enter into agreements that are necessary or convenient to implement the project plan and the reinvestment zone financing plan.[690] Such agreements can pledge or provide for the use of revenue from the tax increment fund and/or provide for the regulation or restriction of land use. These agreements are not subject to the competitive bidding requirements in Chapter 252 of the Local Government Code.[691] If the zone was created by petition, the board, with the approval of the city, may impose certain zoning restrictions within the zone.[692]

With the approval of the city or county that designated the reinvestment zone, the board of directors may establish and provide for the administration of programs for a public purpose of developing and diversifying the economy, eliminating unemployment and underemployment, and developing or expanding transportation, business and commercial activity in the zone.[693] This power includes but is not limited to, programs to make grants and loans from the tax increment fund. Also, the board has all the powers of a city under Chapter 380 of the Local Government Code with the approval of the city or the county. This approval may be granted in an ordinance by a city, or in an order by the county, approving a project plan or reinvestment zone financing plan or approving an amendment to a project plan or reinvestment financing plan.

If the board is pursuing a project to construct public right-of-ways or infrastructure within the zone, the board may enter into an agreement to pledge tax increment fund revenue to pay for land and easements located outside the zone if:

- the zone is or will be served by the rail transportation or bus rapid transit project;

- the land or the development rights or conservation easements in the land are acquired for the purpose of preserving the land in its natural or undeveloped condition; and

- the land is located in the county in which the zone is located.[694]

Also, the board is required to implement a program to enhance the participation of "disadvantaged businesses" in the procurement process in a zone created by petition.[695] The program shall make information concerning the procurement process and the opportunities within the zone available to disadvantage businesses. The board is required to compile an annual report listing the numbers and dollar amounts of contracts awarded to disadvantaged businesses during the previous year as well as the total number and dollar amount of all contracts awarded.[696]

---

[690]   *Id.* § 311.010(b).
[691]   *Id.* § 311.010(g).
[692]   *Id.* § 311.010(c).
[693]   *Id.* § 311.010(h).
[694]   *Id.* § 311.01005 (West 2008).
[695]   *Id.* § 311.0101.
[696]   *Id.* § 311.0101(c).

Step Eight:

The city or county must submit an annual report to the chief executive officer of each taxing unit that levies taxes on property within the zone.[697]

The report must be provided within 150 days of the end of the city's or county's fiscal year. The report must include the following items:

- the amount and source of revenue in the tax increment fund established for the zone;

- the amount and purpose of expenditures from the fund;

- the amount of principal and interest due on outstanding bonded indebtedness;

- the tax increment base and current captured appraised value retained by the zone;

- the captured appraised value shared by the city or county and other taxing units;

- the total amount of tax increments received; and

- any additional information necessary to demonstrate compliance with the tax increment financing plan adopted by the city or county.

A copy of the above report must be sent to the Comptroller's Office.[698]

Central Registry

The Comptroller shall maintain a central registry of:[699]

- reinvestment zones designated under the Tax Increment Financing Act;

- project plans and reinvestment zone financing plans adopted pursuant to the Tax Increment Financing Act; and

- the annual reports the city or county submitted to the chief executive officer of each taxing unit that levies taxes on property within the zone.

A city or county that designates a reinvestment zone or approves a project plan or reinvestment zone financing plan must deliver to the Comptroller's Office a report containing the following information:[700]

- a general description of each reinvestment zone. This description must include the size of the zone, the types of property located in the zone, the duration of

---

[697]   *Id.* § 311.016(a) (West Supp. 2011).
[698]   *Id.* § 311.016(b).
[699]   *Id.* § 311.019(a) (West 2008).
[700]   *Id.* § 311.019(b).

the zone, and the guidelines and criteria established for the zone under section 311.005 of the Tax Code;

- a copy of each project plan or reinvestment zone financing plan adopted; and

- "any other information required by the comptroller" that helps in the administration of the central registry and tax refund for economic development (Tax Code Chapter 111, subchapter F).

The plan must be delivered before April 1 of the year following the year the zone is designated or the plan is approved. A city or county that amends or modifies a project plan or reinvestment zone financing plan must deliver a copy of the amendment or modifications to the Comptroller before April 1st of the year following the year in which the plan was amended or modified.[701]

State Assistance

Cities and counties with concerns about the tax increment financing laws can seek assistance from the state. The Comptroller's Office will provide assistance regarding the administration of the Tax Increment Financing Act upon request of the governing body or the presiding officer.[702] Further, the Governor's Office of Texas Economic Development and Tourism and the Comptroller's Office may provide technical assistance to a city or county regarding the designation of a tax increment financing reinvestment zone or the adoption and execution of project plans or reinvestment zone financing plans.[703]

School Districts

Until September 1, 1999, school districts were able to reduce the value of taxable property reported to the state to reflect any value lost due to tax increment financing participation by the district.[704] The ability of the school district to deduct the value of the tax increment that it contributed prevented the school district from being negatively affected in terms of state school funding. However, the situation is different for tax increment reinvestment zones created after that date. The Comptroller is statutorily prohibited from reducing taxable property value for school districts to reflect tax increment financing losses for zones that are proposed on or after May 31, 1999.[705] This statutory prohibition affects any amendments to or new tax increment financing agreements the school districts make with cities or counties after September 1, 1999.

---

[701] *Id.* § 311.019(c).
[702] *Id.* § 311.020(a).
[703] *Id.* § 311.020(b).
[704] In tax increment financing, value is not actually "lost." Rather, some of the land's increase in value is classified as "captured appraised value" so that an amount of taxes can be forwarded to the tax increment financing board. Such taxes are, in effect, "lost" to the school district because they must be contributed to the tax increment fund and cannot be used for school programs.
[705] *See* TEX. GOV'T CODE ANN. § 403.302(d)-(e) (West Supp. 2011). *See also* Tex. Att'y Gen. Op. GA-549 (2007).

Additionally, some cities may enter into tax increment financing agreements with school districts for certain limited purposes.[706] Cities with a population of less than 130,000 that have territory in three counties may enter into new tax increment financing agreements or may amend existing agreements with a school district located wholly or partially within the reinvestment zone. However, the agreement must be for the dedication of revenue from the tax increment fund to the school district for the purpose of acquiring, constructing or reconstructing an educational facility located inside or outside the tax increment financing reinvestment zone.[707]

Termination of Reinvestment Zone

A tax increment financing reinvestment zone terminates on the earlier of:

1) the termination date designated in the original ordinance or order designating the zone;

2) the earlier or later termination date designated by a subsequent ordinance or order adopted under Section 311.007(c) of the Tax Code;[708] or

3) the date on which all project costs, tax increment bonds and interest on those bonds are paid in full.[709]

If the city or county that created the zone designate a later termination date through a subsequent ordinance or order, the other contributing taxing units are not required to pay any of their tax increment after the original termination date unless those taxing units enter into an agreement to continue to pay their tax increment with the city or county that created the zone.[710] Also, a city or county that created the zone can terminate the zone before all debts and obligations are paid in full.[711] The city or county would have to deposit an amount that would suffice to pay the principal of, premium, and interest on all bonds issued with a trustee or escrow agent. The amount deposited would also have to

---

[706]   TEX. TAX CODE ANN. § 311.0085 (West Supp. 2011).

[707]   *Id.* § 311.0085(c).

[708]   *Id.* § 311.017(a)(1).

[709]   *Id.* § 311.017(a)(2).

[710]   *Id.* § 311.017(a-1) (West Supp. 2011). *See id.* 311.017(a-1) (Different terminations dates for a city that has a population of more than 220, 000 but less than 235,000 or more and is the county seat of a county that has a population of 280,000 or less). *See also* Tex. H.B. 2853 § 22, 82nd Leg., R.S. (2011) (The legislature validates and confirms all governmental acts and proceedings of a city or county, the board of directors of a reinvestment zone, or an entity acting under Section 311.010(f) of the Tax Code that were taken before the effective date of this Act and relate to or are associated with the designation, operation, or administration of a reinvestment zone or the implementation of a project plan or reinvestment zone financing plan under Chapter 311 of the Tax Code including the extension of the term of a reinvestment Zone, as of the dates on which they occurred. The acts and proceedings may not be held invalid because they were not in accordance with Chapter 311 of the Tax Code, or other law. This section does not apply to any matter that on the 30th day after the effective date of this Act: (1) is involved in litigation if the litigation ultimately results in the matter being held invalid by a final judgment of a court; or (2) has been held invalid by a final judgment of a court.).

[711]   TEX. TAX CODE ANN. § 311.017(b) (West Supp. 2011).

cover any other amounts that may become due to the trustee or escrow agent, including compensation of the trustee or escrow agent.

Validation Statute

A governmental act or proceeding of a city or county, the board of directors of a reinvestment zone, or an entity acting under Section 311.010(f) of the Tax Code relating to the designation, operation, or administration or a reinvestment zone financing plan is conclusively presumed, as of the date it occurred, valid and to have occurred in accordance with all applicable statutes and rules if:

1. the 3rd anniversary of the effective date of the act or proceeding has expired; and
2. a lawsuit to annul or invalidate the act or proceeding has not been filed on or before the later of that 2nd anniversary or August 1, 2011.[712]

However, the validation of an action as to the designation, operation, or administration of a reinvestment zone or the implementation of a project plan or reinvestment zone financing plan does not apply to the following:
1. An act or proceeding that was void at the time it occurred;
2. An act or proceeding that, under a statute of this state or the United States, was a misdemeanor or felony at the time the act or proceeding occurred;
3. A rule that, at the time it was passed, was preempted by a statute or this state or the United States, including Section 1.06 or 109.57 of the Alcoholic Beverage Code; or
4. A matter that as of the effective date of Section 311.021 of the Tax Code (June 17, 2011):
   a. Is involved in litigation if the litigation ultimately results in the matter being held invalid by a final judgment of a court; or
   b. Has been held invalid by a final judgment of a court.[713]

Texas Economic Development Act

The Texas Economic Development Act ("the Act'") is another economic development tool used to attract new industries and commercial enterprises. Chapter 313 of the Tax Code authorizes certain property tax incentives for economic development provided by school districts. School districts have the ability to provide tax credits and an eight-year limitation on appraised value of a property for the maintenance and operations portion of the school district property tax to eligible corporations and limited liability companies. The property remains fully taxable or the purpose of any school district debt service tax.

---

[712] *Id.* § 311.021(a).
[713] *Id.* § 311.021(b).

Eligibility Requirements for Limitation on Appraised Values

The Act provides that only particular entities are eligible for limitations on appraised property values. Limitations on appraised values are available to property owned by a corporation or a limited liability company to which a franchise tax pursuant to section 171.001 of the Tax Code applies.[714] These eligible corporations or limited liability companies are required to make investments that create jobs within the state. Further, these corporations and limited liability companies must use the property for:[715]

- manufacturing;[716]

- research and development;[717]

- clean coal project as defined by section 5.001 of the Water Code;

- advanced clean energy project as defined by section 382.003 of the Health & Safety Code;

- renewable energy electric generation;[718]

- electric power generation using integrated gasification combined cycle technology;[719]

- nuclear electric power generation;[720] or

- a computer center[721] primarily used in connection with one or more activities described above.

Creation of Qualifying Jobs

In order for the eligible property of these corporations or limited liability companies to receive a limitation of appraised values, the recipient must make a commitment to create a specified number of new jobs and "qualifying jobs." The number of new jobs and "qualifying jobs" required to be created depends upon whether the school district is considered a non- rural school district or a rural school district

Non-Rural School District Versus Rural School District
The Act has created different investment requirements and minimum limitation requirements for owners of qualified property in rural school districts as opposed to non-rural school districts. A school district is considered a rural school district if:

---

[714] TEX. TAX CODE ANN § 313.024(a) (West Supp. 2011). ("This subchapter [subchapter B] and Subchapters C and D apply only to property owned by a corporation or limited liability company to which Section 171.001 applies.").

[715] *Id.* § 313.024(b).

[716] *See Id.* § 313.024(e)(1) (Definition of manufacturing).

[717] *See Id.* § 313.024(e)(5) (Definition of research and development).

[718] *See Id.* § 313.024(e)(2) (Definition of renewable energy electric generation).

[719] *See Id.* § 313.024(e)(3) (Definition of integrated gasification combined cycle technology).

[720] *See Id.* § 313.024(e)(4) (Definition of nuclear electric power generation).

[721] *See Id.* § 313.024(e)(6) (Definition of computer center).

- the school district has territory in a strategic investment area under Subchapter O of Chapter 171 of the Tax Code immediately before subchapter O expired;[722] or

- the school district is located in a county:[723]

  - with a population of less than 50,000; and

  - in which, from 1990 to 2000, according to the federal decennial census, the population either remained the same, decreased, or increased at a rate not greater than three percent annually.[724]

If a school district qualifies as a rural school district, then that school district can utilize Subchapter C of Chapter 313 of the Tax Code which allows differing amounts with regard to the categorization of rural school districts, minimum amounts of qualified investments, and minimum limitations on appraised values requirements on qualified property. The non-rural school district can utilize Subchapter B.

In non-rural school districts, a property owner is required to create "at least 25 new jobs" on the owner's qualified property.[725] At least 80% of all the new jobs created must be "qualifying jobs."[726] A "qualifying job" for a non-rural school district is defined to mean a permanent full-time job that:[727]

- requires at least 1,600 hours of work a year;

- is not transferred from one area in this state to another area in this state;

- is not created to replace a previous employee;

- is covered by a group health benefit plan for which the business offers to pay at least 80% of the premiums or other charges assessed for employee-only coverage under the plan, regardless of whether an employee may voluntarily waive the coverage; and

- pays at least 110% of:

  - the county average weekly wage for manufacturing jobs[728] in the county or region where the job is located, or

---

722   *Id.* § 313.051(a)(1) (Note: section 171.721(2) of the Tax Code was repealed by the 79th Legislature. A list of counties designated as strategic investment areas at the end of 2008 can be found at: http://www.window.state.tx.us/taxinfo/proptax/ecodev.html under "List of Counties").

723   *Id* § 313.051(a)(2).

724   *See* Population in 1990 and 2000, Numerical and Percent Change in Population 1990 to 2000 in Counties in Texas - Ranked by Percent Change table at: http://txsdc.utsa.edu/Reports/Subject/Population.aspx.

725   TEX. TAX CODE ANN. § 313.021(2)(A)(iv)(b) (West Supp. 2011).

726   *Id.* § 313.024(d).

727   *Id.* § 313.021(3).

728   *See Id.* § 313.021(5) (Definition of county average weekly wage for manufacturing jobs).

- The county average weekly wage for all industries in the county where the job is located, if the property owner creates more than 1,000 jobs in the county.[729]

In rural school districts, a property owner is required to create at least 10 new jobs on the owner's qualified property.[730] At least 80 percent of all the new jobs created must be "qualifying jobs." A "qualifying job" for a rural school district has the same meaning as a qualifying job for a non-rural school district.[731]

Other Eligibility Considerations

In determining an applicant's eligibility for a property limitation, whether located in a non-rural school district or a rural school district, other eligibility considerations are taken into account. These other considerations are:

- land on which a building or component of a building described by Section 313.021(1)(E) of the Tax Code is located is not considered a qualified investment[732];

- property that is leased under a capitalized lease may be considered a qualified investment;

- property that is leased under an operating lease may not be considered a qualified investment; and

- property that is owned by a person other than the applicant and that is pooled or proposed to be pooled with property owned by the applicant may not be included in determining the amount of the applicant's qualifying investment.[733]

Categorization of School Districts

The Act authorizes school districts to make limitations on appraised property values, provided the eligible entity makes qualified investments on qualified property. Non-rural school districts and rural school district are sorted into five categories to determine the minimum amount of qualified investment the entity must make and the minimum amount of limitation the school district may provide on appraised property values. The Comptroller's Website has a complete listing of school district classifications, minimum amounts of qualified investments, and limitations on appraised values at: www.window.state.tx.us/taxinfo/proptax/hb1200/values.html.

---

[729]   *Id.* § 313.021(5).
[730]   *Id.* § 313.051(b).
[731]   *See id.* § 313.021(3) (Definition of qualified jobs).
[732]   *See id.* § 313.021(1) (Definition of qualified investment).
[733]   *Id.* § 313.024(c).

Non-Rural School Districts

Non-rural school districts are categorized according to the taxable value of property within the district in the preceding tax year as determined by chapter 403 of the Government Code.[734] Non-rural school districts are categorized as follows:[735]

I $10 billion or more of taxable property
II $1 billion or more but less than $10 billion of taxable property
III $500 million or more but less than $1 billion of taxable property
IV $100 million or more but less than $500 million of taxable property
V.   less than $100 million of taxable property.

Rural School Districts

Likewise, rural schools districts are categorized according to the taxable value of *industrial* property within the district in the preceding tax year as determined by chapter 403 of the Government Code.[736] Rural school districts are categorized as follows:[737]

I $200 million or more of taxable industrial property
II $90 million or more but less than $200 million of taxable industrial property
III $1 million or more but less than $90 million of taxable industrial property
IV $100,000 or more but less than $1 million of taxable industrial property
V   less than $100,000 of taxable industrial property.

---

[734]   *Id.* § 313.022(b).
[735]   *Id.*
[736]   *Id.* § 313.052.
[737]   *Id.*

Minimum Amount of a Qualified Investment and Limitation on Appraised Values

Non-Rural School Districts

The minimum amounts of qualified investment[738] and the minimum amounts of limitation[739] for each category of non-rural school districts are as follows:

Category	Minimum Amounts Of Qualified Investment	Minimum Amounts Of Limitation on Appraised Values
I	$100 million	$100 million
II	$ 80 million	$ 80 million
III	$ 60 million	$ 60 million
IV	$ 40 million	$ 40 million
V	$ 20 million	$ 20 million

A Non-rural school district, regardless of category, may agree to limitations greater than the minimum amounts.[740]

Rural School Districts

The minimum amounts of qualified investment[741] and minimum amounts of limitation on appraised values [742] for each category of rural school districts are as follows:

Category	Minimum Amounts Of Qualified Investment	Minimum Amounts Of Limitation on Appraised Values
I	$ 30 million	$ 30 million
II	$ 20 million	$ 20 million
III	$ 10 million	$ 10 million
IV	$ 5 million	$ 5 million
V	$ 1 million	$ 1 million

Again, a rural school district, regardless of category, may agree to limitations greater than the minimum amounts.[743]

Limitation Agreement

Any limitation agreement between the school board or a non-rural or a rural school district and the property owner must be in writing.[744] The written agreement must describe with specificity the qualified investment that the person will make on or in

---

[738]   *Id.* § 313.023.
[739]   *Id.* § 313.027(b).
[740]   *Id.* § 313.027(c).
[741]   *Id.* § 313.053.
[742]   *Id.* § 313.054(a).
[743]   *Id.* § 313.054(b).
[744]   *Id.* § 313.027(d).

connection with the person's qualified property that is subject to the limitation on appraised value.[745] Other property of the person that is not specifically described in the agreement is not subject to the limitation agreement unless the school board, by official action, provides that the other property is subject to the limitation. Additionally, the agreement:[746]

- must incorporate each relevant provision of subchapter B of Chapter 313 of the Tax Code and, to the extent necessary, include provisions for the protection of future school district revenues through the adjustment of the minimum valuations, the payment of revenue offsets, and other mechanisms agreed to by the property owner and the school district;

- may provide that the property owner will protect the school district in the event the district incurs extraordinary education-related expenses related to the project that are directly funded in state aid formulas, including expenses for the purchase of portable classrooms and the hiring of additional personnel to accommodate a temporary increase in student enrollment attributable to the project;

- must require the property owner to maintain a viable presence in the school district for at least three years after the expiration of the limitation agreement;

- must provide for the termination of the agreement, the recapture of ad valorem tax revenue lost as a result of the agreement if the owner of the property fails to comply with the terms of the agreement, and payment of penalty, interest or both on the recaptured ad valorem tax revenue;

- may specify any conditions that will require the district and the property owner to renegotiate all or any part of the agreement; and

- must specify the ad valorem tax years covered by the agreement.

A limitation agreement may provide for a deferral of the date on which the qualifying time period[747] for the project is to commence, or an agreement may be amended to provide for such a deferral.[748] A subsequent agreement amending the deferral date may not be construed to permit a qualifying time period that has commenced to continue for more than the number of years applicable to the project.

A limitation agreement many not be entered into under which a person agrees to provide supplement payments to a school district in an amount that exceeds an amount equal to $100 per student per year in average daily attendance, or for a period that exceeds the

---

[745]   *Id.* § 313.027(e).
[746]   *Id.* § 313.027(f).
[747]   *See id.* § 313.021(4) (Definition of qualified time period).
[748]   *Id.* § 313.027(h).

period beginning with the qualified time period and ending with the period described in section 313.104(2)(B) of the Tax Code.[749]

Application for Property Limitation

The owner of qualified property may apply to the school district's board of trustees in which the property is located for a limitation on the appraised value for school district maintenance and operations ad valorem tax purposes of the person's qualified property.[750] An application must be made on the form prescribed by the State Comptroller. A copy of this application may be obtained from the Comptroller's Website at: www.window.state.tx.us/taxinfo/proptax/hb1200/index.html.

Additionally, the application must be accompanied by: [751]

- the application fee established by the school board of trustees;

- information sufficient to show that the real and personal property identified in the application meets the definition of "qualified property"; and

- information relating to each economic impact evaluation criterion.

Application fee, qualified property and economic impact evaluation criterion are discussed below.

Application Fee

The school board by official action shall establish a reasonable, nonrefundable application fee to be paid by property owners who apply to the district for a limitation on the appraised value of the person's qualified property. [752] The amount of an application fee must be reasonable and may not exceed the estimated cost to the district of processing and acting on an application, including the cost of the economic impact evaluation.

Qualified Property

As mentioned above, jobs and qualified jobs have to be created on qualified property. "Qualified property" is defined to mean:[753]

- **land**:

  - that is located in an area designated as a tax increment financing reinvestment zone under Chapter 311 of the Tax Code, a tax abatement reinvestment zone under Chapter 312 of the Tax Code, or an enterprise zone under Chapter 2303 of the Government Code;

---

[749]   *Id.* § 313.027(i) (Note: This limitation does not apply to the amounts described in section 313.027(f)(1) or (2) of the Tax Code).
[750]   *Id.* § 313.025(a).
[751]   *Id.*
[752]   *Id.* § 313.031(b).
[753]   *Id.* § 313.021(2).

- on which a person proposes to construct a new building or erect or affix a new improvement that does not exist before the date the owner applies for a limitation on appraised value;

- that is not subject to a tax abatement agreement entered into by a school district under Chapter 312 of the Tax Code; and

- on which, in connection with the new building or new improvement described above, the owner of the land proposes to:

  - make a qualified investment in an amount equal to at least the minimum amount required by Section 313.023 of the Tax Code; and

  - create at least 25 new jobs;[754]

- **a new building or other new improvement** that a person proposes to construct or affix that does not exist before the date the owner applies for a limitation on appraised value;[755] or

- **tangible personal property** that:

  - is not subject to a tax abatement agreement entered into by a school district under Chapter 312 of the Tax Code;[756] and

  - except for new equipment described in sections 151.318(q) (semiconductor fabrication cleanrooms and equipment) or 151.318(q-1) (pharmaceutical biotechnology cleanrooms and equipment) of the Tax Code, is first placed in service:

    o in the new building or in or on the new improvement that a person proposes to construct or affix that does not exist before the date the owner applies for a limitation on appraised value, or

    o on the land on which that new building or new improvement is located, if the personal property is ancillary and necessary to the business conducted in the new building or in or on the new improvement.[757]

Economic Impact Evaluation

As indicated earlier, an economic impact evaluation must accompany an application for limited appraisal value.[758] The school district must request this evaluation from the

---

[754] *Id.* § 313.021(2)(A)(iv)(b). *But see id.* § 313.051(b) (property owner located in rural school district subject to Subchapter C is "required to create only at least 10 new jobs on the owner's qualified property.").

[755] *Id.* §§ 313.021(2)(A)(ii), .021(2)(B).

[756] *Id.* § 313.021(2)(C)(i). *See also id.* § 312.002(f) (West 2008).

[757] *Id.* § 313.021(2)(C)(ii) (West Supp. 2011).

[758] *Id.* § 313.025(a)(3).

Comptroller's office.[759] The economic impact evaluation must contain the following criteria:[760]

1) the recommendations of the Comptroller;

2) the name of the school district;

3) the name of the applicant;

4) the general nature of the applicant's investment;

5) the relationship between the applicant's industry and the types of qualifying jobs to be created by the applicant to the long-term economic growth plans of this state as described in the strategic plan for economic development submitted by the Texas Strategic Economic Development Planning Commission under Section 481.033, Government Code, as that section existed before February 1, 1999;

6) the relative level of the applicant's investment per qualifying job to be created by the applicant;

7) the number of qualifying jobs to be created by the applicant;

8) the wages, salaries and benefits to be offered by the applicant to qualifying job holders;

9) the ability of the applicant to locate or relocate in another state or another region of this state;

10) the impact the project will have on this state and individual local units and government, including:

   a. tax and other revenue gains, direct or indirect, that would be realized during the qualifying time period, the limitation period, and a period of time after the limitation period considered appropriate by the comptroller; and

   b. economic effects of the project, including the impact on jobs and income, during the qualifying time period, the limitation period, and a period of time after the limitation period considered appropriate by the comptroller;

11) the economic condition of the region of the state at the time the person's application is being considered;

12) the number of new facilities built or expanded in the region during the two years preceding the date of the application that were eligible to apply for a limitation on appraised value; and

13) the effect of the applicant's proposal, if approved, on the number or size of the school district's instructional facilities[761];

---

759   *Id.* § 313.025(b).
760   *Id.* § 313.026.

14)   the projected market value of the qualified property of the applicant as determined by the comptroller;

15)   the proposed limitation on appraised value for the qualified property of the applicant;

16)   the projected dollar amount of the taxes that would be imposed on the qualified property, for each year of the agreement, if the property does not receive a limitation appraised value with assumptions of the projected appreciation or depreciation of the investment clearly stated;

17)   the projected dollar amount of the taxes that would be imposed on the qualified property, for each year of the agreement, if the property received a limitation appraised value with assumptions of the projected appreciation or depreciation of the investment clearly stated;

18)   the projected effect on the Foundation School Program of payments to the district for each year of the agreement;

19)   the projected future tax credit if the applicant also applies for school tax credits under section 313.103 of the Tax Code; and

20)   the total amount of taxes projected to be lost or gained by the district over the life of the agreement computed by subtracting the projected taxes stated in number 17 from the projected taxes stated in number 16.

The comptroller's recommendation is based on number 5 thorough 20 of the list above.[762]

Approval Process for Application for Property Limitation

The school district board of trustees is not required to consider an application for a limitation on appraised value.[763] Should the school board elect to consider the application, the school district must submit three copies of the application to the Comptroller's office within seven days of receiving each document and request an economic impact evaluation of the application.[764]

Upon receipt of the application from the school district, the Comptroller shall conduct an economic impact evaluation and provide a copy of it to the school district as soon as practicable. The school district will provide a copy of the economic impact evaluation to the applicant on request. The comptroller will make a recommendation to the school district on whether to accept or reject the application, based on the criteria in the economic impact evaluation, input for the Texas Education Agency[765] and any other

---

[761]   *See* TEX. EDUC. CODE ANN. § 46.001 (West 2006) (Definition of instructional facilities).

[762]   TEX. TAX CODE ANN. § 313.026(b) (West Supp. 2011).

[763]   *Id.* § 313.025(b).

[764]   *Id.* § 313.025(a-1), (b) (Note: Section 313.025(a-1) requires the school district to submit "a copy of the application and agreement" to the Comptroller, while section 313.025(b) requires the school district to submit "three copies of the application" to the Comptroller).

[765]   *Id.* § 313.025(b-1).

information available to the Comptroller, including information provided by the school district.[766] The Comptroller has no more than 91 days to review and give a recommendation concerning the approval or disapproval of an application after receiving it from the school district.[767]

The school board must approve or disapprove the application before the 151st day after the date the application is filed, unless an extension is agreed to by the school board and the applicant.[768] The school district must make a written finding as to each economic impact evaluation criterion before approving or disapproving the application. Further, the school board is required to deliver a copy of those findings to the applicant.[769] Also, in determining whether to grant an application, the school board must consider any recommendations made by the Governor's Office of Texas Economic Development and Tourism.[770] The Governor's Office of Texas Economic Development and Tourism is authorized to recommend that a school district grant a person a limitation on appraised values. Further, the school board is entitled to request and receive assistance in deciding whether to grant an application from: (1) the Comptroller; (2) the Governor's Office of Texas Economic Development and Tourism; (3) the Texas Workforce Investment Council; and (4) the Texas Workforce Commission.[771]

---

[766]   *Id.* § 313.026(b).
[767]   *Id.* § 313.025(d).
[768]   *Id.* § 313.025(b).
[769]   *Id.* § 313.025(e).
[770]   *Id.* § 313.025(g).
[771]   *Id.* § 313.025(c).

**Texas Comptroller of Public Accounts:
Economic Development and Analysis
Division**
111 E. 17th Street
Austin, Texas 78774
Phone: (512) 463-4679
Toll Free: (800) 531-5441 ext. 3-4679
Fax: (512) 475-0664

**Governor's Office of Texas Economic
Development and Tourism**
P.O. Box 12428
Austin, Texas 78711
Phone: (512) 936-0101
Fax: (512) 936-0303

Texas Workforce Commission
101 E. 15th Street
Austin, Texas 78778
Phone: (512) 463-2222

**Texas Workforce Investment Council:
Office of the Governor**
P.O. Box 12428
Austin, Texas 78711
Phone: (512) 936-8100
Fax: (512) 936-8118

Once the school district has received its recommendations from the Comptroller and any other recommendations concerning the application for limitation on the appraised value of the person's qualified property, the school board may approve an application only if the school board finds that: [772]

- the information in the application is true and correct;

- the applicant is eligible for the limitation on the appraised value of the person's qualified property; and

- determine that granting the application is in the best interest of the school district and the State of Texas.

The school district may approve an application that the Comptroller has recommended should be disapproved only if: [773]

- the school board holds a public hearing for the sole purpose to consider the application and the comptroller's recommendation; and

- at a subsequent meeting of the school board held after the public hearing, at least two-thirds of the members of the school board vote to approve the application.

Limitation on Appraised Values

If a person's application is approved by the school board, for each of the first eight tax years that begin after the applicable qualifying time period, the appraised value of the

---

[772]   *Id.* § 313.025(f).
[773]   *Id.* § 313.025(d-1).

person's qualified property, as described in the agreement may not exceed the lesser of:[774]

- the market value of the property; or
- an amount agreed to by the school board of trustees, in accordance with the following:

Category	Non-Rural School Districts Minimum Amount Of Limitation [775]	Rural School Districts Minimum Amount Of Limitation [776]
I	$100 million	$ 30 million
II	$ 80 million	$ 20 million
III	$ 60 million	$ 10 million
IV	$ 40 million	$5 million
V	$ 20 million	$ 1 million

The "qualifying time period" generally begins the date the school district approves an application, and ends December 31st of the second complete tax year following that date except for nuclear electric power generation facilities or advanced clean energy projects.[777]

When appraising a person's qualified property that is subject to a limitation on appraised value, the chief appraiser of the appraisal district where the qualified property is located shall determine the market value of the property and include in the appraisal records both the market value and the appropriate value agreed to by the school board subject to the minimum limitation amounts listed above.[778]

Recapture of Lost Revenue of Ad Valorem Taxes

A person with whom the school district enters into an agreement of limitation on appraised value of qualified property must make the minimum amount of qualified investment during the qualifying time period and create the required number of qualifying jobs during each year of the agreement.[779] If in any tax year a property owner fails to meet the obligations of the agreement, the property owner is liable to the state for a penalty for a certain amount.[780] If the penalty is not paid by February 1st of the

---

[774]   *Id.* § 313.027(a).
[775]   *Id.* § 313.027(b).
[776]   *Id.* § 313.054(a).
[777]   *Id.* § 313.021(4).
[778]   *Id.* § 313.027(g).
[779]   *Id.* § 313.0275(a).
[780]   *Id.* § 313.0275(b) (The penalty is the amount computed by subtracting from the market value of the property for that tax year the value of the property as limited by the agreement and multiplying the difference by the maintenance and operations tax rate of the school district for that tax year).

following tax year, it becomes delinquent in accordance with section 33.01 of the Tax Code.[781]

Tax Credits

In addition to the limitation on appraised values under either subchapter B or C of the Act, a person is entitled to receive a tax credit from the school district that approved the limitation. The amount of the tax credit is an amount equal to the amount of ad valorem taxes paid to that school district that were imposed on the portion of the appraised value of the qualified property that exceeds the amount of the limitation agreed to by the school board in each complete tax year of the applicable qualifying time period.[782] Should the person relocate the business outside the school district, the person would not be entitled to the tax credit in or after the year in which the person relocated the business.[783]

Application for Tax Credit

An application for the tax credit must be made to the school board to which the ad valorem taxes were paid. The application for the tax credit must be:[784]

- made on the form prescribed for that purpose by the State Comptroller and verified by the applicant. A copy of the application for tax credit may be obtained at the Comptroller's Website at:

  http://www.window.state.tx.us/taxinfo/proptax/hb1200/index.html;

- accompanied by:

  - a tax receipt from the collector of taxes for the school district showing full payment of school district ad valorem taxes on the qualified property for the applicable qualifying time period; and

  - any other document or information that the comptroller or the school board considers necessary for a determination of the applicant's eligibility for the credit or the amount of the credit.

Action on Application and Grant of Tax Credit

Before granting an application for tax credit, the school board must:[785]

- determine the person's eligibility for a tax credit; and

- if the person's application is approved, by order or resolution direct the collector of taxes for the school district:

---

781   *Id.* § 313.0275(c).
782   *Id.* § 313.102(a).
783   *Id.* § 313.102(b).
784   *Id.* § 313.103(a).
785   *Id.* § 313.104.

- in the second and subsequent six tax years that begin after the date the application is approved, to credit against the taxes imposed on the qualified property by the district in that year an amount equal to one-seventh of the total amount of tax credit to which the person is entitled under Section 313.102 of the Tax Code, except that the amount of a credit granted in any of those tax years may not exceed 50% of the total amount of ad valorem school taxes imposed on the qualified property by the school district in that tax year; and

- in the first three tax years that begin on or after the date the person's eligibility for the limitation under Subchapter B or C expires, to credit against the taxes imposed on the qualified property by the district an amount equal to the portion of the total amount of tax credit to which the person is entitled under Section 313.102 of the Tax Code that was not credited against the person's taxes under the above section in a tax year covered by the above section, except that the amount of a tax credit granted under this paragraph in any tax year may not exceed the total amount of ad valorem school taxes imposed on the qualified property by the school district in that tax year.

Remedy for Erroneous Tax Credit

If the State Comptroller and the school board determine that a person who received a tax credit was not entitled to the credit or was entitled to a lesser amount of credit, an additional tax will be imposed on the qualified property equal to the full credit or the amount of the credit to which the person was not entitled, as applicable, plus interest at an annual rate of 7%. The interest rate is calculated from the date the credit was issued.[786] Further, a tax lien can be attached to the qualified property to secure payment of the additional tax and interest imposed and any penalties incurred. A person delinquent in the payment of an additional tax cannot submit a subsequent application or receive a tax credit in a subsequent year.[787]

Disclosure of Appraised Value Limitation Information

The Comptroller shall post on the comptroller's website each document or item of information the comptroller designates as substantive before the 15th day after the date the document or item of information is received or created.[788] Each document or item of information must continue to be posted until the appraised value limitation expires. The comptroller shall designate the following as substantive:[789]

- Each application requesting a limitation on appraised value;

- The economic impact evaluation made in connection with the application; and

---

[786]   *Id.* § 313.105(a).
[787]   *Id.* § 313.105(b).
[788]   *Id.* § 313.0265(a).
[789]   *Id.* § 313.0265(b).

- Each application requesting school tax credits.

If the school district maintains a generally accessible website, the district shall maintain a link on its website to the area of the Comptroller's website where the information on each district's agreements to limited appraised value is maintained.[790]

Confidentiality of Business Information

Information provided to a school district in connection with an application for a limitation on appraised value that describes the specific processes or business activities to be conducted or the specific tangible personal property to be located on real property covered by the application shall be segregated in the application from the other information in the application and is confidential and not subject to public disclosure unless the school board approves the application.[791] Other information in the custody of the school district or the comptroller in connection with the application, including information related to the economic impact of a project or the essential elements of eligibility under this Act, such as the nature and amount of the projected investment, employment, wages, and benefits, may not be considered confidential business information if the school board agrees to consider the application. Information in the custody of the school district or the comptroller is not confidential if the school district approves the application. Also, applications for tax credit or any information provided to the school district to the Texas Education Agency under section 42.2515 of the Education Code is not confidential.[792]

Tax Abatement Agreements

Section 313.030 of the Tax Code provides that if property receives a limitation on appraised value in a particular tax year then the property is not eligible for a tax abatement agreement by the school district under Chapter 312 of the Tax Code in the same tax year.[793] Pursuant to Section 312.002(f) of the Tax Code, school districts are no longer authorized to enter into tax abatement agreements.[794]

Impact Fees

A city or county may impose and collect from the owner of a qualified property a reasonable impact fee to pay for the cost of providing improvements associated with or attributable to property that receives a property tax limitation.[795]

---

[790]   *Id.* § 313.0265(c).
[791]   *Id.* § 313.028.
[792]   *Id.* § 313.103(b).
[793]   *Id.* § 313.030.
[794]   *Id.* § 312.002(f).
[795]   *Id.* § 313.006(b).

Adopting the Freeport and Goods-in-transit Exemptions

Introduction

A constitutional amendment authorizes a type of property tax exemption for items classified as "Freeport property."[796] Freeport property includes various types of goods that are detained in Texas for a short period of time (175 days or less). The goods must be in Texas only for a limited purpose, such as storage or factory processing. This exemption was proposed to enhance the ability of certain areas to attract warehouse and distribution center facilities by offering a special property tax exemption for the goods they typically handle.

Another constitutional amendment authorizes an additional type of property tax exemption for items classified as "Goods-in-transit property."[797] The Goods-in-transit exemption is similar to the Freeport exemption with two key differences:

1) the Goods-in-transit exemption may apply to goods traveling inside the state; and

2) the Goods-in-transit exemption is only available for goods stored at locations, typically warehouses, owned by someone other than the owner of the goods themselves.

Freeport Exemption

The constitutional amendment was unusual from the standpoint that no action was necessary by taxing units that wanted to exempt Freeport property from taxation. The exemption was self-enacting unless the taxing units took specific action to continue to tax the property. If a city decided to override the Freeport exemption and continue taxing the property, the governing body of the city had to take official action to tax the property by April 1, 1990. The official action that was required was not defined under the law. It would likely have been in the form of a resolution, order or ordinance of the taxing unit to retain its right to tax Freeport property. Most cities and other taxing units took the necessary action at that time to continue to be able to tax the Freeport property.

A taxing unit is free to change its decision and choose to exempt Freeport property in order to promote economic development. Such a decision would be made by the governing body of the taxing unit by repealing the original resolution or ordinance to tax Freeport property. It must be emphasized, however, that if a taxing unit such as a city now chooses to exempt Freeport property, the exemption may not be repealed later. In other words, once the taxing unit chooses to exempt Freeport property, this type of property remains exempt from property taxation by that taxing unit forever.[798]

---

796   TEX. CONST. art. VIII § 1-j.
797   TEX. CONST. art. VIII § 1-n.
798   TEX. CONST. art VIII, § 1-j(b).

The Freeport exemption, if adopted, applies throughout the local taxing entity's jurisdiction. For example, if a city adopts the Freeport exemption, it applies throughout the entire city. Similarly, if a county or school district adopts the Freeport exemption, it applies throughout the entire taxing jurisdiction of that county or school district. A local government may not choose to exempt Freeport property in only a portion of its territory.

Freeport property includes goods, wares, merchandise, ores, and certain aircraft and aircraft parts.[799] It does not include oil, natural gas and other petroleum products. Petroleum products are defined as "liquid and gaseous materials that are the immediate derivatives of the refining of oil or natural gas."[800] Freeport property qualifies for an exemption from ad valorem taxation only if it has been detained in the state for 175 days or less for the purpose of assembly, storage, manufacturing, processing or fabricating.[801]. Some types of companies currently receiving Freeport tax exemptions include auto makers, computer manufacturers, beverage producers, iron works, warehousing and distribution facilities, and medical supply companies.

Even when goods are sold to an in-state purchaser rather than shipped directly out of state, they may qualify for the Freeport exemption. To receive the exemption in such a case, the property must qualify under the above requirements as Freeport property and must be transported out of the state within 175 days after it was first acquired in or imported into the state.[802]

Goods-in-transit Exemption

Like the Freeport exemption, the Goods-in-transit exemption is self-enacting unless taxing units hold a hearing and then take official action to tax the goods prior to January 1 of the first tax year in which the unit wishes to tax the goods. Unlike the Freeport exemption, taxing units are free to postpone their decision to tax Goods-in-transit goods until any future tax year.[803] For example, if a taxing unit failed to act to tax Goods-in-transit goods prior to January 1, 2008 (the first tax year the exemption went into effect), they could act again prior to January 1, 2009, to tax goods in that tax year, or likewise in any future year.

Goods-in-transit means tangible personal property that:

---

[799] TEX. CONST. art. VIII, § 1-j(a).

[800] TEX. TAX CODE ANN. § 11.251(j) (West 2008).

[801] *Id.* § 11.251(e); TEX. CONST. art. VIII. § 1-j(a).

[802] Op. Tex. Att'y Gen. No. DM-463 (1997) (Article VIII, section 1-j of the Texas Constitution establishes an exemption from ad valorem tax for "freeport" goods, that is, certain property destined for shipment out-of-state within 175 days after the date the property was acquired in or imported into the state. The freeport exemption is available to property where it is acquired or imported in this state by a person who detains it in the state "for assembling, storing, manufacturing, processing, or fabricating purposes," even though the property is not sold or transported out of the state by that person, but is instead sold to an in-state purchaser who uses the property in manufacturing other items which are then transported out of state within 175 days of the time the first owner acquired it.).

[803] TEX. TAX CODE ANN. § 11.253(j) (West Supp. 2011).

- is acquired in or imported into this state to be forwarded to another location in this state or outside the state;

- is stored under a contract of bailment by a public warehouse operator[804] at one or more public warehouse facilities in this state that are not in any way owned or controlled by the owner of the personal property for the account of the person who acquired or imported the property;

- is transported to another location in this state or outside this state not later than 175 days after the date the person acquired the property in or imported the property into this state; and

- does not include oil, natural gas, petroleum products, aircraft dealer's motor vehicle inventory, dealer's vessel and outboard motor inventory, dealer's heavy equipment inventory, or retail manufactured housing inventory.[805]

Additionally, if a taxing unit wants to tax Goods-in-transit on or after January 1, 2012, the taxing unit must take action to continue to tax on or after October 1, 2011 in the manner required for official action by the governing body.[806] The official action to tax the Goods-in-transit must be taken before January 1 of the first tax year in which the taxing unit proposes to tax Goods-in-transit. Before acting to tax the exempt property, the governing body of the taxing unit must conduct a public hearing as required by Section 1-n(d) of Article VIII of the Texas Constitution. If the governing body of a taxing unit provides for the taxation of the Goods-in-transit, the exemption does not apply to that unit unless the governing body by official action rescinds or repeals its previous action to tax Goods-in-transit. Also, if the governing body that took action to provide for the taxation of Good-in-transit and pledged the taxes imposed for payment of a debt of the taxing unit, the tax official of the taxing unit may continue to impose the taxes against the good-in-transit until the debt is discharged, if cessation of the imposition would impair the obligation of the contract by which the debt was created.[807]

Also, unlike the Freeport exemption, taxing units that repeal the decision to continue taxing Goods-in-transit goods (reinstating the exemption, in other words) apparently may choose to again tax the goods at some time in the future, provided they do so prior to January 1st of the first tax year they intend to again tax the goods.[808]

The Goods-in-transit exemption, if applicable, applies throughout the local taxing entity's jurisdiction. For example, if the Goods-in-transit exemption applies to a city, it applies throughout the entire city. Similarly, if a Goods-in-transit exemption applies to a county or school district, it applies throughout the entire taxing jurisdiction of that county or

---

[804]   *Id.* § 11.253(a)(6) (Definition of public warehouse operator). *See also id.* § 11.253(a)(5) (Definition of bailee and warehouse).
[805]   *Id.* § 11.253(a)(2).
[806]   *Id.* § 11.253(j-1).
[807]   *Id.* § 11.253(j-2).
[808]   *Id.* § 11.253(j).

school district. A local government may not choose to exempt Freeport property in only a portion of its territory.

Goods-in-transit property includes goods, wares, merchandise, ores and certain aircraft and aircraft parts.[809] It does not include oil, natural gas and other petroleum products.[810] The constitutional amendment that authorized the Goods-in-transit exemption would have permitted legislation allowing the goods to remain at a location for up to 270 days tax-free,[811] but the enabling legislation adopted a narrower, 175-day window that mirrors the Freeport exemption.[812]

---

[809] TEX. CONST art. VIII, § 1-n(a), (b)(1).

[810] *Id.* art. VIII, § 1-n(a). *See* TEX. TAX CODE ANN. § 11.253(a)(4) (West Supp. 2011) (Definition of petroleum product).

[811] TEX. CONST. art. VIII, § 1-n(a)(3).

[812] TEX. TAX CODE ANN. § 11.253(a)(2)(C) (West Supp. 2011).

IV. Economic Development Through Tourism

The Local Hotel Occupancy Tax

Economic development for many Texas cities and some counties is a matter of tourism. Texas consistently ranks along with California and Florida as one of the top three destinations for U.S. travelers. To fund the promotion of tourism, more than 500 Texas cities and 60 counties levy a local hotel occupancy tax generating over a billion dollars per year in revenue for these cities and counties. It is clear that the amount of money spent on tourism in Texas is growing and communities are increasingly looking to tourism for much needed revenue. The local hotel occupancy tax can provide an important source of funding for maintenance of a city's and county's tourism program and can translate into economic development for the entire area.

Authorized Entities and Procedures

Both general law cities and home rule cities are authorized to adopt a hotel occupancy tax ("HOT") within the city boundaries.[813] Implementing such a tax is optional. A city may implement a hotel occupancy tax by adopting an ordinance calling for the levy of the tax. The ordinance needs to be approved by a simple majority of the members of the governing body at an open meeting. Unlike a local sales tax, the adoption of a local hotel occupancy tax does not require voter approval. Although not mandated by state statute, a city may hold a public hearing to give the public an opportunity to express its views regarding the implementation and potential uses of the tax. Home rule cities (cities over 5,000 population that have adopted a home rule charter) should check their city charter for any additional requirements that the charter may impose.

Most cities are eligible to adopt a hotel occupancy tax rate of up to seven percent of the consideration paid for the use of a hotel room.[814] A city with a population of under 35,000 may also adopt the hotel occupancy tax within that city's extraterritorial jurisdiction (ETJ).[815] If a city adopts the hotel occupancy tax within its ETJ, the combined state, county and municipal hotel occupancy tax rate may not exceed 15%.

Some counties have received legislative approval to adopt a county hotel occupancy tax.[816] Generally, counties are authorized to adopt a rate not to exceed seven percent of the consideration paid for a hotel room for areas outside of the jurisdiction of a city.[817] Within the city limits, counties are generally capped at a county hotel tax rate of 2 percent.[818] The State of Texas also imposes a six percent hotel occupancy tax rate that applies throughout the state.[819]

---

[813] TEX. TAX CODE ANN.§§ 351.001 (West Supp 2011) (Definition of "municipality"); .002 (West 2008) (Municipal hotel occupancy tax authorized).
[814] *Id.* § 351.003(a) (West Supp 2011).
[815] *Id.* § 351.0025 (West 2008).
[816] *Id.* § 352.002.
[817] TEX. TAX CODE ANN. § 352.003(a) (West Supp. 2011).
[818] *Id.* § 352.003(b) (Note: County hotel occupancy tax can range from one percent to seven percent within a city. Counties that are authorized to have hotel occupancy tax should check section 352.003 of the Tax Code for the exact percentage rate that can be charged).
[819] *Id.* § 156.052 (West 2008).

Issues to Consider before Adopting the Tax

A local government will want to consider a number of issues before it implements a local hotel occupancy tax. These concerns include:

- Would the expenditure of hotel occupancy tax be likely to attract out-of-town tourists that would stay overnight or otherwise conduct business at area lodging facilities? Hotel occupancy tax revenues may not be used to establish or enhance facilities or programs that would not attract out-of-town visitors and directly promote the hotel and convention industry.[820]

- How does the proposed hotel occupancy tax rate compare to the hotel occupancy tax rates of neighboring communities? Will the proposed rate be above, in line with, or below nearby areas that compete for available tourism business?

- What revenues can be expected by the imposition of a hotel occupancy tax? Projected revenues can be roughly estimated by applying the proposed local hotel occupancy tax rate against the taxable revenues of the hotels in the locale during prior years. Hotels report their taxable revenues each year to the Comptroller when they submit the state hotel occupancy tax. The information from this report to the Comptroller can be adjusted to get a basic estimate of the amount of revenue a city could anticipate if it adopted a local hotel occupancy tax. Cities may obtain information and make special requests by logging onto the Comptroller's Website at www.window.state.tx.us. If a city has any other questions about hotel occupancy tax, it can call the Comptroller at (800) 252-1385.

- How would the proposed tax fit into the city's future plans and goals? What types of programs and improvements that are authorized under the hotel tax laws will be possible with the anticipated revenues? Would the proposed programs and expenditures be possible without the imposition of a hotel occupancy tax and how soon would they be possible? What existing or new facilities and programs would qualify for funding? To qualify for funding, each of the facilities or programs must fit into one of the statutory categories for expenditures which are discussed in detail later in this chapter.[821] Each expenditure also must be likely to result in increased tourism by out-of-town visitors to the city and must have some impact on hotel and/or convention activity.

- How will the city measure the benefits of expenditures of the hotel occupancy tax? For example, a city could ask recipients of hotel occupancy tax proceeds to keep a log of out-of-town visitors or business transactions that took place after the enhancement of their program or facility with hotel occupancy tax money. Many visitor centers and tourist attractions have a guest book that out-of-town visitors are encouraged to sign. The visitor logs could include a box to check if the visitor is "staying at an area hotel." The city could use this information later to estimate the effectiveness of the various expenditures at promoting increased tourism and hotel activity.

- What local entities would be encouraged to participate in the decisions regarding administration of a local hotel occupancy tax? Will the city involve local citizens, the chamber of commerce, and representatives of the local hotels to review potential uses of the hotel occupancy tax proceeds? Involving area hotel representatives in the allocation

---

[820] *Id.* § 351.101(a)-(b) (West Supp. 2011).

[821] *Id.* §§ 351.101(a)(1)-(12), .110 (West 2008).

decisions has helped many communities avoid opposition to the types of programs that are ultimately funded. Area hoteliers can also help the community accurately assess how much of an impact the hotel tax funded programs have on area hotel activity.

Who Charges the Tax

The following businesses are considered "hotels" and are required to charge the tax:[822]

- a hotel,
- motel,
- tourist home,
- tourist court
- lodging house,
- inn,
- rooming house, or
- bed and breakfast.

Hospitals, sanitariums, nursing homes, dormitories and other non-hotel housing facilities owned by institutions of higher education, and oilfield portable units[823] may not charge the tax. While recreational vehicles (RVs) and RV rental spaces are not expressly listed in the statute, the Comptroller's Office has interpreted the statute to exclude RVs and RV lots from taxation.

The hotel occupancy tax may be imposed against any "person" (including corporations and other legal entities) who pays for the use of a hotel room that is ordinarily used for sleeping.[824] The price of the room does not include the cost of food served by the hotel or the cost of other personal services.[825] Unlike the state hotel occupancy tax, local hotel occupancy tax does not apply to the cost of renting meeting rooms, banquet or event space within a hotel since these rooms are not considered "sleeping rooms."[826]

Exemptions From the Tax

State law exempts the following individuals from payment of the state and local hotel occupancy tax, if they are traveling on official business:

1) federal employees[827];

2) foreign diplomats with a tax exempt card issued by the U.S. Department of State[828];

---

[822]   *Id.* § 351.001(4) (West Supp. 2011), 352.001(1) (West 2008). *See id.* § 156.001(1) (West Supp. 2011) (The term "hotel" has the meaning assigned by Section 156.001 of the Tax Code which is defined as "a building in which members of the public obtain sleeping accommodations for consideration."). *See also* 34 TEX. ADMIN. CODE § 3.161(3) (West 2012).

[823]   *See id.* § 152.001(20) (West Supp. 2011) (Definition of "oilfield portable unit").

[824]   TEX. TAX CODE ANN § 351.002(a) (West 2008). *See* TEX. GOV'T CODE ANN. § 311.005(2) (West 2005) (Definition of "person" as used in any Texas code).

[825]   TEX. TAX CODE ANN. §§ 351.002(b), 156.051(b) (West 2008) (Note: The price of a room could also not include the cost of beverages. However, if the food and beverages prices are not separately stated from the room rental prices, those cost could be included in the price of the room. This is often demonstrated when a hotel has a single "package" price that includes room and food/services.).

[826]   *Id.* § 156.051(a).

[827]   *Id.* §§ 351.006(a), 352.007(a), 156.103(a). *See also* 34 TEX. ADMIN. CODE §3.161(3) (West 2012).

[828]   34 TEX. ADMIN. CODE § 3.161(b)(4) (West 2012).

3) a very limited number of state officials with a hotel tax exemption card (heads of state agencies, state legislators and legislative staff, members of state boards and commissions, and state judges)[829]; and

4) persons or businesses who have the right to use or possess a hotel room at least 30 consecutive days.[830]

Employees of Texas institutions of higher education (colleges) are exempt from the state hotel occupancy tax, but must pay local hotel occupancy tax.[831] Additionally, employees of secondary schools (grade schools and high schools) from Texas and outside of Texas are exempt from state hotel occupancy tax, but must pay local hotel tax.[832] All individuals claiming one of the above exemptions are required to show appropriate identification and to fill out a Hotel Occupancy Tax Exemption Certificate. A certificate form that can be used for this purpose is available on the Comptroller's Website at www.window.state.tx.us/taxinfo/taxforms/12-forms.html. Lodging operators and other interested parties can also access an internet searchable list of all of the entities that have been granted a letter of exemption from the state hotel occupancy tax. This site can be accessed at: www.window.state.tx.us/taxinfo/hotel/index.html.

Officers or employees of a state agency, institution, board or commission who are traveling on official business must pay the tax, but are entitled to a refund from the involved governmental taxing entities.[833] The state and the local government refund the hotel occupancy tax to the exempt employee through a separate process. For information on how the state handles refunds of the state hotel occupancy tax, contact the Comptroller's Office at (800) 531-5441, extension 6-5913 or (512) 466-5913. A city or county may want to request a copy of the Comptroller's refund application form for the state hotel occupancy tax and adapt that form for handling refunds of the municipal or county hotel occupancy tax.

City and county officers and employees are not exempt from the state or local hotel occupancy tax even if the officers or employees are traveling on official business. Further, cities may not authorize additional exemptions from the hotel occupancy tax. For example, the attorney general ruled in JM-865 (1988) that neither cities nor counties have the authority to grant an exception to the hotel occupancy tax for religious, charitable or educational organizations without new constitutional or statutory authority to do so. It is important to reiterate that there are many entities, including educational, charitable, and religious entities, that are or may be exempt from the state hotel occupancy tax, but must pay the city and county hotel occupancy tax.

How the City or County Receive the Tax

The local hotel occupancy tax is paid by the hotel customer to the hotel. The tax is then remitted by the hotel to the city or county on a regular basis, to be established by the city or county. The Comptroller's Office is not involved in the collection of the local hotel occupancy tax. The state

---

[829]   *Id.* § 3.161(b)(2).

[830]   TEX. TAX CODE ANN. §§ 351.002(c), 156.101 (West 2008). *See also* 34 TEX. ADMIN. CODE § 3.161(b)(6) (West 2012).

[831]   *Id.* §§ 156.102(b)(2), .103(b), 351.006(b), 352.007(b). *See also* 34 TEX. ADMIN. CODE §§ 3.161(a)(2), (b)(1) (West 2012).

[832]   *See* 34 TEX. ADMIN. CODE §§ 3.161(a)(2), (b)(1) (West 2012).

[833]   TEX. TAX CODE ANN. § 351.006(b), 352.007(b), 156.103(b) (West 2008).

requires hotels to turn over collected hotel occupancy taxes on a monthly basis. Some hotels in smaller communities, however, petition the Comptroller for permission to turn over the tax proceeds on a quarterly basis. For the convenience of hotel operators, many cities and counties use the same reporting and collection schedule used by the state for collection of the state hotel occupancy tax.

Cities and counties that levy the hotel occupancy tax should send a tax return form to each hotel operator two to four weeks before the taxes are due. Regardless of the reporting period used, cities and counties should require hotels to include as part of their report a copy of the hotel's tax report done for the Comptroller. The state report data can be used to check the completeness of the local report provided by the hotel to the city or county. Cities and counties should be aware that, in certain cases, the state and local tax are subject to different exemptions and, as a result, the revenues may not exactly coincide.

A city or county may request hotel occupancy tax audit information from the Comptroller.[834] However, the city or county must keep such information confidential and use the information only for enforcement or administration of the city's or county's hotel tax. To obtain such information, a city or county must make a written request to:

> Open Records Division
> Comptroller of Public Accounts
> P.O. Box 13528
> Austin, Texas 78711-3528.

The request must be on official letterhead and be signed by a high-level local official, preferably the mayor or county judge. A city or county may also fax a written request for this information to the Open Records Division of the Comptroller's Office at (512) 475-1610.

Cities and counties can also obtain from the Comptroller's Office a copy of the latest quarterly state report listing all of the hotels that currently remit state hotel occupancy taxes. The easiest and fastest way to get this report is to log onto the Comptroller's Website at www.window.state.tx.us and click on the topic, "Texas Taxes." Alternatively, a city or county may request a copy of the report by calling the Comptroller's Office at (800) 252-1385 or sending an e-mail to open.records@cpa.state.tx.us.

Reimbursement of Hotel Operator for Collection Expenses

Cities by ordinance or counties by order or resolution may allow hotel operators to retain up to one percent of the amount of hotel occupancy taxes collected as reimbursement for the costs of collecting the tax.[835] Neither cities nor counties are permitted to retain any of the collected tax to cover the cost of imposing or collecting the tax. However, cities or counties that undertake responsibility for administering a facility or event funded by the local hotel occupancy tax may be reimbursed from the tax revenues for actual expenses incurred in operating the facility or event, if the expenditure directly promotes tourism and local convention and hotel activity.

---

[834]   *Id.* § 111.006(d) (West Supp. 2011).
[835]   *Id.* §§ 351.005(a), 352.005 (West 2008).

Penalties and Enforcement for Failure to Report or Collect the Tax

The local hotel occupancy tax statutes provide for specific penalties that may be assessed against hotel operators who fail to file a tax report or pay the tax when due.[836] A city may impose a 15% penalty if the tax has been delinquent for at least one complete city fiscal quarter and collect reasonable attorney's fees against any hotel operator who does not file their report or pay the taxes due.[837] The city can conduct an audit of each hotel for which a tax report was not filed to determine the amount of taxes that are due.[838] The city shall provide at least 30 days' written notice to the person who is required to collect the tax with respect to a hotel before conducting an audit of the hotel.[839] If, as a result of an audit, the city obtains documentation or other information showing a failure to collect or pay city and state hotel occupancy tax when due, the city shall notify and submit the relevant information to the comptroller.[840] The comptroller shall review the information submitted by the city and determine whether to proceed with collection and enforcement efforts. If the information results in the collection of delinquent state hotel occupancy tax and the assessment has become administratively final, the comptroller shall distribute a percentage of the amount collected to the city to defray the cost of the city audit. The city can charge for the cost of the audit but only if the tax has been delinquent for at least two complete municipal fiscal quarters at the time that the audit was conducted and the city has not received a disbursement from the comptroller in accordance with an audit of concurrent tax delinquency.[841] The city can adopt a hotel occupancy tax ordinance that includes a provision that makes it a misdemeanor offense if the hotel operator fails to file the tax report or remit the taxes.[842]

Additionally, cities are given the authority to take the following actions against a hotel operator who fails to report or collect the local hotel occupancy tax:

- require the forfeiture of any revenue the city allowed the hotel operator to retain for its cost of collecting the tax;[843]

- bring a civil suit against the hotel operator for noncompliance;[844]

- ask the district court to enjoin operation of the hotel until the report is filed and/or the tax is paid; and

- any other remedies provided under Texas law.[845]

The most noteworthy of these remedies is the ability of the city to request that the district court close down the hotel if the hotel occupancy taxes are not paid. Often, a city can gain compliance simply by informing the hotel operator of the possibility of such a closure.

---

[836]   *Id.* §§ 351.004(a) (West Supp. 2011), 352.004.
[837]   *Id.* § 351.004(a)(1), (3).
[838]   *Id.* § 351.004(a-1)(1), (a-3).
[839]   *Id.* § 351.004(a-3).
[840]   *Id.* § 351.008.
[841]   *Id.* § 351.004(a)(2). *See id.* §§ 156.2513, 351.008.
[842]   *Id.* § 351.004(c).
[843]   *Id.* § 351.005(b) (West 2008).
[844]   *Id.* § 351.004(a) (West Supp. 2011).
[845]   *Id.* § 351.004(d).

Also, counties can assess penalties against a hotel operator for failing to file the tax report or paying the taxes that are due.[846] If the hotel operator fails to file the report or pay the taxes due, the county shall be paid a penalty of five percent of the amount of the taxes due. Thirty days after the date the report should have been filed or taxes should have been paid and the hotel operator still has failed to do either, the county can add another penalty of five percent of the amount of the taxes due. If the taxes are not paid within 60 days, delinquent taxes and accrued penalties draw interest at a rate of ten percent a year.[847]

Counties have the authority to take certain actions against a hotel operator who fails to report or collect the local hotel occupancy tax. These actions include:

- bring a civil suit against the hotel operator for noncompliance;

- ask the district court to enjoin operation of the hotel until the report is filed and/or the tax is paid; and

- any other remedies provided under Texas law.[848]

Just like a city, the county can request the district court to close down the hotel if the hotel occupancy taxes are not paid.

Counties can perform an audit on each hotel in relation to the person who did not file their reports in order to determine the amount of tax due.[849] The county shall provide 30 days' written notice to the person who was required to file the reports with the county.[850] If as a result of the audit, the county obtains documentation or other information showing the failure to collect or pay county and state hotel occupancy tax when due, the county shall notify and submit the relevant information to the comptroller.[851] The comptroller shall review the information submitted by a county and determine whether to proceed with collection and enforcement efforts. If the information results in the collection of delinquent state hotel occupancy taxes and the assessment becomes administratively final, the comptroller shall distribute a percentage of the amount collected to the county to defray the cost of the county audit.

A city and county may also require that persons buying a hotel retain out of the purchase price an amount sufficient to cover any delinquent hotel occupancy taxes that are due to the city.[852] If the buyer does not remit such amount to the city and county (where applicable) or show proof that the hotel is current in remitting its hotel occupancy taxes, the buyer becomes liable for any delinquent hotel occupancy taxes due on the purchased hotel.

The purchaser of a hotel may request that the city and county provide a receipt showing that no hotel occupancy tax is due (a "Letter of No Tax Due") on the property to be purchased.[853] The city and county is required to issue the statement not later than the 60th day after the request. If

---

[846]   *Id.* § 352.004(b).
[847]   *Id.* § 352.004(c).
[848]   *Id.* § 352.004(d).
[849]   *Id.* § 352.004(e), .006(a).
[850]   *Id.* § 352.004(e).
[851]   *Id.* § 352.008.
[852]   *Id.* §§ 351.0041 (West 2008), 352.0041.
[853]   *Id.* §§ 351.0041(c); 352.0041(c).

the city or county fails to issue the statement within the deadline, the purchaser is released from the obligation to withhold the amount due from the purchase price for that local governmental entity.[854]

Use of Local Hotel Occupancy Tax Revenues for Cities

There is a two-part test that every expenditure of local hotel occupancy tax revenue must pass to be valid. First, the expenditure must directly enhance and promote tourism and the convention and hotel industry.[855] In other words, the expenditure must be likely to attract visitors from outside the city into the city or its vicinity and must have some impact on convention and hotel activity. If the expenditure is not reasonably likely to accomplish this result, it cannot be funded by hotel occupancy tax revenues. The hotel occupancy tax may not be used for general revenue purposes or to pay for governmental expenses not directly related to increasing tourism.[856]

Second, every expenditure must clearly fit into one of the statutory categories for the expenditure of local hotel occupancy tax revenues. These categories are as follows:[857]

1. **Funding the establishment, improvement or maintenance of a convention center or visitor information center.**[858]

Simply naming a facility a convention center or visitor information center does not bring it under this section. State law specifies that the facility must be one that is primarily used to host conventions and meetings.[859] The term "convention center" is defined to include civic centers, auditoriums, exhibition halls and coliseums that are owned by the city or another governmental entity or that are managed in whole or in part by the city. It also includes parking areas in the immediate vicinity of other convention center facilities. It does not include facilities that are not of the same general characteristics as the structures listed above.

The attorney general has specifically ruled against the expenditure of local hotel occupancy taxes for a city recreational facility such as a golf course or a tennis court.[860] However, the Legislature has provided additional statutory authority that allows the use of local hotel occupancy tax for certain sporting related expenses if they meet certain criteria discussed below. It is possible that facilities that are not considered convention centers may still be able to receive funding if the expenditure can be justified under the categories described below for promotion of the arts or for historical preservation or restoration projects. A city may pledge the hotel occupancy tax revenue for the payment of bonds that are issued under Chapter 1504 of the Government Code for convention center facilities, as authorized under the hotel occupancy tax law.[861]

---

[854]   *Id.* §§ 351.0041(d); 352.0041(d).
[855]   *Id.* § 351.101(a) (West Supp 2011). *See* Op. Tex. Att'y Gen. No. GA-0124 (2003).
[856]   TEX. TAX CODE ANN. § 351.101(b) (West Supp. 2011).
[857]   *Id.* §§ 351.101(a), .0035 .110 (West 2008).
[858]   *Id.* § 351.101(a)(1) (West Supp. 2011).
[859]   *Id.* § 351.001(2) (West Supp. 2011).
[860]   *See* Op. Tex. Att'y Gen. Nos. JM-184 (1984), JM-965 (1988).
[861]   TEX. TAX CODE ANN. § 351.102 (West Supp. 2011).

2.   Paying the administrative costs for facilitating convention registration.[862]
This provision applies only to administrative costs that are actually incurred for assisting in the registration of convention delegates or attendees. It may include covering the facility costs, personnel costs, and costs of materials for the registration of convention delegates or attendees.

3.   Paying for tourism-related advertising and promotion of the city or its vicinity. [863]
This provision is strictly limited to expenditures for a solicitation or promotional program or advertising which is directly related to attracting conventions or tourism. The attorney general has ruled that this provision does not authorize advertising to attract new businesses or permanent residents to a city.[864] Again, the purpose of the expenditure must be directly related to increasing tourism and the convention and hotel industry.

4.   Funding programs that enhance the arts. [865]
This section authorizes the expenditure of hotel occupancy tax revenues for a variety of arts-related programs. It allows funding for the encouragement, promotion, improvement and application of the arts including instrumental and vocal music, dance, drama, folk art, creative writing, architecture, design and allied fields, painting, sculpture, photography, graphic and craft arts, motion pictures, radio, television, tape and sound recording, and other arts related to the presentation, performance, execution and exhibition of these major art forms. The fact that a program directly promotes the arts is not in itself sufficient to justify expenditure of the local hotel tax. The funded event/facility must also have the impact of directly promoting both tourism and the hotel and convention industry.

5.   Funding historical restoration or preservation programs. [866]
This category allows a city to spend its hotel occupancy tax revenues to enhance historical restoration and preservation projects or activities that encourage tourists and convention delegates to visit the city's preserved historic sites or museums. This funding can include the costs for rehabilitation or preservation of existing historic structures. Also, the costs of advertising, conducting solicitations and promotional programs to encourage tourists and convention delegates to visit such preserved historic structures or museums can be funded under this category. The tax can be used on historic sites or museums that are in the immediate vicinity of the convention center facilities or visitor information centers, or anywhere else in the city where tourist and convention delegates frequently visit. The fact that a program results in historical restoration or preservation is not in itself sufficient to justify expenditure of the local hotel tax. The funded event/facility must also have the impact of directly promoting both tourism and the hotel and convention industry.

6.   Funding costs to hold sporting events in certain municipalities.[867]
Cities located in a county with a population of one million or less may use hotel occupancy tax proceeds for expenses, including promotional expenses, directly related to sporting events in

[862]   *Id.* § 351.101(a)(2).
[863]   *Id.* § 351.101(a)(3).
[864]   *See* Op. Tex. Att'y Gen. No. JM-690 (1987) ([Chapter 351 of the Tax Code] does not authorize the use of hotel/motel occupancy tax funds for advertising which is not related to attracting conventions, visitors or tourists).
[865]   TEX. TAX CODE ANN. § 351.101(a)(4) (West Supp. 2011).
[866]   *Id.* § 351.101(a)(5).
[867]   *Id.* § 351.101(a)(6).

which the majority of participants are tourists. Such funding is permissible provided the sporting event substantially increases economic activity at hotels and motels within the city or its vicinity. This provision is intended to allow communities to fund the event costs for sporting tournaments that result in substantial hotel activity. For example, if a city had to pay an application fee to seek a particular sporting event or tournament, it could use this authority if the event would substantially increase economic activity at hotels and the city was within a county of one million or less population. The requirement that a majority of the participants must be "tourists" is included to prohibit the use of local hotel tax for sporting related facilities or events that are purely local (e.g., local recreation centers, local little league and parks events, etc.).

7.   Enhancing   and   upgrading   existing   sport   facilities   or   fields   for   certain municipalities.[868]

This expenditure authorizes certain cities to use hotel occupancy tax revenue to upgrade certain existing sports facilities. Existing sports facilities or fields for baseball, softball, soccer, and flag football may be upgraded with hotel occupancy tax revenue if the facility is: 1) owned by the city;[869] and 2) the sports facility or field has been used in preceding calendar year a combined total of more than 10 times for district, state, regional, or national sports tournaments.[870] The cities that are authorized to use hotel occupancy tax revenue for this expenditure are:

1)   those with a population of 80,000 or more that are located in a county with a population of 350,00 or less;

2)   those with a population of between 75,000 and 95,000 that are located in a county with a population of less than 200,000 but not more than 160,000;

3)   those with a population of between 36,000 and 39,000 that are located in a county with a population of 100,000 or less that is not adjacent to a county with a population of more than 2 million;

4)   those with a population of at least 13,000 but less than 39,000 and is located in a county that has a population of at least 200,000;

5)   those with a population of at least 70,000 but less than 90,000 and no part of the city is located in a county with a population greater than 150,000;

6)   those located in a county that has a population of at least 500,000, adjacent to the Texas-Mexico border and the county does not have a city with a population greater than 500,000; or

7)   Has a population of at least 25,000 but not more tha[n] 26,000 and is located in a county that has population of 90,000 or less.[871]

If hotel tax revenues are spent on enhancing or upgrading a sports facility, the city must determine the amount of "area hotel revenue" that was generated by hotel activity from sports events that were held at the hotel tax funded facility for five years after the upgrades to the sport facility are complete.[872] The area hotel revenues that were generated from sports events at the

---

[868]   *Id.* § 351.101(a)(7).
[869]   *Id.* § 351.101(a)(7)(A).
[870]   *Id.* § 351.101(a)(7)(C).
[871]   *Id.* § 351.101(a)(7)(B)(i)-(vii).
[872]   *Id.* § 351.1076(a) (West 2008).

hotel tax-funded facility over that five year period must at least equal the amount of hotel tax that was spent to upgrade the sports facility.[873] If the amount of hotel tax that was spent on the facility upgrades exceeds hotel revenue attributable to the enhancements over that five-year period, the city must reimburse the hotel occupancy tax revenue fund any such difference from the city's general fund.[874] For example, if a city spent $400,000 on improvements to its soccer fields, it would have to show at least $400,000 in hotel night revenue, including hotel banquet revenue, directly attributable to events held at that soccer field over the five year period after the soccer field improvements were completed. If the city could only show $300,000 in hotel industry revenue due to events held at that soccer field, the city would have to reimburse the city hotel tax for the $100,000 difference from the city's general fund.

8. Signage to sights and attractions.[875]
Cities are allowed to use hotel occupancy tax to erect signage to direct the public to sights and attractions that are visited frequently by hotel guests in the city.

9. Funding transportation systems for tourists.[876]
With conventions and large meetings, there is often a need to transport the attendees to different tourism venues. Cities are allowed to use of hotel occupancy tax to cover the costs for transporting tourists from hotels in and near the city to any of the following destinations:

- the commercial center of the city;
- a convention center in the city;
- other hotels in or near the city; and
- tourist attractions in or near the city.

The reimbursed transportation system must be owned and operated by the city, or privately owned and operated and financed in part by the city. The law specifically prohibits the use of the local hotel occupancy tax to cover the costs for transporting the general public by any such system.

Use of Local Hotel Occupancy Tax Revenues for Counties
Just like cities, counties that are authorized to impose hotel occupancy tax have to follow a two-part test to determine that every expenditure of the tax is valid.[877] First, the expenditure must directly enhance and promote tourism and the convention and hotel industry. The expenditure must be likely to attract visitors from outside the county into the county or it vicinity and must have some impact on convention and hotel activity. If the expenditure is not reasonably likely to accomplish this result, it should not be funded by hotel occupancy tax revenues. The hotel occupancy tax may not be used for general revenue purposes or general governmental operations of a county.[878]

---

[873] *Id.*
[874] *Id.* § 351.1076(b).
[875] *Id.* § 351.101(a)(9) (West Supp. 2011).
[876] *Id.* § 351.110 (West 2008).
[877] *Id.* § 352.1031(a) (This statute refers to Tax Code § 351.101).
[878] *Id.* § 352.1031(b).

Second, a county can only spend hotel occupancy tax revenue on those categoriesof expenditures that the county has specifically been given permission by statute to do so.[879] Usually, this depends on either the population of the county or where the county is geographically located or both.

Use of Tax Proceeds to Cover Administrative Expenses

The implementation of programs or improvements under the above categories may involve certain administrative costs. State law allows proceeds of the tax to be used to cover the portion of administrative costs that are directly attributable to work on facilities or events that may be funded by the tax.[880] For example, efforts to promote the city or county as a tourist and convention locale often involve some travel expenses. There are two circumstances under which cities or counties may spend hotel occupancy tax revenues for travel-related expenditures.[881]

- First, tax revenues may be spent to pay for travel to attend an event or to conduct an activity that is directly related to the promotion of tourism and the convention and hotel industry. "Tourism" is defined in the Tax Code as guiding or managing the travel of individuals from their residence to a different city or county for pleasure, recreation, education or culture.[882]

- Second, local hotel occupancy tax revenues may be spent on travel that is directly related to the performance of the person's job in an efficient and professional manner. This travel should facilitate the acquisition of skills and knowledge which will promote tourism and the convention and hotel industry.

Entities that manage activities funded by the hotel occupancy tax may spend some of the tax for certain day-to-day operational expenses. These expenses may include supplies, salaries, office rental, travel expenses and other administrative costs. These costs can be reimbursed if they are incurred directly in the promotion and servicing of expenditures authorized under the hotel occupancy tax laws. The portion of the administrative costs that are covered may not exceed the percentage of the cost that is attributable to the activity funded by the hotel occupancy tax. In other words, administrators who spend 33 percent of their time overseeing hotel occupancy tax funded programs could seek funding for no more than 33 percent of their salary or 33 percent of other related overhead costs.[883]

Additional Limits on Expenditures

Texas statutes provide certain additional rules regarding the percentage of hotel occupancy tax revenues that may be spent on each of the categories of expenditures discussed above. The rules differ according to the population of the city or the description of the county in the Tax Code.

---

[879] *Id.* §§ 352.101-.106; .108; .110 (West 2008 & West Supp. 2011).
[880] *Id.* §§ 351.101(e)-(f) (West Supp. 2011), 352.1015(c)-(d) (West 2008).
[881] *Id.*
[882] *Id.* §§ 351.001(5), (6)(West Supp. 2011), 352.001(3), (4) (West 2008).
[883] *Id.* §§ 351.101(e)(West Supp. 2011), 352.1015(c)(West 2008).

General Rules of Allocation of Hotel Occupancy Tax Revenue

Minimum Expenditure That Must be Spent on Advertising and Promotion

A city with a population of 200,000 or greater is required to spend at least 50 percent of the hotel occupancy tax collected by the city on advertising and conducting solicitations and promotional programs to attract tourists to the city or its vicinity.[884] However, it should be noted that if a city takes in over $2 million annually in hotel taxes, it is not subject to this 50 percent requirement.[885]

If the city has a population of less than 200,000, the amount that the city can spend on advertising and conducting solicitations and promotional programs depends on the hotel occupancy tax rate adopted by the city. If the city adopted a hotel occupancy tax rate of not more than three percent, at least one-half of one percent of the rate must be spent on advertising and promotion of the city and its vicinity.[886] If the city adopted a hotel occupancy tax rate that exceeds three percent, at least one percent of the rate must be spent on advertising and promotion of the city and its vicinity. [887] For example, if a city has a seven percent hotel occupancy tax rate, at least one-seventh of the hotel occupancy tax proceeds must be spent on advertising and promoting the city and its vicinity to attract tourists and hotel and convention activity.

Maximum Expenditure for the Arts

Generally, cities with populations of less than 1.6 million are limited to a set percentage with regard to art programs. Such cities may not spend on art programs more than 15 percent of their hotel occupancy tax revenues or no more than the amount of tax generated by the city at the tax rate of one percent of the cost of a room, whichever is greater.[888] If the city has a population of more than 1.6 million (Houston), then not more than 19.30 percent of hotel occupancy tax revenue or no more than the amount of tax generated by the city at the tax rate of one percent of the cost of a room, whichever is greater, can be spent on art programs.

Maximum Expenditure For Historical Restoration and Preservation

Cities with a population of more than 125,000 may not spend more than 15 percent of their tax revenue for historical restoration and preservation projects and activities.[889] Additionally, a city, in certain cases, may allocate at least some of its hotel occupancy tax money for acquiring, constructing, improving, maintaining or operating a convention center or visitor information center. If a city fails to allocate money for a convention center purpose, the Tax Code prohibits that city from allocating more than 50 percent of its hotel occupancy tax for historical restoration or preservation projects.[890] If a city under 125,000 population does spend some of its hotel occupancy tax on a convention center, there is no statutory limitation on expenditures for historic preservation and restoration.

---

[884]   *Id.* § 351.103(a).

[885]   *Id.* § 351.103(b). *See also* Op. Tex. Att'y Gen. No. JC-105 (1999) (Pursuant to section 351.103(b) of the Texas Tax Code, the allocation restriction of section 351.103(a) of the Tax Code does not apply to a municipality which has collected in excess of $2 million in hotel occupancy tax revenue in the most recent calendar year).

[886]   TEX. TAX CODE ANN. § 351.103(a)(1) (West 2008).

[887]   *Id.* § 351.103(a)(2).

[888]   *Id.* § 351.103(c).

[889]   *Id.*

[890]   *Id.* § 351.103(d).

Delegating the Management of Funded Activities

The governing body of a city and county may, by written contract, delegate the management or supervision of programs and activities funded with revenue from the hotel occupancy tax.[891] This delegation may be made to a person, another governmental entity or to a private organization.[892] The delegation of this authority is often made to the local chamber of commerce or to the convention and visitor bureau.

There are a number of procedural requirements that the Legislature has imposed on entities that undertake management of these funds. For example, a city or county is required to approve in writing the portion of an entity's annual budget that involves expenditure of hotel occupancy tax funds. This approval must be sought in advance of the expenditures. Hotel tax funded entities also must submit at least quarterly reports to the city council or the commissioners court on their expenditures of the tax revenues. The reports must list all expenditures made by the entity from the hotel occupancy taxes provided by the city or county.[893] The entity is required to keep complete and accurate financial records of each expenditure of hotel occupancy tax revenue.[894] These records must be made available for inspection and review upon the request of the governing body or upon a request from any other person.

The entity delegated authority to manage these funded programs undertakes a fiduciary duty with respect to this revenue. Such entities are required to maintain the city hotel occupancy tax revenue in a separate bank account established for that purpose. This account may not be commingled with any other account.[895]

Documenting Activities Funded by the Hotel Occupancy Tax

Before making a hotel occupancy tax expenditure, a city, county or other hotel occupancy tax funded entity must specify each scheduled activity, program or event that is directly funded by hotel occupancy tax proceeds or has its administrative costs funded in whole or in part by the tax. The activity or program must directly relate to enhancing and promoting tourism and the convention and hotel industry.[896]

If the city or county delegates to another entity the management or supervision of an activity or event funded by the local hotel occupancy tax, each entity that is funded by the tax shall, before making an expenditure, specify each scheduled activity, program or event that is directly funded by the tax or has its administrative costs funded in whole or in part by the tax. Further, the list must indicate the activities and programs that are directly enhancing and promoting tourism and

---

[891] *Id.* §§ 351.101(c) (West Supp. 2011), 352.1015 (West 2008).

[892] *Id.* (Please note that a legislative body such as a city council is limited in the degree to which it may delegate its authority to another entity. See, for example, *Texas Boll Weevil Eradication Foundation, Inc. v. Lewellen*, 952 S.W.2d 454 (Tex. 1997). *See also Andrews v. Wilson*, 959 S.W.2d 686 (Tex. App. -- Amarillo, 1998)).

[893] *Id.* §§ 351.101(c) (West Supp. 2011), 352.1015(a) (West 2008).

[894] *Id.* §§ 351.101(d) (West Supp. 2011), 352.1015(b) (West 2008).

[895] *Id.* §§ 351.101(c) (West Supp. 2011), 352.1015(a) (West 2008).

[896] *Id.* §§ 351.108(b) (West 2008), 352.109(b).

the convention and hotel industry.[897] For cities, this list of expenditures should be provided to the city secretary or the city secretary's designee.[898]

County Development District

The Texas Legislature has recognized that it is sometimes advantageous to pursue economic development at the county level. The County Development District Act provides counties that have a population of 400,000 or less with a means to generate sales tax funds for local economic development and tourism-related projects. Such districts are initiated by a petition of landowners in the proposed district. Upon approval of the petition by the county, an election is called to gain the voters' consent to create the district and to levy a sales tax to fund district projects. A county development district may acquire or dispose of the same sorts of projects and pay the same sorts of costs as a Type B economic development corporation. However, a county development district project must promote and develop tourism within the county.[899]

The statutes governing the creation and administration of county development districts are found in Chapter 383 of the Texas Local Government Code.[900]

Powers and Duties of a County Development District

A county development district has broad authority to establish projects related to economic development and promotion of tourism in the district. Unlike economic development corporations, which are ultimately overseen by the city or county's governing body, Texas law does not require a county development district to get approval from the county before it commits to various projects or expenditures.

The district has the following general powers and duties:

Expenditure of Tax Proceeds. If a sales and use tax was approved by the voters in the district and is being collected, the district can use the tax for projects that promote and develop tourism within the county and to pay bonds issued by the district.[901]

---

897   *Id.* §§ 351.108(c), 352.109(c).
898   *Id.* § 351.108(d).
899   *See* TEX. LOC. GOV'T CODE ANN. §§ 383.002 (West 2005) ("This chapter furthers the public purpose of developing and diversifying the economy of this state by providing incentives for the location and development of projects in certain counties to **attract visitors and tourists**."); 383.003(a) ("[s]mall and medium-sized counties in this state need incentives for the development of public improvements to **attract visitors and tourists** to those counties..."); 383.003(b) ("[t]he means and measures authorized by this chapter are in the public interest and serve a public purpose of this state ... by providing incentives for the location and development in certain counties of this state of projects that **attract visitors and tourists** ..."); 383.023(5) (a petition proposing a county development corporation must state that the district "will serve the public purpose of **attracting visitors and tourists** to the county.")(emphasis added). *See also,* Op. Tex. Att'y Gen. No. JC-291 (2000) at 7 - 10 (A county development district created under chapter 383 of the Local Government Code is not authorized to levy ad valorem taxes. A county development district may undertake a project only if it is consistent with the purpose of chapter 383 – "providing incentives for the location and development of projects in certain counties to attract visitors and tourists.").
900   TEX. LOC. GOV'T CODE ANN. §§ 383.001 *et seq.* (West 2005 & West Supp. 2011).
901   *Id.* §§ 383.002, .105 (West 2005). *See also,* Op. Tex. Att'y Gen. No. JC-291 (2000).

Power of the County to Adopt a Hotel Occupancy Tax and of the District to Expend Hotel Occupancy Tax Revenue. A commissioners court may impose a hotel occupancy tax of up to seven percent within the boundaries of a county development district.[902] The tax can only be imposed outside of the city limits. Such a tax would be collected by the hotel operators and remitted to the county. Within 10 days of its receipt of such tax proceeds, the county must remit the proceeds to the development district. Such hotel tax money may be used by a county development district for any purpose for which the district may use its sales tax proceeds. The county is not authorized to retain a portion of the tax revenues. This tax is in addition to the state hotel occupancy tax.

Ability to Pursue Type B Projects that Promote Tourism. The district may acquire and dispose of projects consistent with the purpose of the district. The definition of "project" in this chapter refers to the same types of projects available to Type B economic development corporations under the Development Corporation Act.[903] Such projects could include athletic facilities, tourism and entertainment facilities, parks and certain public facility and public space improvements, improvements related to commercial businesses, and related transportation and infrastructure improvements that promote tourism.

Limited Application of Competitive Bidding Laws. Competitive bidding provisions apply to county development district contracts,[904] unless the contract is with a governmental entity or a nonprofit corporation created under the Development Corporation Act (Type A and Type B economic development corporations).[905]

Ability to Exercise Powers of Municipal Management District. The district has and may exercise all powers and rights of a municipal management district under Chapter 375 of the Local Government Code [906] except the power to impose ad valorem taxes, unless such a power or right would be inconsistent with Chapter 383 of the Local Government Code. [907]

Limited Eminent Domain Power. A district located outside of a municipality may exercise the power of eminent domain to acquire land or interests in land for water or sewer purposes.[908]

Financial Transaction Powers. The district may disburse money by check, draft, order or other instrument. Disbursement requires the signature of three board directors unless the board has adopted an agreement that the signature of a specific employee or other officer is sufficient. [909]

---

902 TEX. TAX CODE ANN. § 352.107 (West 2008).

903 TEX. LOC. GOV'T CODE ANN. § 383.004(8) (West Supp. 2011) ("Project" has the meaning assigned by TEX. LOC. GOV'T CODE ANN. §§ 505.151-.156).

904 *Id.* § 383.111 (West 2005).

905 *Id.* § 383.112.

906 *Id.* § 383.061(b).

907 *See* Op. Tex. Att'y Gen. No. JC-291 (2000) (Concluding county development districts do not have the power to levy ad valorem taxes).

908 TEX. LOC. GOV'T CODE ANN. § 383.063 (West 2005).

909 *Id.* § 383.064.

Ability to Sue or be Sued. The district may sue or be sued in the name of the district in any court in the state. [910]

Application of reporting, disclosure, and ethics requirements. Chapter 49 of the Water Code applies in part to county development districts. A district must adopt an ethics policy, must conduct an annual audit, must file certain reports at the Texas Commission on Environmental Quality, and appoint an investment officer. [911]

Ability to Borrow. The district can borrow money for purposes related to the district's functions. [912]

The directors may pay all necessary costs and expenses that were incurred in the creation and organization of the district. The district can also pay the cost related to the district's investigation of and planning for district projects, the cost of an engineer's report, project design fees, legal fees and other necessary expenses. [913] Also, the district can use the same definition of what is a permissible "cost" that is used by a Type B development corporations. [914]

If a district decides to issue bonds, the bonds can be used to defray all or part of the costs of the district's projects. [915] To pay the principal and interest on the bonds, the district may use its sales tax revenue, designated project revenues, or any grants, donations or other funds. [916] Bond proceeds can be used by the district to pay interest on the bonds during the acquisition or construction of a project, to pay administrative and operating expenses of a project, to create a reserve to repay the bonds, and to pay all expenses that were incurred during the issuance, sale and delivery of the bonds. [917]

Eligibility and Procedure to Create a County Development District

A county development district can be created only in a county with a population of 400,000 or less. [918] Also, a county development district sales tax cannot be imposed if the combined sales tax rate in any part of the proposed district would exceed the two percent statutory cap for local sales tax. [919]

A county cannot initiate a county development district on its own motion. Rather, establishment of a district must be requested by a petition filed with the commissioners court of the county in which all of the land in the proposed district is located. The petition must include a sworn

---

[910]   *Id.* § 383.062.
[911]   *See id.* § 383.003(c) (West 2005), TEX. WATER CODE ANN. §§ 49.001(a)(1), .002(a) (West 2008).
[912]   TEX. LOC. GOV'T CODE ANN. § 383.065 (West 2005).
[913]   *Id.* § 383.066.
[914]   *Id.* § 383.004(4) (West Supp. 2011).
[915]   *Id.* § 383.081 (West 2005).
[916]   *Id.* § 383.082.
[917]   *Id.* § 383.083.
[918]   *Id.* § 383.021(a).
[919]   *Id.* § 383.106(a).

statement by all of the landowners indicating consent to the creation of the proposed district.[920] The petition must also meet the following requirements:

- describe the boundaries of the proposed district by metes and bounds or by lot and block number if there is a recorded map or plat survey of the area;

- name of the district, which must include the name of the county followed by "Development District No. _____";

- name five persons who will serve on a temporary board of directors;

- state the general nature of work to be done and provide a current estimate of the cost of the project; and

- state the necessity and feasibility of the proposed district and indicate whether the district will take actions that will attract visitors and tourists to the county and the district.[921]

Once a petition requesting the creation of the district is submitted to the commissioners court, a public hearing must be scheduled to allow testimony for or against the proposed district.[922] The date, time and place of this hearing must be set by the county within 60 days of the county's receipt of the petition.[923] The county must publish notice of the hearing in a newspaper of general circulation in the county no later than 30 days before the hearing.[924] Additionally, notice of the hearing must be mailed to all of the landowners in the proposed district and to the developer of the project.[925] Finally, notice of the meeting must be properly posted at the county courthouse 72 hours in advance in compliance with the Texas Open Meetings Act.[926]

At the required public hearing, the commissioners court must examine the sufficiency of the petition requesting creation of the development district.[927] Also, any interested person who wishes to speak about the sufficiency of the petition or about whether the district should be created must be allowed to do so. Lastly, in conducting the required public hearing, the commissioners court should comply with all the requirements of the Texas Open Meetings Act.[928]

After the required public hearing, the commissioners court must make two findings regarding the petition. First, it must determine whether the petition meets statutory requirements. Second, the commissioners court must find that the district and its proposed projects would be feasible, necessary, and serve the public purpose of attracting visitors or tourists to the county.[929] If the commissioners court grants the petition, the order creating the district may specify that the cost to the county of publishing notice, conducting the hearings for the creation of the district, and conducting the sales and use tax election are to be borne by the district.[930] Further, the county

---

[920]   *Id.* § 383.022.
[921]   *Id.* § 383.023.
[922]   *Id.* § 383.024.
[923]   *Id.*
[924]   *Id.* § 383.025.
[925]   *Id.*
[926]   TEX. GOV'T CODE ANN. §§ 551.041, .049 (West 2004), .043 (West Supp. 2011).
[927]   TEX. LOC. GOV'T CODE ANN. § 383.026 (West 2005).
[928]   TEX. GOV'T CODE ANN. §§ 551.001 *et seq.* (West 2004 & Supp. 2011).
[929]   TEX. LOC. GOV'T CODE ANN. § 383.027(a) (West 2005).
[930]   *Id.* § 383.027(b).

may require the petitioner to pay to the county the amounts specified in the order creating the district at the time the order becomes final.[931]

If the commissioners court finds that the petition does not meet statutory requirements, it must enter an order denying the petition. The petition must also be denied if the commissioners court finds that the creation of the district and the proposed project is not feasible and necessary and would not serve the purpose of attracting visitors and tourists to the county.[932]

Initiating an Election to Adopt a County Development District

If the commissioners court finds that the petition meets statutory requirements and that the district would promote the required public purposes, it must approve the petition and appoint five temporary directors to the board for the proposed district.[933] This temporary board then must call an election on the creation of the district and the adoption of a sales tax to fund district projects.[934] The permissible rates for a local sales tax under this authority are one-fourth of one percent, three-eighths of one percent, or one-half of one percent.[935] In no case may the sales tax be imposed if the combined local sales tax rate in any part of the district would exceed the two percent statutory cap for local sales tax.[936] The order calling for an election on the district and on the imposition of a sales tax to fund district projects (a combined proposition) must include the following information:

- the nature of the election, including the proposition that is to appear on the ballot;
- the date of the election;
- the hours during which the polls will be open;
- the location of the polling places; and
- the proposed rate of the sales and use tax for the district.[937]

The temporary directors of the development district must publish a substantial copy of the election order for two consecutive weeks in a newspaper with general circulation in the county. The first notice must be published prior to the 14th day before the election.[938] The notice must also include the wording of all the ballot propositions. The entire notice must generally be provided both in English and in Spanish.[939]

The election ballot must give the voters the opportunity to approve or reject the proposed development district. The ballot must use the following wording:

---

931   *Id.*
932   *Id.* § 383.027(c).
933   *Id.* §§ 383.027(a), .028(a).
934   *Id.* § 383.030.
935   *Id.* § 383.103.
936   *Id.* § 383.106(a).
937   *Id.* § 383.031.
938   *Id.* § 383.032.
939   *See* TEX. ELEC. CODE ANN. §§ 272.001 *et. seq.* (West 2010 & Supp. 2011).

The creation of _____ County Development District No. _____ and the adoption of a proposed local sales and use tax rate of (*the rate specified in the election order*) to be used for the promotion and development of tourism. [940]

Conducting an Election to Approve a County Development District

When the board of a county development district orders an election for the levy of a sales tax, it must follow all applicable requirements for special elections contained in the Election Code, the County Sales and Use Tax Act (Chapter 323 of the Tax Code), and any other Texas statutes regarding elections. Specifically, the following requirements must be met:

Potential Dates for the Election. The election must be held on a uniform election date as provided by Chapter 41 of the Election Code. There are uniform election dates in May and November. The current uniform election dates are:

- the second Saturday in May in an odd-numbered year;
- the second Saturday in May in an even-numbered year, for an electionheld by a politica, subdivision other than a county; or
- the first Tuesday after the first Monday in November. [941]

Time Frame for Ordering the Election. The district should order the election at least 71 days prior to the date of the election, unless the election is the general election for state and county officers. [942] If the election is the general election for state and county officers, then the district should order the election at least 78 days prior to the date of the election. [943] Section 383 of the Local Government Code does not address how far in advance the election must be ordered by the board. [944] Nonetheless, it is advisable to provide at least 71 or 78 days' notice, since this is the requirement applicable to most other special elections in Texas, and it allows time to comply with other Election Code requirements, such as early voting. Also, the Legislature added a provision noting the Election Code provision "supersedes a law outside this code to the extent of any conflict." [945]

Joint Elections. Chapter 271 of the Election Code allows two or more political subdivisions to enter into an agreement to hold the elections jointly in the election precincts that can be served by common polling places, subject to certain other provisions in the Election Code. This provision allows small governmental units, including county development districts, to share the costs of conducting elections, which can otherwise be a fiscal burden. For example, a county development district can pay a fee to the county in which it is located to pay for the use of the election personnel at the polling place closest to the district.

Other Procedural Requirements. The board must follow all other applicable procedural requirements under the Election Code for special elections. For further information about the

---

[940]   TEX. LOC. GOV'T CODE ANN. § 383.033(b) (West 2005).
[941]   TEX. ELEC. CODE ANN. § 41.001(a) (West Supp. 2011).
[942]   *Id.* § 3.005(c).
[943]   *Id.*
[944]   TEX. LOC. GOV'T CODE ANN. § 383.031 (West 2005).
[945]   TEX. ELEC. CODE ANN. § 3.005(b) (West Supp. 2011).

requirements contained in the Election Code, contact the Secretary of State's Office, Elections Division, at (800) 252-8683.

Reporting Results of a County Development District Election

The Election Code requires that, no earlier than the eighth day and no later than the eleventh day[946] after an election, the temporary board of the county development district must canvass the ballots and enter the results of the election into the minutes of a meeting.[947] If a majority of the votes cast are in favor of the district, the temporary board, by order, declares the district created and the amount of the tax adopted and enters the results in the minutes.[948] If the outcome is the opposite, then the temporary board, by order, declares the proposition to create the district failed and enter the results in the minutes.[949]

Whether the results of the election create the district or not, the board must send a certified copy of the order by certified or registered mail to the commissioners court, the Comptroller, and to any other taxing entity with jurisdiction over the property within the district.[950] The order must include the following:

- the date of the election;
- the proposition on which the vote was held;
- the total number of votes cast for and against the proposition; and
- the number of votes by which the proposition was approved.[951]

In addition to the certified copy of the order, the board must send the Comptroller a map of the district clearly showing the district's boundaries. After receiving the documents, the Comptroller has 30 days to notify the board that the Comptroller's Office will administer the tax.

Unlike economic development corporations, which must wait one year between holding certain elections, the board of a county development district may call for another election at any time if the election should fail.[952]

Effective Date of County Development District Sales Tax

The change in the sales tax rate becomes effective on the first day of the first calendar quarter after the expiration of the first complete calendar quarter occurring after notice of the election has been provided to the Comptroller.[953] The new tax rate applies to purchases on or after the effective date as provided under Section 323.102(c) of the Tax Code.

---

[946] TEX. ELEC. CODE ANN. § 67.003 (West 2010).

[947] In contrast to the Election Code, Section 383.034 of the Local Government Code does not address the time limit the development district's temporary board has to canvass an election to confirm the district and to adopt the sales tax. It is recommended that district boards follow the provisions of the Election Code and canvass the election between 8 and 11 days after it has taken place.

[948] TEX. LOC. GOV'T CODE § 383.034(b) (West 2005).

[949] *Id.*

[950] *Id.* § 383.034(c).

[951] *Id.*

[952] *Id.* § 383.102(a) (Excluding Section 323.406 of the Tax Code which imposed a one year waiting period between elections).

[953] TEX. TAX CODE ANN. § 323.102(c) (West 2008).

May Election: Send notice to the Comptroller no later than the last week in June. On October 1ˢᵗ, the new tax rate will take effect. The district will receive its first payment in December.

November Election: Send notice to the Comptroller no later than the last week in December. On April 1ˢᵗ, the new tax rate will take effect. The district will receive its first payment in June.

If adopted, the sales tax would apply to the retail sale of all sales taxable items within the district after the effective date of the tax.[954]

Allocation of the Sales Tax Proceeds by the Comptroller

Once the sales tax is effective, retailers collect it along with any other applicable sales taxes including the state sales tax, and remit the revenues to the Comptroller. The Comptroller remits the proceeds to the district. The County Sales and Use Tax Act (Chapter 323 of the Tax Code) governs the imposition, computation, administration and use of the tax, except where it is inconsistent with the County Development District Act.[955]

Limitations on District Sales Tax Rates

A county development district may levy a sales tax only if the combined sales tax rate in any part of the proposed district would not exceed the two percent statutory cap for local sales tax.[956] Other factors also may influence the rate at which a development district can impose a sales tax. For example, if the city in which a district is located imposes or increases its sales tax rate, the county development district's tax rate is automatically reduced to stay below the two percent cap.[957] If a city annexes a district and this results in the combined local sales tax climbing over two percent, the district's tax rate is also reduced to stay under the local sales tax limit.[958] In either circumstance, the city must reimburse the development district the difference in the amount of taxes the district would have collected before the tax rate was reduced and the amount the district is able to charge after the reduction.[959] The city has 10 days to reimburse the development district after the city receives its funds from the Comptroller, and the city must reimburse the district as long as the district has outstanding bonds to pay.[960]

Power of the District to Increase, Decrease or Abolish the County Development District Sales Tax

In addition to the automatic sales tax reductions discussed above, a county development district may increase, decrease or abolish its sales tax in two ways. First, the district's board, on its own motion, may vote to decrease or abolish the tax.[961] Alternatively, the board may call for an

---

[954]   Tᴇx. Lᴏc. Gᴏv'ᴛ Cᴏᴅᴇ § 383.101(b) (West 2005).

[955]   *Id.* § 383.102(a).

[956]   *Id.* § 383.106(a).

[957]   *Id.* § 383.106(b).

[958]   *Id.*

[959]   *Id.* § 383.106(c).

[960]   *Id.*

[961]   *Id.* § 383.104(a).

election to increase, decrease or abolish the tax. [962] The election must be conducted using the same procedures that were followed for the creation of the tax. [963] The ballots must read as follows:

> **To Increase or Decrease the Tax:** "The increase (decrease) in the local sales and use tax rate of (*name of district*) to (*percentage*) to be used for the promotion and development of tourism;" or

> **To Abolish the Tax:** "The abolition of the district sales and use tax used for the promotion and development of tourism." [964]

There is no statutory authorization for a voter-initiated petition to decrease or abolish the tax. An election on these issues is called at the discretion of the county development district board of directors.

Additionally, the county development district's sales and use tax will automatically discontinue by operation of law if no sales tax revenue is collected within the district before the first anniversary of the date the sales tax took effect. [965]

Board of Directors of a County Development District

The operation of the county development district is managed by its board of directors. Upon voter approval of the district, the temporary board of directors automatically becomes the district's permanent board of directors. [966]

To be qualified to serve on the board, a director must be at least 21 years of age, a resident citizen of Texas, and a registered voter in the county in which the district is located. [967] A developer of property within the district, as well as certain relatives, employees and independent contractors of that developer, may be disqualified from serving on the board. [968]

The directors of a county development district serve staggered terms of four years, with two or three board position terms expiring on September 1 of every other year. [969] Each director, whether temporary or permanent, must execute a bond in the amount of $10,000 and take the oath of office required for public officers under the Texas Constitution. [970] Temporary and permanent board members are not entitled to compensation for their service. The board members, however, are entitled to be reimbursed by the district for their actual expenses. [971]

A quorum of the board consists of three members. [972] Once the directors have taken their oaths of office, the board votes to elect a president, a vice president, a secretary and any other officer the

---

[962]   *Id.*
[963]   *Id.* § 383.104(b).
[964]   *Id.*
[965]   *Id.* § 383.104(c).
[966]   *Id.* § 383.041(a).
[967]   *Id.* § 383.042.
[968]   *See Id.* § 383.043.
[969]   *Id.* § 383.041(b).
[970]   *Id.* §§ 383.029(a), .046 (Section 383.046 refer to Local Government Code § 375.067).
[971]   *Id.* §§ 383.029(a), .046 (Section 383.046 refer to Local Government Code § 375.070).
[972]   *Id.* § 383.048(a).

board considers necessary.[973] The board president presides at all meetings, with the vice president fulfilling this duty in the absence of the president.[974] Regular meetings are held to conduct the business of the district,[975] with notice of the meetings posted in accordance with the Open Meetings Act at an accessible place in the district.[976] The county clerk also must post a copy of the notice in the county courthouse. The board is required to establish a district office in the county in which the district is located.[977] The board has control over the management of the district and has the authority to employ any person or any company that the board deems necessary to conduct district business,[978] so long as that employment or appointment does not violate other provisions of law.[979]

The board of directors may vote to adopt bylaws to govern the affairs of the board.[980] Any director who has an interest in a contract with the district, or who is employed by a company that has a financial interest must disclose this interest to the board. An interested board member can neither discuss nor vote on acceptance of such a contract.[981] A contract entered into without disclosure of a director's financial interest is invalid.[982] The County Development District Act does not specify whether a contract would be invalidated if a board member with an interest in the contract disclosed that interest to the board but then proceeded to discuss or vote on the contract. Board members must file disclosure statements if they have certain relationships with vendors that the district does business with,[983] and must receive Public Information Act and Open Meetings Act training because they are local government officials.[984]

Replacements to the board are made by appointment of the commissioners court.[985] If a majority of the other board directors petition the court for removal of a board member, the commissioners court may remove a director after notice and a hearing.[986] There is no statutory authority for the commissioners court to remove a director except pursuant to a request by a majority of the existing board members.

Approval of an Expansion or Decrease in the Area of the District

The board of directors for the district may ask the commissioners court to add or exclude land from the district.[987] Also, an interested landowner may ask the commissioners court to approve such a change.[988] It is then within the discretion of the commissioners court whether to approve

---

[973] *Id.* § 383.047.
[974] *Id.* § 383.048(b).
[975] *Id.* § 383.053(a).
[976] *Id.* § 383.053(b)-(c).
[977] *Id.* § 383.052.
[978] *Id.* § 383.050.
[979] *See, for example,* Ch. 573 of the Government Code (Nepotism) and Ch. 171 of the Local Government Code (Conflict of Interest).
[980] TEX. LOC. GOV'T CODE ANN. § 383.049 (West 2005).
[981] *Id.* § 383.051(a)-(b).
[982] *Id.* § 383.051(c).
[983] *Id.* §§ 176.001–.012 (West 2008 & Supp. 2011).
[984] TEX. GOV. CODE ANN. §§ 551.005, 552.012 (West Supp. 2011).
[985] TEX. LOC. GOV'T CODE ANN. § 383.045 (West 2005).
[986] *Id.* § 383.044.
[987] *Id.* § 383.084(a).
[988] *Id.*

the proposed expansion or decrease in the area. Any such approval must be by a unanimous vote of approval by the commissioners court.[989] There is no statutory requirement for a public vote to either increase or decrease the size of the district. However, the size of the district can only be expanded or reduced prior to the issuance of any bonds.[990]

Dissolution of a County Development District

There are three ways in which a county development district can be dissolved. Those 3 ways are either:

1) a petition from the board to the commissioners court asking to dissolve the district because the majority of the board has found the proposed projects cannot be accomplished and no bonds or credit have been issued;

2) a petition from the board to the commissioner court asking to dissolve the district because the majority of the board has found that all bonds or other debts of the district have been paid and the purpose of the district have been accomplished; [991] or

3) an agreement to dissolve the district between the board and a city because the district is located wholly within the city or is wholly annexed by the city.[992]

If the dissolution is being done by a petition of the board because of either the first or second reasons above, the commissioners court must provide notice and a public hearing as required under Section 383.024 of the Local Government Code.[993] At the public hearing, the commissioners court must determine whether it is in the best interests of the county and the district landowners to dissolve the district. If the commissioners court unanimously finds dissolution is in the best interest of the county, the finding is entered in the court records, and all funds and property of the district are transferred to the commissioners court.[994]

As mentioned above, dissolution of the district can be accomplished by an agreement between the district and a city if the district is located wholly within or is wholly annexed by the city. This form of dissolution requires the district to turn over to the city all money, property and other assets of the district.[995] In turn, the city is required to assume all contracts, debts, bonds and other obligations of the district. If such an agreement is made to dissolve the district, the taxes levied by the district end at the same time the district is dissolved.

There is not a provision for dissolution of the district pursuant to a petition and/or election of the landowners.[996]

---

[989]   *Id.* § 383.084(b).
[990]   *Id.* § 383.084(a).
[991]   *Id.* § 383.122(a).
[992]   *Id.* § 383.123.
[993]   *Id.* § 383.122(b).
[994]   *Id.* § 383.122(c).
[995]   *Id.* § 383.123.
[996]   *Id.* § 383.121.

V.   City, County, Cooperative and Regional Efforts

A City's Authority to Make Grants and Loans

Chapter 380 of the Local Government Code provides significant legislative authority for Texas municipalities in the area of economic development. When a city wants to provide a grant or a loan of city funds or services in order to promote economic development, it generally cites its powers under Chapter 380. Cities have utilized provisions under this law to provide a myriad of incentives that have drawn businesses and industries to locales throughout Texas. The text of Chapter 380 is very short but its importance to economic development cannot be overstated. Provided below is the text of its main provision, Section 380.001.

LOCAL GOVERNMENT CODE
TITLE 12. PLANNING AND DEVELOPMENT
SUBTITLE A. MUNICIPAL PLANNING AND DEVELOPMENT

CHAPTER 380. MISCELLANEOUS PROVISIONS RELATING TO MUNICIPAL PLANNING AND DEVELOPMENT

Sec. 380.001. ECONOMIC DEVELOPMENT PROGRAMS.

(a) The governing body of a municipality may establish and provide for the administration of one or more programs, including programs for making loans and grants of public money and providing personnel and services of the municipality, to promote state or local economic development and to stimulate business and commercial activity in the municipality. For purposes of this subsection, a municipality includes an area that:

  (1) has been annexed by the municipality for limited purposes; or

  (2) is in the extraterritorial jurisdiction of the municipality.

(b) The governing body may:

  (1) administer a program by the use of municipal personnel;

  (2) contract with the federal government, the state, a political subdivision of the state, a nonprofit organization, or any other entity for the administration of a program; and

  (3) accept contributions, gifts, or other resources to develop and administer a program.

(c) Any city along the Texas-Mexico border with a population of more than 500,000 may establish not-for-profit corporations and cooperative associations for the purpose of creating and developing an intermodal transportation hub to stimulate economic development. Such intermodal hub may also function as an international intermodal transportation center and may be collocated with or near local, state, or federal facilities and facilities of Mexico in order to fulfill its purpose.

What this statute allows is the provision of loans and grants of city funds, as well as the use of city staff, city facilities or city services, at minimal or no charge. Whether a city provides any such incentive is completely discretionary. The provision of grants and loans should be used with caution and with attention to necessary safeguards.

A home rule city may grant public money from authorized sources to a Type A or Type B economic development corporation under a contract authorized by Section 380.002 of the Local Government Code. The Type A or Type B economic development corporation is required to use the money for "the development and diversification of the economy of the state, elimination of unemployment or underemployment in the state, and development and expansion of commerce in the state."[997]

To establish a loan or grant, or to offer discounted or free city services, a city must meet the requirements contained in the Texas Constitution and in applicable Texas statutes. Additionally, a city must review its city charter and any other local provisions that may limit the city's ability to provide such a grant or loan. A discussion of these issues follows.

Ensuring that a Public Purpose Is Served by the Incentive

First, any expenditure in the form of a grant, loan or provision of city services at less than fair market value involves a donation of public property. Article III, Section 52-a of the Texas Constitution sets up the constitutional framework for public funding of economic development efforts. It provides that economic development is a public purpose. However, a city may not simply write out checks to interested businesses in order to promote economic development. The city must ensure that the public purpose of economic development will be pursued by the business. For example, if a city provides a grant or a loan to an industry, the city should enter into a binding contract with the funded industry that outlines what steps the business will take that justify the provision of public funding (creation of jobs, expansion of the tax base by construction or enhancement of the physical facilities, etc.). The city should include a recapture provision in the agreement so that if the business does not fulfill its promises, the city will have a right to seek reimbursement of the incentives that were provided. Any such agreement should also include tangible means for measuring whether the industry has met its obligations under the contract. Without these safeguards and a demonstrable benefit to the municipality, such incentives may not pass constitutional muster for serving a public purpose.[998]

Requirements Under the Local Government Code

Any grant or loan must also meet certain statutory requirements. Chapter 380 of the Local Government Code requires that in order for a city to provide a grant or a loan, it must "establish a program" to implement the incentive. The program may be administered by city personnel, by contract with the federal government, the state, or a political subdivision or by contract with any other entity. The applicable statutes do not indicate specifically how such a program is to be administered. It is safe to expect that the program should be planned and outlined in a written document that includes, at a minimum, the safeguards discussed above.

Additionally, any such grant or loan must meet the requirements under the budget law contained in Chapter 102 of the Local Government Code. Specifically, any economic development-related expenditure of city funds must be made pursuant to consideration and approval of the item at an

---

[997]   TEX. LOC. GOV'T CODE ANN. § 380.002(b) (West Supp. 2011).

[998]   *See* Op. Tex. Att'y Gen. No. GA-529 (2007) (City may fund housing project if it finds the project will promote economic development). *See also* Tex. Att'y Gen. LO-94-037 at 3, LO-97-061 at 4 (These two opinions do not concern the establishment of economic development programs under the authority of Local Government Code Chapter 380. However, their reasoning applies to any grant or loan of public money for economic development, regardless of the authority under which such a grant or loan is made.).

open meeting of the city council. If the expenditure was not included within the original budget, the city council would need to pursue a budget amendment.[999]

Compliance with Applicable City Charter Provisions and Local Policies

Home rule cities (cities with a population of over 5,000 that have adopted a city charter) generally may take any actions that are authorized by their city charter and that are not inconsistent with the Texas Constitution, Texas statutes or federal law.[1000] A home rule city must always review its city charter to determine whether it contains any limitations on the ability of the city to make various expenditures. Sometimes a city charter will be more restrictive than state law or will require a super-majority vote for the approval of certain types of expenditures.

Cities with a population of 5,000 or less are usually general law cities. General law cities do not have a city charter and are limited by state law in terms of what expenditures may be made and how to approve them. Accordingly, general law cities must be able to cite a statute that authorizes the type of expenditure or action they are contemplating as part of their economic development program. In certain circumstances, Chapter 380 of the Local Government Code may provide that authority. If a general law city cannot find any statutory authority for the action it wants to take, it does not have authority to take the action. Of course, the city council of a general law city may impose additional local restrictions on the ability of the city to expend money for certain purposes. The city would then have to comply with any such self-imposed limitations or rights.

Review for Conflict with City Bond and Grant Documents

If a city endeavors to offer its city services on a reduced or no-cost basis, the city must review any bond documents that may have been executed with regard to those services. The bond documents must be analyzed to ensure that providing reduced or no-cost service is permitted. For example, if a city has issued bonds to fund a municipal utility system or to fund some other type of public facility, the bond documents may prohibit the city from giving away its utility services or otherwise limiting any other revenue stream until the bonds are fully repaid. Before the city agrees to any type of incentive that involves a gift of public services or funds, it should have its bond counsel and local city attorney review any existing bond and other debt instruments in this regard. This type of limitation may also be part of the conditions placed on a city if it is a recipient of a state or federal grant. Accordingly, the city should review any grant documents it has in its possession to determine if there is any such limitation.

With regard to utility service in particular, Chapter 1502 of the Government Code generally prohibits city-owned utilities from providing free utility services except to city public schools or

---

[999] *See* TEX. LOC. GOV'T. CODE ANN. § 102.009 (West 2008) (Authorizes an amendment to the original city budget only in the case of "grave public necessity."). *See Rains v. Mercantile National Bank of Dallas*, 188 S.W.2d 798, 803 (Tex. Civ. App. - El Paso 1945), aff'd on other grounds, 191 S.W.2d 850 (Tex. 1946); *Bexar County v. Hatley*, 150 S.W.2d 980 (Tex. 1941).

[1000] *See generally, Dallas Merchant's and Concessionaire's Ass'n v. City of Dallas*, 852 S.W.2d 489, 491 (Tex.1993); *City of Richardson v. Responsible Dog Owners*, 794 S.W.2d 17, 19 (Tex.1990).

to buildings and institutions operated by the city.[1001] Also, that chapter requires that the rates charged for utility services be equal and uniform.

Executing Debt Versus Using Current Funds

It is clear from Chapter 380 of the Local Government Code that a city may provide "loans and grants of public money" from the city's current funds. However, Chapter 380 does not provide any express authorization for the city to finance such a program through the issuance of debt or bonds. Texas courts have long required a city to cite specific legal authority for the issuance of any debt instrument. Debt is defined as any obligation that is not completely paid within the current fiscal year from budgeted revenue.[1002]

If the city is a home rule city, it can look to the provisions of its city charter for authority to issue debt as long as those provisions are not inconsistent with state law. A home rule city has the power to issue bonds to the extent provided in the city charter, assuming that the bonds have first been authorized by voters at an election held on the issue.[1003] Often, however, a city charter is silent as to the authority of the city to issue bonds or other debt instruments to promote economic development. If this is the case, the city will need to find other authority within Texas statutes that allows for the issuance of bonds or debt to finance economic development.

If the city is a general law city, it may not issue debt except when there is specific statutory authority that permits the issuance of debt for that purpose. A general law city is limited to taking only those actions that are specifically authorized under the general statutes of Texas. Accordingly, a general law city may be able to fund economic development programs with current city funds under Chapter 380 of the Local Government Code. However, such cities cannot issue debt or bonds without finding specific legislative authority for that type of transaction. For further discussion on the ability of general law cities and home rule cities to issue debt, see the chapter in this handbook titled "Issuing Debt To Finance Economic Development."

Use of Dedicated Tax Funds for Economic Development

A home rule city may grant public money to a Type A or Type B economic development corporation under a contract authorized by Section 380.002 of the Local Government Code. However, as the statute provides, the funds granted by the city to the Type A or Type B corporation must be derived from any source lawfully available to the municipality under its charter or other law other than from the proceeds of bonds or other obligations of the municipality payable from ad valorem taxes.[1004] Creating a program or making a loan or grant through Chapter 380 that is not secured by a pledge of ad valorem taxes or financed by the issuance of bonds or other obligations payable from ad valorem taxes does not constitute or

---

[1001] TEX. GOV'T CODE ANN. § 1502.057(b) (West 2000) (Which prohibits a city from providing free electric, water, sewer or other utility system services except for municipal public buildings, or buildings and institutions operated by the city).

[1002] *See McNeill v. City of Waco*, 89 Tex. 83, 33 S.W. 322 (1895) (Long term debt is any contractual obligation that creates a liability that cannot be paid out of current budget year revenues).

[1003] TEX. GOV'T CODE ANN. § 1331.052(b) (West 2000). *See* Op. Tex. Att'y Gen. No. DM-185 (1992).

[1004] TEX. LOC. GOV'T CODE ANN. § 380.002(c) (West Supp. 2011).

create an unconstitutional debt for purposes of the Texas Constitution.[1005] If a city is using funds other than the property tax, care must be taken to ensure that the city is complying with any limitations imposed on the use of such funds by statute (e.g., statutory provisions relating to dedicated funds, such as the economic development sales tax, hotel occupancy tax, etc., that limit the purposes for which those funds may be used). A city should consult any applicable law to be certain the revenues are used as permitted.

Providing Land to Promote Economic Development

Often, cities try to obtain sites that they can show to businesses that may relocate to the area. Such a site may be a tract of land that is ready for development. In certain cases, a city may find it beneficial to construct a basic structure that can be altered or developed to meet the new business' needs. There are certain legal requirements regarding the procedure for a city to acquire such real property and limitations on the city's ability to sell or grant the land to a business entity.

Procedures for Acquiring Real Property

Chapter 273 of the Local Government Code provides a list of purposes for which a city may purchase property.[1006] A local government could certainly facilitate economic development by purchasing property for one of the uses set forth in Chapter 273. Some of the permissible purposes for the purchase of property under that statute include purchases for municipal water systems, sewage plants and systems, municipal airports, city streets, etc. For instance, if the roads leading to the industrial park needed to be widened, a city could purchase the necessary right-of-way for such an improvement. However, there is no authority in Chapter 273 for a city to purchase land for use by a private entity. Economic development itself is not one of the listed purposes.

Eminent domain may also be an option for acquiring real property. A local government should consult with its legal counsel and any affected landowners before pursuing this course of action.

Finally, if a city decides to purchase real property; it must follow the applicable budgetary laws contained in Chapter 102 of the Local Government Code. A home rule city must also comply with any further requirements contained in the city charter. Unlike the purchase of personal property or the purchase of certain services, expenditures by a city for real property are not required to be competitively bid.[1007]

Procedure for the Sale of Real Property by a City

Once a city has obtained a piece of real property, Chapter 272 of the Local Government Code controls how that property may be sold or transferred. Chapter 272 states that the sale of real property owned by a city must be accomplished through advertisement of the property and acceptance of competitive bids. Accordingly, if a city wants to sell or transfer a property to a business to promote economic development, the city needs to comply with the requirements of Chapter 272. Specifically, Section 272.001(a) states that, with certain exceptions:

[1005] TEX. CONST. art.III, §52-a.
[1006] TEX. LOC. GOV'T CODE ANN. § 273.001 (West 2005).
[1007] *Id.* § 252.022(a)(6).

". . . before land owned by a political subdivision of the state may be sold or exchanged for other land, notice to the general public of the offer of the land for sale or exchange must be published in a newspaper of general circulation in either the county in which the land is located or, if there is no such newspaper, in an adjoining county. The notice must include a description of the land, including its location, and the procedure by which the sealed bids to purchase the land or offers to exchange the land may be submitted. The notice must be published on two separate dates and the sale or exchange may not be made until after the 14th day after the date of the second publication."[1008]

There are certain exceptions to the sale-by-bid requirement. Sale of real property by bid is not required if the real property fits into any of the following categories:

1) narrow strips of land, or land that because of its shape, lack of access to public roads, or small area cannot be used independently under its current zoning or under applicable subdivision or development control ordinances;

2) streets or alleys owned in fee or used by easement;

3) land or a real property interest originally acquired for streets' right-of-way, or easements that the political subdivision chooses to exchange for other land to be used for streets, right-of-ways, easements, or other public purposes, including transactions partly for cash;

4) land that the political subdivision wants to have developed by contract with an independent foundation;

5) a real property interest conveyed to a governmental entity that has the power of eminent domain;

6) city land that is located in a reinvestment zone that has been designated as provided by law and that the city desires to have developed under a project plan adopted by the city for the zone;

7) a property interest owned by a defense base development authority established under Chapter 378 of the Local Government Code;[1009] or

8) land that is owned by a municipally owned utility (under certain circumstances).[1010]

If real property fits into one of the above categories, it does not have to be sold pursuant to notice and competitive bids. These parcels may be sold through a private sale agreement between the city and an interested buyer. Additionally, property under either of the first two categories may be sold to the abutting property owners only as provided under Section 272.001(c) of the Local Government Code, and the city is not required to receive fair market value for the property.

Also, a city can donate or sell property for less than fair market value, without following the notice and bidding process, to another political subdivision if:

1) The land or interest will be used by the political subdivision to which it is donated or sold in carrying out a purpose that benefits the public interest of the city;

[1008]   *Id.* § 273.001 (West Supp. 2011).
[1009]   *Id.* § 272.001(b).
[1010]   *Id.* § 272.001(k).

2) The donation or sale is made under terms that effect and maintain the public purpose for which the donation or sale is made; and

3) The title and right to possession of the land or interest reverts to the city if the acquiring political subdivision ceases to use the land or interest in carrying out the public purpose.[1011]

Additionally, there is a special statutory exception allowing a private sale of city-owned property if the real property is acquired by the city with economic development funds from the community development block grant nonentitlement program. Land acquired with these funds may be leased or conveyed without the solicitation of bids. To convey the land in this manner, the city must adopt a resolution stating the conditions for the conveyance and the public purpose that will be achieved.[1012] If the city exercises this option, the land may be leased or sold to a private for-profit entity or to a nonprofit entity that is a party to a contract with the political subdivision. The land must be used by the receiving entity to carry out the purpose of the entity's grant or contract as provided under Section 272.001(i) of the Local Government Code.

Texas law allows a political subdivision of the state, including a city, to convey an interest in real property to an institution of higher education to promote a public purpose related to higher education.[1013] Under this statutory provision, a city may donate, exchange, sell or lease land or improvements to an institution of higher education, as that term is defined by Section 61.003 of the Education Code. The city conveying the land must determine the conditions and terms of the conveyance so as to ensure that the desired public purpose is served and that it meets the constitutional requirements of article III, sections 51 and 52, of the Texas Constitution. A conveyance of land is not required to comply with the normal competitive bidding and notice requirements of Chapter 272 of the Local Government Code. In addition, the city (or other political subdivision) is not required to receive fair market value for the land. An economic development corporation also may convey property to an institution of higher education.[1014]

Under certain circumstances, a city may convey land to an economic development corporation created by the city without complying with the notice and bidding requirements of Chapter 272.[1015] Under this provision of the law, city land may be sold to a city-created economic development corporation for fair market value if the land meets both of the following criteria:

1) the land was a gift to the city or was received by the city as part of a legal settlement; and

2) the land is adjacent to an area designated for development by the economic development corporation.

In order to sell land under this provision, the city must adopt an ordinance describing the property to be conveyed and must require that the conveyance comply with Section 5.022 of the Property Code (except that a covenant of general warranty is not required) and must state the consideration paid by the corporation for the land.

[1011] *Id.* § 272.001(l).
[1012] *Id.* § 272.001(i).
[1013] *Id.* § 272.001(j).
[1014] *Id.* § 501.154.
[1015] *Id.* § 253.009.

Also, a city with a population under 20,000 or less, may transfer real property or an interest in real property to and economic development corporation governed by Chapter 504 or 505 of the Local Government Code without complying with the notice and bidding requirements of Chapter 272.[1016] The consideration for this transfer is an agreement between the city and the economic development corporation.[1017] The economic development corporation will agree to use the property that promotes a public purpose of the city. If, at any time, the economic development corporation fails to use the property in accordance with the agreement, the property will automatically revert to the city. These provisions shall be in the appropriate instrument that transfers the property to the economic development corporation.[1018] However, if the city acquired the property through eminent domain, it may not transfer the property to an economic development corporation.[1019]

Finally, for cities under 1.9 million, a transfer of title or interest in land to a federally-exempt nonprofit organization is also exempt from the notice and bidding requirements of Chapter 272 of the Local Government Code.[1020] An agreement with the nonprofit organization must require use of the land in a manner that primarily promotes a public purpose of the city. Failure to use the property in this manner results in reversion of the property to the city. These two provisions of public use and reversion must be included in the legal instrument of transfer.

Municipal Agreements Not to Annex

To attract a business into an area, a city may choose to encourage the business to locate in the city's extraterritorial jurisdiction. If the business locates in the city's extraterritorial jurisdiction, the city may enter into an agreement not to annex the business property for a set period of time. In this way, the city gets the benefit of having the business locate in the area and the creation of additional jobs. The business in turn is freed from ad valorem taxation of its property by the city for the designated period of time. This approach is termed an "agreement not to annex" and is authorized under Section 42.044 of the Local Government Code.

Section 42.044 allows the governing body of any city to designate a portion of its extraterritorial jurisdiction as an industrial district. The statute does not define the phrase "industrial district" except to indicate that the term has the "customary meaning" and to specify that it includes an area where tourist-related businesses and facilities are located.[1021] Within an industrial district, the city may enter into written contracts to guarantee a business that its property will not be annexed by the city for a period of up to 15 years.[1022] Also, any such agreement may contain other lawful terms and considerations that the parties agree to be reasonable, appropriate and not unduly restrictive of business activities.

The parties to such a contract may renew or extend the agreement not to annex for successive

---

[1016] *Id,* § 253.012(a)-(c).
[1017] *Id.* § 253.012(d).
[1018] *Id.* § 253.012(e).
[1019] *Id.* § 253.012(f).
[1020] *Id.* § 253.011 (West 2005).
[1021] *Id.* § 42.044(a) (West 2008).
[1022] *Id.* § 42.044(c).

periods not to exceed 15 years for each extension.[1023] In the event any owner of land in an industrial district is offered an opportunity to renew or extend a contract, then all owners of land within the district must be offered the same opportunity to renew or extend the agreement.

A city is permitted to provide fire-fighting services within an industrial district that is subject to an agreement not to annex the area.[1024] The services can be performed directly by the city and paid for by the property owners of the district. Alternatively, the city may contract for the provision of the fire-fighting services by an outside source. However, if certain property owners contract to provide their own fire-fighting services, they may not be required to pay any part of the cost of the fire-fighting services provided by the city within the district.[1025]

The law provides several other protections to the city and to the business during the time a property is subject to an agreement not to annex. It provides that a political subdivision may not be created within an industrial district designated under Section 42.044 unless the city gives its written consent by ordinance or resolution.[1026] The city is required to give or deny its consent within 60 days of receiving such a written request. Failure to give or deny consent within the allotted time constitutes the city's consent to the initiation of that political subdivision's creation proceedings. If the city gives its consent or its consent is presumed by the city's failure to act, the political subdivision must initiate its creation within six months and must be finally completed within 18 months. Failure of the proposed political subdivision to comply with these time requirements terminates the consent for the proceedings.

Use of Interlocal Agreements

All levels of local government are interested in securing a stable tax base and sound economic growth for their residents. The ability of local governments to participate in economic development varies according to the statutes that control their operations. Currently, cities and counties are the only types of local governments that are authorized to undertake economic development programs. Accordingly, city and county leaders have often used their respective powers to work together to try to attract and retain business development within their regions.

This regional approach is prevalent in both the rural areas of Texas, where communities may not have the funds to do a great deal of individual marketing of their locales, and the most populous areas of Texas, where a regional approach can maximize the efforts to recruit larger businesses to an urban area. In certain cases, this cooperation is formalized into a written agreement that outlines each of the governmental entities' respective duties. This type of agreement is termed an "interlocal agreement" and is authorized under the Interlocal Cooperation Act contained in Chapter 791 of the Government Code.

The purpose of the Interlocal Cooperation Act is to increase the efficiency and effectiveness of local governments by authorizing them to be able to contract with one another to accomplish their mutual goals.[1027] The Act allows local governments to contract with the State or with other

---

[1023]   *Id.* § 42.044(d).
[1024]   *Id.* § 42.044(e).
[1025]   *Id.* § 42.044(f).
[1026]   *Id.* § 42.045.
[1027]   TEX. GOV'T CODE ANN. § 791.001 (West 2004).

corporate entities organized under state law,[1028] such as development corporations, councils of government (also known as COGs or regional councils), or industrial commissions, to accomplish shared goals. The subject of an interlocal contract must be to perform a "governmental function or services" as outlined under the Act.[1029] Within the Act, there is a category allowing the joint pursuit of "other governmental functions in which the contracting parties are mutually interested."[1030] It is this category that is usually cited as authority for interlocal agreements regarding economic development. However, any contract that is executed by a governmental entity may only require the performance of functions or services that each of the entities would be authorized to perform individually under state law.[1031]

If a city and a county enter into an interlocal agreement regarding economic development efforts, the agreement must meet the applicable requirements under the Act and any requirements under other laws or restrictions that apply to that type of governmental entity. For example, each entity would need to follow the applicable budget laws for that type of governmental entity. Additionally, a home rule city would need to be sure that any agreement that is adopted is consistent with the city's charter.

The Interlocal Cooperation Act contains a number of requirements. It states that any contract under the Act must:

- be authorized by the governing body of each party to the contract;[1032]

- state the purpose, terms, rights and duties of the contracting parties;[1033]

- specify that each party paying for the performance of governmental functions or services must make those payments from current revenues available to the paying party;[1034]

- fairly compensate the performing party for the services or functions performed under the contract;[1035] and

- may have a specified term of years that may be renewed.[1036]

The parties to an interlocal contract may create an administrative agency or designate an existing local government to supervise the performance of the contract.[1037] The agency or designated local government may employ personnel, perform administrative activities, and provide services necessary to perform the interlocal contract.[1038] Additionally, local governments may provide in an interlocal contract for the submission of disputes to alternative dispute resolution.[1039]

[1028]   *Id.* § 791.003(4)-(5) (West Supp. 2011) (Defines "local government" and "political subdivision").
[1029]   *Id.* § 791.003(3) (Defines "governmental functions and services").
[1030]   *Id.* § 791.003(3)(N).
[1031]   *Id.* § 791.011(c)(2).
[1032]   *Id.* § 791.011(d)(1).
[1033]   *Id.* § 791.011(d)(2).
[1034]   *Id.* § 791.011(d)(3).
[1035]   *Id.* § 791.011(e).
[1036]   *Id.* § 791.011(f).
[1037]   *Id.* § 791.013(a) (West 2004).
[1038]   *Id.* § 791.013(b).
[1039]   *Id.* § 791.015.

If the contract involves construction or other public works-type activities by a county, it must be given specific written approval by the commissioners court of the county, as provided under Section 791.014 of the Government Code. Any property that is held and used for a public purpose under an interlocal agreement is exempt from taxation in the same manner as if the property were held and used by the participating political subdivisions.[1040] An interlocal agreement, like any contract, should be produced in consultation with local legal counsel for each of the governmental entities.

Economic Development Activities by Councils of Government

A council of governments is a voluntary association of local governments formed under Chapter 391 of the Local Government Code and constitutes a political subdivision of the state. These associations are also known as COGs, regional councils, development councils or regional planning commissions. Currently, Texas is divided into 24 state planning regions, and each region has a corresponding regional council. All 254 Texas counties and most Texas cities are members of their local regional council.

Technical Assistance by Councils of Government

Councils of government are authorized by statute to undertake a number of functions, including assisting local governments in their planning efforts so that the needs of agriculture, business and industry are recognized.[1041] Because of the myriad functions that COGs are authorized to undertake, they can be indirectly and directly helpful in economic development efforts. For instance, COGs can provide technical assistance to local governments by training officials on economic development issues and providing help in the preparation of related grant applications. COGs may also help local government with funding for certain infrastructure needs that would certainly impact economic development. For example, at least seven COGs have received designation as Metropolitan Planning Organizations under the Federal Aid Highway Act of 1973.[1042] This designation allows the COG to receive federal funds to help in planning and implementing responses to local transportation needs.

Economic Development District Designation; Planning and Revolving Loan Fund Resources

Councils of government have also undertaken other types of economic development initiatives. Perhaps the most common of such initiatives involves gaining designation of the local COG region as an "economic development district" (EDD) under federal law.[1043] Such districts help local governments combine their resources in planning and developing programs to improve the region's economic conditions, primarily by developing strategies and implementing programs that combat high unemployment and increase the per capita income of the region's workforce. Additionally, an EDD is eligible for technical assistance from the regional office of the federal Economic Development Administration. Of the 24 councils of government in Texas, 23 have gained designation as EDDs.

[1040]   *Id.* § 791.013(c).
[1041]   TEX. LOC. GOV'T. CODE ANN. § 391.001(a)(2)(c) (West 2005).
[1042]   23 U.S.C.A. § 101, *et seq.*
[1043]   42 U.S.C.A. § 3121, *et seq.* (Public Works and Economic Development Act of 1965).

Upon designation as an EDD, certain federal funds become available to aid these districts in their planning efforts to develop and administer a Comprehensive Economic Development Strategy, which is a 5-year plan developed by the EDD that acts as a road map for achieving the region's economic goals and objectives. An effort to digitize the strategy is underway by each EDD.

Also, councils of government develop and administer revolving loan funds provided by the federal Economic Development Administration and can leverage these funds with both private and other public financing resources in order to maximize the public benefit and return on investment to the region.

Support to Texas Workforce Development

Councils of government are eligible for federal funds that are administered by the Texas Workforce Commission. These funds are used primarily for employment and training programs through participation in the Workforce Investment Act of 1998.[1044] The COGs may provide administrative support to the region's Workforce Development Board and/or staff to the Workforce Development Centers to provide planning, implementation and program administration services to the Workforce Development Board and the region's workforce constituents.

Small Business Administration Certified Development Corporations and 504 Loan Program

Some councils of government have formed Small Business Administration (SBA) Section 53 Certified Development Corporations. These corporations are authorized to make long-term financing available through SBA's 504 Loan Program which allows eligible businesses to construct and/or acquire commercial real estate with favorable interest rates, long-term financing and low down payments.

Regional Reviews and Texas Community Development Block Grant Program

Councils of government have helped local governments obtain Community Development Block Grant funds from the Texas Community Development Block Grant Program administered by the Texas Department of Agriculture. Some COGs facilitate the regional review committees that develop application scoring criteria and conduct application reviews. Others regions provide technical assistance and grant administration for their communities. Councils of government ensure that applications are ranked and funded based on funding allocations to each of the 24 COGs.

Competitive Grant Activities

Councils of government can assist local jurisdictions in obtaining competitive grants under the Brownfields Program administered by the U.S. Environmental Protection Agency, the Weatherization Assistance Program and the Energy Efficiency and Renewable Energy programs both funded by the U.S. Department of Energy, the Texas Department of Housing and Community Affairs, and the State Energy Conservation Office. Councils of government may

---

[1044]   29 U.S.C.A.§ 2801, *et seq.*

assistant jurisdictions to find targeted funding opportunities that maximize regional impact and avoid duplication.

To obtain more information about COGs and their role in economic development, contact your local COG or contact the Texas Association of Regional Councils (TARC) at (512) 478-4715. Also, you may want to visit the TARC website at: www.txregionalcouncil.org.

County Economic Development Powers

County governments are limited to the statutory powers given to them by the Texas Legislature. In order for a county to take an action, it must be able to cite a statute that authorizes the type of initiative that is being pursued. There are several statutes that provide counties with methods for facilitating economic development initiatives.

County Industrial Commissions

Section 381.001 of the Local Government Code specifically authorizes counties to promote economic development through county industrial commissions. The commission's aims are to "investigate and undertake ways of promoting the prosperous development of business, industry, and commerce in the county."[1045] It may assist in the location, development and expansion of business enterprises, and is required to cooperate with the Governor's Division of Texas Economic Development and Tourism.[1046]

A county industrial commission consists of at least seven county residents appointed by the county judge.[1047] Members serve two-year terms without pay, although the county may pay for "necessary expenses."[1048]

County Boards of Development

Section 381.002 of the Local Government Code authorizes counties to create county boards of development to promote the growth and development of the county. These boards are created only if county residents have voted at an election to dedicate a portion of the property tax for this purpose.[1049] If a majority of the voters approve such a dedication at an election on the issue, the commissioners court may set aside part of the county's ad valorem tax revenue (a maximum of five cents per $100 assessed valuation) as a board of development fund. This money is to be used to "advertise and promote the growth and development of the county."[1050]

The fund is administered by a county board of development consisting of five members appointed to two-year terms by the commissioners court.[1051] As with the county industrial commission, the members are unpaid. The board is responsible for preparing and submitting a budget for the ensuing year to the commissioners court in the same manner that county budgets

---

[1045] TEX. LOC. GOV'T CODE ANN. § 381.001(f) (West Supp. 2011).
[1046] *Id.* § 381.001(g).
[1047] *Id.* § 381.001(a)-(b).
[1048] *Id.* § 381.001(d)-(e).
[1049] *Id.* § 381.002(a) (West 2005).
[1050] *Id.* § 381.002(a)-(b).
[1051] *Id.* § 381.002(c).

are administered.[1052] Although a county may operate under another law authorizing the appropriation of money or the levy of a tax for advertising and promotion purposes, the county may not appropriate more funds for those purposes than the five cent per $100 assessed valuation permitted under Chapter 381 of the Local Government Code.[1053]

Direct County Economic Development Efforts

Another provision in Chapter 381 of the Local Government Code authorizes counties to contract with a broad range of entities, including state and federal agencies, cities, school districts, nonprofit organizations and even "any other person," to stimulate business and commercial activity. Under Section 381.004, a commissioners court may develop and administer programs in several areas:

- state or local economic development;[1054]

- small or disadvantaged business development;[1055]

- development of business locations within the county;[1056]

- promotion or advertisement of the county and its vicinity to attract conventions, visitors and businesses;[1057]

- encouragement of county contract awards to businesses owned by women and minorities;[1058]

- support comprehensive literacy programs for the benefit of county residents;[1059] and

- encouragement and promotion of the arts.[1060]

Section 381.004 allows the county to use county employees or funds to pursue the above programs.[1061] Additionally, the law allows counties to accept contributions, gifts or other resources.[1062] It should be noted that the County Purchasing Act allows the county to exempt these program contracts from competitive bidding requirements.[1063]

The attorney general has concluded that Section 381.004 does not authorize a county to simply provide funds to existing non-county programs, even if those programs are directed at economic development. Rather, any program funded under this section must be initiated by the county and must be administered either by the county or by an entity under contract with the county.[1064] The

---

[1052]   *Id.* § 381.002(d).
[1053]   *Id.* § 381.002(g).
[1054]   *Id.* § 381.004(b)(1).
[1055]   *Id.* § 381.004(b)(2).
[1056]   *Id.* § 381.004(b)(3).
[1057]   *Id.* § 381.004(b)(4).
[1058]   *Id.* § 381.004(b)(5).
[1059]   *Id.* § 381.004(b)(6).
[1060]   *Id.* § 381.004(b)(7).
[1061]   *Id.* § 381.004(c)(3).
[1062]   *Id.* § 381.004(c)(4).
[1063]   *Id.* § 262.024(a)(10) (West Supp. 2011).
[1064]   Tex. Att'y Gen. LO-98-007 (1998).

commissioners court is authorized to make loans, grant public money, or provide county personnel and services to permissible Chapter 381 economic development programs.[1065]

Also, counties may form a county alliance corporation under state law through the Development Corporation Act.[1066] A county alliance corporation is simply a nonprofit corporation formed by a county alliance of two or more counties to pursue economic development.[1067] The corporation is governed by a board of directors who are appointed by and serve at the pleasure of the commissioners court of each county in the alliance.[1068] Unlike cities with economic development corporations, counties do not have the authority to levy a sales tax for economic development for the corporation's use.

County Ability to Provide Loans or Grants

Counties are constitutionally prohibited from granting "public money or any thing of value in aid of, or to any individual, association or corporation whatsoever"[1069], unless the Legislature authorizes a county to undertake programs to provide for loans and grants of public money.[1070] The purpose of these programs can be for the: development and diversification of the state's economy, elimination of unemployment, stimulation of agricultural innovation, and development of transportation or commerce.

Chapter 381 of the Local Government Code allows counties to make loans or grant public monies for permissible Chapter 381 economic development programs.[1071] Like cities, counties must maintain sufficient control over the way these funds are spent. To ensure such control, a county would be well advised to execute a formal contract between the county and the entity that spends the funds, outlining the respective rights and duties under the agreement. Additionally, the county would want to include a recapture provision outlining how the county would be reimbursed for any incentives it provided if the funded entity is ultimately unable to meet its commitments.

[1065]   TEX. LOC. GOV'T CODE ANN. § 381.004(h) (West 2005).

[1066]   *See* Chapter 506 of the Local Government Code which allows a county to create a county alliance corporation under the Development Corporation Act.

[1067]   TEX. LOC. GOV'T CODE ANN. §§ 506.001, .002 (West Supp. 2011).

[1068]   *Id.* §§ 506.051, .053.

[1069]   TEX. CONST. art. III, § 52(a).

[1070]   TEX CONST. art. III, § 52-a.

[1071]   TEX. LOC. GOV'T CODE ANN. § 381.004(h) (West 2005).

VI. Issuing Debt to Finance Economic Development

Legal Authority to Issue Bonds

Occasionally, cities may not have sufficient current funds to pay for certain economic development incentives. Consequently, the city may look to its ability to issue debt to finance such incentives. The power to issue debt, however, is quite different for home rule cities than it is for general law cities. Either type of city will want to be certain that it has the authority to issue bonds or other forms of indebtedness before it commits itself to such an incentive. Provided below is a discussion of the basic authority for cities to issue debt to finance economic development projects.

Legal Authority to Issue Bonds for Economic Development

Even though a city has the power to generally manage its own financial affairs, Texas courts have held that cities do not have an inherent right to issue bonds. In order to issue bonds, a city must be able to point to a statute or city charter provision which specifically authorizes the issuance of bonds for the proposed purpose. A statute or charter provision that which a city the power to borrow money does not in itself provide the city with the authority to issue bonds.[1072]

Presently, there are several sources of statutory authority which provide for the issuance of bonds for economic development purposes. Chapter 311 of the Tax Code allows the issuance of tax increment bonds to finance a tax increment economic development project.[1073] Chapter 1509 of the Government Code allows cities to finance certain manufacturing and commercial facilities, and Chapters 501 – 507 of the Local Government Code (the Development Corporation Act) authorize development corporations to issue bonds for certain economic development.

Bonds for Certain Commercial Projects

Under Chapter 1509 of the Government Code, a city may issue revenue or general obligation bonds to finance the construction or purchase of a facility for the purpose of leasing the facility to a private entity for use in a manufacturing or another commercial activity.[1074] A city may also issue these bonds to obtain a building or other facility that subsequently will be leased to a political subdivision of the state or to a state agency for public use.[1075] For example, a city could issue bonds to finance the construction of a facility to house a regional state office in order to bring government jobs to a particular area. In this circumstance, the bonds would be payable from the lease revenue. Additionally, a city could provide that such bonds are payable from ad valorem taxes if the bonds are approved by a majority of the voters at an election held for that

---

[1072] *City of Brenham v. German-American Bank*, 144 U.S. 173, 12 S. Ct. 559 (1892) (The city charter of Brenham, which allowed the city to borrow money for general purposes on the credit of the city, only included authority to borrow money for ordinary governmental purposes; this did not include the power to issue bonds).

[1073] TEX. TAX CODE ANN. §§ 311.010(h), .015 (West Supp. 2011).

[1074] TEX. GOV'T CODE ANN. §§ 1509.001(a)(2) (West Supp. 2011), .003 (West 2000), .004 (West Supp. 2011).

[1075] *Id.* § 1509.001(a)(1) (West Supp. 2011) (In addition, in 2005, the Legislature added (a)(3) allowing leases to the federal government to enhance the military value of a military facility located in or near a municipality that is a defense community under Section 397.001 of the Local Government Code).

purpose.[1076] A city that utilizes this authority will want to visit with its local bond counsel to determine the applicable legal requirements.

Economic Development Corporation Bonds

Under the Development Corporation Act, bonds can be issued to finance certain economic development projects authorized by that statute.[1077] These bonds are issued by the economic development corporation (not by the city) and are payable from the economic development sales tax proceeds or lease revenues which the corporation receives from the user of the financed project. The city is not the issuer of the debt and cannot be held liable for any obligations of this corporation.[1078] The types of projects that may be funded by the economic development sales tax are covered in detail in Chapter I of this handbook addressing Type A and Type B sales tax.

Which Obligations Must Receive Attorney General Approval

Section 1202.003(a) of the Government Code requires that public securities and the record of proceedings relating to the authorization of public securities must be submitted to the Office of the Attorney General (hereinafter, the "OAG") for review and approval .[1079] With limited exceptions, public securities must be approved by the OAG before they can be issued.

Public securities are defined to mean certain instruments, including bonds, notes, certificates of obligation, certificates of participation, or other instruments evidencing a proportionate interest in payment due by an issuer that are incurred under the issuer's borrowing power and are in the appropriate form.[1080] Exempted from the approval requirement are certain time warrants, leases, lease-purchase agreements, installment sale contracts, and bonds that are payable only from current revenues or taxes collected in the year of issuance.[1081] However, it is important to note that each of these obligations may be required to receive approval under other law. Notes given to banks to evidence a commercial bank loan are not generally considered securities that have to be approved by the OAG and, in most instances, cannot be approved by the OAG even if such approval is desired. As discussed later in this handbook, however, there is no clear general authorization to execute such notes.

Authority under Local Government Code Chapter 380

Many cities cite Section 380.001 of the Local Government Code for their authority to offer grants or loans of city funds as an incentive to new or expanding businesses. Although Chapter 380 allows the provision of city grants and loans to promote economic development, this chapter does not specifically authorize the issuance of any type of bonds or other long term general or special obligations to finance such a program.

[1076]   *Id.* § 1509.005 (West 2000).

[1077]   TEX. LOC. GOV'T CODE ANN. §§ 501.006, 505.104, .302(2) (West Supp. 2011).

[1078]   *Id.* § 501.207.

[1079]   In addition to the requirements for Attorney General approval contained in Chapter 1202 of the Texas Government Code (West 2000 & Supp. 2011), a number of statutes contain their own requirements for Attorney General approval. A local government should always consult the specific statute which it cites as authorization to issue debt for any restrictions or requirements relating to that debt.

[1080]   TEX. GOV'T CODE ANN. § 1202.001(3) (West Supp. 2011).

[1081]   *Id.* §1202.007.

Attorney General Opinion DM-185 (1992) concluded that Section 380.001 did not specifically authorize the issuance of bonds to fund city grant and loan programs. Such authorization, however, may be contained in a city charter of a home rule city. Accordingly, a home rule city can issue general obligation bonds to provide grants or loans under its economic development program if two conditions are met. First, there must be a specific provision in the city charter that allows the issuance of bonds for that purpose. Second, the voters must approve the bond issuance at an election held on the issue. Attorney General Opinion DM-185 does not address what specific charter language would be necessary to authorize bonds to fund a loan or grant program.

Attorney General Opinion DM-185 also concluded that any grant of funds made under the authority of Chapter 380 must comply with the constitutional requirement that public resources be used for the direct accomplishment of a public purpose. Thus, any program to provide grants or loans under Chapter 380 must contain sufficient controls to ensure that the funds involved are actually used to carry out the intended public purpose.

Procedures for Issuing Bonds for Economic Development

If an economic development project involves the issuance of bonds, a city may obtain for assistance from experts on the financial and legal aspects of a bond financing. With regard to the financial implications, a city usually hires a financial advisor who is available through any of a number of investment banking firms in Texas. For assistance in complying with the legal requirements of a bond financing, bond counsel should be hired.

The chosen financial advisor and bond counsel will review the proposed structure of the bond financing. If there are unusual legal issues associated with the issuance of the bonds, bond counsel may contact the Public Finance Division of the Office of the Attorney General to resolve these issues. Ordinarily, these issues will be settled prior to submission of the financing instrument to the OAG for approval. If bond counsel is satisfied with the legal aspects of the proposed financing, the financial advisor can complete the analysis of the financial feasibility of the financing. Financial issues could include consideration of the likely market reaction to the proposed bonds and the strength of the sources of repayment of the bonds.

When bond counsel and the financial advisor are satisfied that all legal requirements have been met and that the bonds will be marketable at a reasonable price, the bonds are sold. The bond sale can be made pursuant to competitive bids or through a negotiated sale with a preselected "underwriter," as provided by law. The financial advisor is responsible for advising the city as to the best approach for selling the bonds. The financial advisor, in conjunction with bond counsel, must also determine that all federal regulations are met regarding the issuance of the bonds.

The OAG's review of public securities is strictly a legal one, not a financial one, though the OAG does review whether the public securities can apparently be paid within any statutory or constitutional limits on taxation or historical or reasonable projected revenues. The OAG approval does not address the wisdom or advisability of the financing techniques employed or the expenditures which the bonds are intended to finance.

The minimum time requirement for the review of bonds by the OAG is 10 to 12 working days, depending upon the type of issuer, for economic development-related financing. Additional time will be required if all of the necessary documentation is not provided at the time the bonds are submitted. In a complex financing, the OAG may require certain revisions to the documents or may seek the resolution of legal issues that arise. If so, the review process may take substantially longer than the minimum time period. Once the attorney general has approved the bonds, they are registered with the Comptroller and can then be delivered to the purchaser in return for the purchase price. The financing then "closes" and the bond proceeds are considered available for the construction or acquisition of the facilities.

If questions arise concerning the constitutionality of a transaction or the legal basis upon which a transaction is predicated, the OAG will require that a formal OAG opinion be obtained or that a bond validation judgment be sought by the filing of a bond validation lawsuit pursuant to Chapter 1205 of the Government Code. Once the OAG has approved the bonds, they are registered with the Comptroller and can then be delivered to the purchaser in return for the purchase price.

Effect of Attorney General Approval of Bonds

The significance of OAG approval of bonds is that once bonds are approved, they are incontestable for any reason[1082] except for unconstitutionality.

Other Instruments to Finance Infrastructure Improvements

There are a number of financial instruments other than bonds that are typically used by cities to finance public improvements. Whether such instruments may be used to fund economic development-related expenditures depends on the relevant statutory authority and any authorization provided by the city charter. The OAG has promulgated rules requiring a public entity to demonstrate coverage for its dept from a portion of the entity's constitutional tax limit, described as the "bond allowable".[1083] Those rules prevent most local governments from incurring debt that would require more than two-thirds of the issuer's property tax rate to be dedicated to debt service. Further, under the OAG's rules, a home rule city with the maximum legal property tax rate of $2.50 per $100 of valuation may not incur an amount of debt that would require more than $1.50 of that rate for debt service. Occasionally, other law, such as the city charter of a home rule city, may place stricter limits on the amount of debt that a city may incur.

Bank Loans and Other Forms of Indebtedness

Long-term bank notes (notes for more than one year) may be executed by cities if such borrowing is authorized under the city charter or under other statutory authority. Accordingly, a home rule city could borrow money from a bank or enter into other forms of indebtedness to further economic development to the extent authorized by the city charter and the Texas Constitution.

General law cities have limited authority to borrow money. Section 101.005 of the Local Government Code states that in order to meet the infrastructure needs of the city, the governing body may borrow money based on the credit of the city. This provision, however, does not

---

[1082]   *Id.* § 1202.006 (West 2000).
[1083]   1 TEX. ADMIN. CODE § 53.5 (2012).

provide authority for these cities to issue long-term notes (obligations that are payable beyond the current fiscal year.)[1084]

[1084]   *See McNeill v. City of Waco*, 33 S.W. 322 (1895) (For Constitutional purposes, "debt" is any contractual obligation that creates a liability that cannot be paid out of current budget year revenues). *See also Andrus v. Crystal City*, 253 S.W. 557 (Tex. Civ. App. -- San Antonio 1923), *aff'd*, 265 S.W.550 (Tex. Comm'n App. 1924) (municipal debts may be created without tax levy when they are to be paid out of funds for current year).

VII. Other Economic Development Initiatives

Public Improvement Districts

Cities and counties often need to make certain improvements to their infrastructure to facilitate economic growth within an area. New businesses may choose not to locate where there are inadequate streets, substandard utility services, or other public facilities or services that are inferior. It is also difficult for existing businesses to prosper in areas that have poor public infrastructure. Texas law provides a number of ways to finance needed public improvements, including the use of special assessments. Public Improvement Districts (PIDs) offer cities and counties a means for undertaking such projects.

The Public Improvement District Assessment Act allows any city to levy and collect special assessments on property that is within the city or within the city's extraterritorial jurisdiction (ETJ).[1085] Further, counties may levy and collect special assessments on property located within the county unless, within 30 days of a county's action to approve the public improvement district, a home rule city objects to its establishment within the home rule city's corporate limits or ETJ.[1086] The statute authorizing the creation of PIDs is found in Chapter 372 of the Local Government Code. The public improvement district may be formed to accomplish any of the following improvements:[1087]

1) landscaping;

2) erection of fountains, distinctive lighting and signs;

3) acquiring, constructing, improving, widening, narrowing, closing or rerouting sidewalks, streets or any other roadways or their rights-of-way;

4) construction or improvement of pedestrian malls;

5) acquisition and installation of pieces of art;

6) acquisition, construction or improvement of libraries;

7) acquisition, construction or improvement of off-street parking facilities;

8) acquisition, construction, improvement or rerouting of mass transportation facilities;

9) acquisition, construction, or improvements of water, wastewater or drainage improvements;

10) the establishment or improvement of parks;

11) projects similar to 1 through 10 listed above;

12) acquisition, by purchase or otherwise, of real property in connection with an authorized improvement;

13) special supplemental services for improvement and promotion of the district, including services relating to advertising, promotion, health and sanitation, water and wastewater,

---

[1085] TEX. LOC. GOV'T CODE ANN. § 372.003(a) (West Supp. 2011).
[1086] *Id.* § 372.003(d).
[1087] *Id.* § 372.003(b).

public safety, security, business recruitment, development, recreation, and culture enhancement;

14) payment of expenses incurred in the establishment, administration, and operation of the district, including expenses related to the operation and maintenance of mass transportation facilities[1088]; and

15) the development, rehabilitation, or expansion of affordable housing.

Below are the ten steps necessary to create a public improvement district and levy assessments.

Step One:

The governing body or a group of the affected property owners must initiate a petition that calls for a defined area of the city or county to be declared a public improvement district.[1089]

The petition must state:[1090]

- the general nature of the proposed improvements;

- the estimated cost of the improvements;

- the boundaries of the proposed assessment district;

- the proposed method of assessment, which may specify included or excluded classes of assessable property;

- the proposed apportionment of costs between the public improvement district and the municipality or county as a whole;

- whether the district will be managed by the municipality or county, by the private sector, or by a partnership of the two;

- that the persons signing the petition request or concur with the establishment of the district; and

- that an advisory board may be established to develop and recommend an improvement plan to the governing body of the municipality or the county.

The petition is sufficient if it meets two conditions. First, it must be signed by owners of more than 50 percent of the appraised value of taxable real property subject to assessment under the proposal.[1091] Second, the petition must also be signed by record owners of real property liable for assessment under the proposal who:[1092]

- Constitute more than 50 percent of all record owners of property that is liable for assessment under the proposal; or

- own taxable real property that constitutes more than 50 percent of the area of all taxable real property that is liable for assessment under the proposal.

[1088]   *Id.* § 372.003(b-1).
[1089]   *Id.* § 372.002 (West 2005). *See also* Tex. Att'y Gen. LO-96-129 (Concluding a petition is a prerequisite for the establishment of a public improvement district).
[1090]   TEX. LOC. GOV'T CODE ANN. § 372.005(a) (West 2005).
[1091]   *Id.* § 372.005(b)(1).
[1092]   *Id.* § 372.005(b)(2).

The petition may be filed with the city secretary or an officer performing the city secretary's functions.[1093]

Step Two:

After receiving a petition to establish a public improvement district, the governing body of the city or county may appoint an advisory board to develop and recommend an improvement plan for the PID.[1094]

The membership of the board must be sufficient to meet the same criteria that made the petition sufficient. First, the board must be composed of owners of more than 50 percent of the appraised value of taxable real property subject to assessment under the proposal.[1095] Second, it must include representation by record owners of real property liable for assessment under the proposal who:[1096]

- Constitute more than 50 percent of all record owners of property that is liable for assessment under the proposal; or

- own taxable real property that constitutes more than 50 percent of the area of all taxable real property that is liable for assessment under the proposal.

Step Three:

After receiving a petition to establish a public improvement district, the governing body of the city or county should prepare a feasibility report.[1097]

The purpose of the report is to determine whether an improvement should be made as proposed by the petition, or in combination with other improvements authorized under Chapter 372 of the Local Government Code. The report may be conducted using the services of municipal employees, county employees or outside consultants.

Step Four:

A public hearing on the advisability of the improvements must be conducted after meeting statutory notice requirements.[1098]

After the feasibility report is completed, a public hearing must be held by the governing body of the city or county to determine the advisability of the proposed improvements. Notice of the public hearing must be published in a newspaper of general circulation in the city, or county and the city's extraterritorial jurisdiction where the district is to be located.[1099] Notice must be published more than 15 days prior to the date of the hearing. Additionally, notice of the PID must be mailed more than 15 days prior to the date of the hearing to the owners of property within the proposed PID.[1100] The notice must contain the following information:[1101]

[1093]   *Id.* § 372.005(c).
[1094]   *Id.* § 372.008(a).
[1095]   *Id.* § 372.008(b)(1)
[1096]   *Id.* § 372.008(b)(2).
[1097]   *Id.* § 372.007(a).
[1098]   *Id.* § 372.009.
[1099]   *Id.* § 372.009(c).
[1100]   *Id.* § 372.009(d).
[1101]   *Id.* § 372.009(c).

1) the time and place of the hearing;

2) the general nature of the proposed improvements;

3) the estimated cost of the improvements;

4) the boundaries of the proposed assessment district;

5) the proposed method of assessment; and

6) the proposed apportionment of cost between the improvement district and the municipality or county as a whole.

By resolution, the city or county must make findings regarding the advisability of the proposed improvements and Items 2 through 6 above based on the public hearing.[1102]

Step Five:

The governing body of the city or county must adopt a resolution by majority vote authorizing the creation of a PID.[1103]

The authorization of the PID must be done within six months of the public hearing on the PID. The authorization is effective once notice of the resolution is published in a newspaper of general circulation in the city or county and the city's extraterritorial jurisdiction (ETJ) where the district is to be located.[1104]

Step Six:

Twenty days after authorization of the PID has taken effect, the city or county may begin construction of the improvements.[1105]

If within the 20 day period, a protest petition is filed, construction may not begin. Such a petition must be signed by owners representing at least two-thirds of total area of the district or by two-thirds of all the land owners in the district. However, the statute does not set out a procedure for cities or counties to follow once they have received this protest petition.

Step Seven:

A five-year on-going service plan and assessment plan must be developed.[1106]

The on-going service plan must define the annual indebtedness and projected costs of the improvements for the PID. The plan may be prepared by the PID advisory board or another entity, if an advisory board is not appointed. The plan must be reviewed and approved by the city or county. Also, the service plan must be reviewed and updated annually for purposes of determining an annual budget for improvements.

An assessment plan must be included in the annual service plan.[1107] The assessment plan is based upon the assessments made by the city or the county.[1108] The city or county shall apportion the

---

[1102]   *Id.* § 372.009(b).
[1103]   *Id.* § 372.010(a).
[1104]   *Id.* § 372.010(b).
[1105]   *Id.* § 372.010(c).
[1106]   *Id.* § 372.013.
[1107]   *Id.* § 372.014(a).

cost of the improvements assessed against the property in the PID. The apportionments are based upon the special benefits that accrue to the property because of an improvement.[1109] The city or county may establish by ordinance or order:[1110]

1) Reasonable classification and formulas for the apportionment of the cost between the city or county and the area to be assessed; and

2) The methods of assessing the special benefits for carious classes of improvements.

Costs for improvements may be assessed either by:[1111]

1) Equally per front foot or square foot;

2) According to the value of the property as determined by the city or county, with or without regard to improvements on the property; or

3) In any other manner that results in imposing equal shares of the cost on similarly benefitted properties within the PID.

Assessments may be adjusted annually upon review of the service plan.[1112] Also after the findings of the city or the county, the area of the PID to be assessed can be less than the area described in the proposed boundaries on the original notice.[1113] The city and county are responsible for payment of assessments against exempt municipal or county property within the district.[1114] Payment of assessments by other tax exempt jurisdictions must be established by contract.

Step Eight:

The city or county must prepare a proposed assessment roll and provide notice and a hearing on the proposed assessment roll.[1115]

If the city forms the district, a copy of the proposed assessment roll must be filed with the city secretary. If the county forms the district, the proposed assessment roll must be filed with the county tax assessor-collector.[1116] Notice of a public hearing on the proposed assessment roll must be published in the newspaper of general circulation at least 10 days before the date of the hearing. The notice must state:

1) the date, time, and place of the hearing;

2) the general nature of the improvement;

3) the cost of the improvement;

1108   *Id.* § 372.015(a).
1109   *Id.*
1110   *Id.* § 372.015(c).
1111   *Id.* § 372.015(b).
1112   *Id.* § 372.015(d).
1113   *Id.* § 372.012. (Note: the city or county cannot assess property that was not in the original proposed boundaries. This can only be allowed if notice and a hearing to include that property is done in accordance with section 372.009).
1114   *Id.* § 372.014(b).
1115   *Id.* § 372.016.
1116   *Id.* § 372.016(b).

4) the boundaries of the assessment district; and

5) that written or oral objections will be considered at the hearing.

Also, notice of the public hearing on the roll must be mailed to affected property owners.[1117] At the public hearing, the governing body must hear and rule on any objections that are raised.[1118] Also, the governing body may amend a proposed assessment on any parcel.

Step Nine:

After all the objections have been heard and considered, the governing body may levy, by ordinance or order, the special assessment against the taxable properties within the district.[1119]

The ordinance or order must include the method of payment and may provide for installment payments. The city or county must approve an interest rate and a period of time for the installment payments. Also, the installment payments must be an amount necessary to meet annual costs[1120] and must continue for a period that either retires the indebtedness for the improvements within the district or is the period that was approved by the city or county for the payment of installments. Also, the city or county may defer an assessment until a date specified in the ordinance or order.[1121] Additionally, the city or the county can contract with another taxing unit or the board of directors of the appraisal district to collect the special assessments.[1122]

As mentioned above, the city or county specifies the interest rate in the installment payments on assessments. If the city or county issue general obligation bonds, revenue bonds, time warrants or temporary notes to finance the improvements, the interest rate may not exceed a rate that is one-half of one percent higher than the actual rate paid on the debt.[1123] Also, the interest that accrues between the effective date of the assessment ordinance or order and the payment of the first installment must be added to the first installment payment.

The assessment is a first and prior lien against the property; superior to all other liens and claims except liens for state, county, school district or city ad valorem taxes; and is a personal liability of a charge against the owners of the property regardless of whether the owners are named.[1124] The assessment lien is effective from the date of the assessment ordinance or order until the assessment is paid and it runs with the land.[1125] The lien may be enforced by the city or the county in the same manner that an ad valorem tax lien against real property may be enforced.[1126] Foreclosure of accrued installments does not eliminate the outstanding principal balance of the assessment and any foreclosure purchaser of the property is subject to the assessment lien and any associated obligations.

[1117]   *Id.* § 372.016(c).

[1118]   *Id.* § 372.017(a) (West Supp. 2011).

[1119]   *Id.* § 372.017(b).

[1120]   *See id.* § 372.023(h).

[1121]   *See id.* § 372.0055 (If the proposed improvement includes a deferred assessment, the city or county must estimate the appraised value of taxable real property liable for assessment in the district; and the cost of improvement before holding the public hearing).

[1122]   *Id.* § 372.0175.

[1123]   *Id.* § 372.018(a).

[1124]   *Id.* § 372.018(b).

[1125]   *Id.* § 372.018(c)-(d).

[1126]   *Id.* § 372.018(e).

Delinquent installments of assessments shall incur interest, penalties and attorney's fees in the same manner as delinquent ad valorem taxes.[1127] The interest on any delinquent installment shall be added to each subsequent installment until all delinquent installments are paid.[1128] However, a special assessment is not considered a tax as that term is used in the Texas Constitution.[1129] Thus, this office held that a homestead may not be subjected to forced sale for nonpayment of a public improvement district assessment. However, this office then qualified that conclusion by stating that an assessment may be enforced by foreclosure provided that the statutory lien associated with the assessment attached to the real property prior to the date the property became a homestead.[1130]

Step Ten:

The governing body may make additional assessments against property within the district to correct omissions or mistakes regarding the costs of the improvements.[1131]

Before such an additional assessment may be made, the city or county must provide the same type of notice and public hearing that was required for the original assessment.

Payment of Costs of Improvements

Costs of improvements must be paid in specified ways.[1132] If the cost is payable by the city or county, the city or county may use general funds available for the purpose of improvement or other available general funds.[1133] Cost that is payable from special assessments that have been paid in full must be paid from that assessment.[1134] Costs payable from a special assessment that is payable in installments may be paid by any combination of the following:[1135]

1) under an installment sales contract or a reimbursement agreement between the city or county and the person who acquires, installs, or constructs the improvement;

2) as provided by a temporary note or time warrant issued by the city or county and payable to the person that acquires, installs, or constructs the improvement; or

3) by the issuance and sale of revenue or general obligation bonds[1136].

An installment sales contract, reimbursement agreement, temporary note, or time warrant may be assigned by the payee without consent of the city or the county.[1137]

The cost of more than one improvement may be paid either (1) from a single issue and sale of bonds without other consolidation proceedings before the bond issue; or (2) under a single installment sales contract, reimbursement agreement, temporary note, or time warrant.[1138]

[1127]   *Id.* § 372.018(f).
[1128]   *Id.* § 372.018(a).
[1129]   Op. Tex. Att'y Gen. No. JC-386 (2001).
[1130]   Op. Tex. Att'y Gen. No. GA-237 (2004). *See id.* at 2 n. 2.
[1131]   *Id.* § 372.019 (West 2005).
[1132]   *Id.* § 372.023 (West Supp. 2011).
[1133]   *Id.* § 372.023(b).
[1134]   *Id.* § 372.023(c).
[1135]   *Id.* § 372.023(d).
[1136]   *See id.* § 372.024 (West 2005).
[1137]   *Id.* § 372.023(d-1) (West Supp. 2011).

If bonds are issued, the city or county must create a separate PID fund in the treasury to which the proceeds from the sale of bonds, temporary notes, time warrants or other sums appropriated are credited.[1139] The fund may be used solely to pay cost incurred in making an improvement. When an improvement is completed, the balance of the part of the assessment that is for improvements must be transferred to the fund established for the retirement of bonds.

Dissolution of a Public Improvement District

A public improvement district may be dissolved if a petition requesting dissolution is filed and contains the signatures of at least the same number of property owners required to create the PID.[1140] Public notice and a public hearing must be held in the same manner as those required to create a PID.[1141] If the district is dissolved, the PID stays in effect until it has paid off any indebtedness that remains for the improvements.

Municipal Management Districts

Municipal management districts allow commercial property owners to enhance a defined business area. The districts, also called downtown management districts, are created within an existing commercial area to finance facilities, infrastructure and services beyond those already provided by individual property owners or by the municipality. The improvements may be paid for by a combination of self-imposed property taxes, special assessments and impact fees, or by other charges against property owners within the district. The creation of such a district does not relieve a city from providing basic services to an area included within the district. A district is created to supplement, not to supplant, the municipal services available to the area. A number of Texas cities have used municipal management districts to provide much-needed funding to enhance the economic vitality of the business centers within the municipality.

The general statutes governing municipal management districts are located in Chapter 375 of the Local Government Code.[1142]
A municipal management district is considered a governmental agency and a political subdivision of the state.[1143] The creation of a municipal management district within an eligible commercial area involves five steps.

[1138] *Id.* § 372.023(g) (West Supp. 2011).
[1139] *Id.* § 372.022.
[1140] *Id.* §§ 372.011, .005 (West 2005) (Section 372.005(c) of the Local Government Code provides that the "petition may be filed with the municipal secretary or other officer performing the functions of the municipal secretary." This section does not note the county official with whom a petition to dissolve a county PID should be filed with.).
[1141] *Id.* § 372.011.
[1142] There are specific municipal management district that have there own statute. These statutes can be found in the Special District Local Law Code.
[1143] TEX. LOC. GOV'T CODE ANN. § 375.004(a) (West 2005).

Step One:

The owners of a majority of the assessed value of the real property in the proposed district, or 50 persons who own real property in the proposed district, must sign a petition asking for the creation of a district.[1144]

This petition must include:[1145]

1) the proposed district boundaries;

2) specific purposes for which the district will be created;

3) general nature of the work, projects or services to be provided, the necessity for those services, and the estimated cost;

4) name of the district which must start with a general description of the location of the district followed by the term "Management District" or "Improvement District";

5) names of the proposed initial directors that include the directors' experience and length of initial service; and

6) resolution of the city in support of the creation of the district.

The description of the boundary of the proposed district must be by metes and bounds, verifiable land marks, or by lots and block numbers if there is a recorded map or plat and survey of the area.[1146] All of these documents, along with the petition requesting creation of the district, must be submitted to the Texas Commission on Environmental Quality for approval of the district.[1147]

Step Two:

The Texas Commission on Environmental Quality (TCEQ), or a person authorized by the TCEQ, sets a date, time and place for a public hearing to consider the petition.[1148]

The notice must state that each person has a right to appear and present evidence and testify for or against the allegations in the petition, the form of the petition, the necessity and feasibility of the district's project, and the benefits to accrue.

TCEQ must publish notice of the hearing once a week for two consecutive weeks in a newspaper of general circulation in the city in which the district is to be located.[1149] The first publication must occur not later than the 31st day before the date on which the hearing will be held. TCEQ must mail the notice to the county where the district is proposed if the county has requested notice.[1150] Also, the city may request for TCEQ notice of creation of a district.[1151] A city may make such a request in January of each year to receive these notices by mail.

[1144]   *Id.* § 375.022(b) (West Supp. 2011) (Determining the owners of a majority of the assessed value of the real property or 50 persons who own real property must be in accordance with the most recent certified county property tax rolls).

[1145]   *Id.* § 375.022(c).

[1146]   *Id.* § 375.022(c)(1).

[1147]   *Id.* § 375.022(a).

[1148]   *Id.* § 375.023 (West 2005).

[1149]   *Id.* § 375.024(a).

[1150]   *Id.* § 375.024(b).

Step Three:

The petitioner has a duty to send a notice of the public hearing to each property owner in the proposed district who did not sign the petition.[1152]

The notice must be sent at least 30 days prior to the hearing. The petitioner must send the notice by certified mail with return receipt requested. The notice must include all of the information noted in the Step Two.

Step Four:

TCEQ must hold the public hearing and consider the need for the district and the sufficiency of the underlying documentation.[1153]

At the hearing, TCEQ examines the petition and hears testimony from any interested person on the sufficiency of the petition, whether the district is feasible and necessary, and whether the district would be a benefit to all or any part of the land to be included. Also, while considering the petition, TCEQ has to determine if the project is feasible, necessary and a public benefit.[1154] TCEQ considers the availability of comparable services from other systems and the reasonableness of the proposed public projects and services when making that determination. If after the hearing, TCEQ finds that the district is feasible, necessary and a public benefit, TCEQ, by order, shall make that finding and grant the petition. The order must state the specific purpose for the district is created[1155] and the boundaries of the district[1156].

After granting the petition, TCEQ will appoint the initial board of directors.[1157] The board of directors is composed of at least five but not more than 30 directors who serve staggered four years.[1158] TCEQ will divide the initial board into two groups where one group will serve four-year terms and the other group will serve two-year terms.[1159] To be qualified to serve as a director, a person must be 18 years of age and either:[1160]

- be a resident of the district;

- own property within the district;

- own stock of a corporate entity within the district;

- be the beneficiary of a trust that owns property in the district; or

- be an agent, employee, or tenant of any of the aforementioned entities.

[1151]   *Id.* § 375.024(c).
[1152]   *Id.* § 375.024(e).
[1153]   *Id.* § 375.025.
[1154]   *Id.* § 375.025(c).
[1155]   *Id.* § 375.026.
[1156]   *Id.* § 375.041.
[1157]   *Id.* § 375.026.
[1158]   *Id.* § 375.061 (West Supp. 2011).
[1159]   *Id.* § 375.062 (West 2005).
[1160]   *Id.* § 375.063.

Step Five:

Upon approval of the petition by TCEQ, the municipal management district board appoints its officers.[1161]

Each of the appointed directors must execute a bond of $10,000 and take a written and oral oath of office.[1162] Once the directors are appointed and qualified by executing a bond and taking the oath, the board members themselves must elect a president, a vice-president, a secretary and any other officers the board considers necessary.[1163] One-half of the serving directors constitutes a quorum, and a concurrence of a majority of a quorum of directors is required for any official action of the district.[1164] However, if the board wants to authorize the levy of assessments, the levy of taxes, the imposition of fees or the issuance of bonds, the board must have the written consent of two-thirds of the board. Generally, a director may not vote on matters that affect property owned by the director or that affects the director's employer.[1165]

Directors are not compensated for their service, but are reimbursed for necessary expenses incurred in carrying out the duties and responsibilities of a director.[1166] Also, the director's position is not considered a civil office of emolument.[1167]

The initial and succeeding board of directors must recommend to the governing body of the city persons to serve on subsequent boards.[1168] The city will review the recommendations and will approve or disapprove the recommendations. If the city is not satisfied with the recommendations, the city can request the board to submit additional recommendations.
Directors may serve successive terms. After public notice and a public hearing, a director may be removed by the governing body of the city for misconduct or for failure to carry out duties on petition by a majority of the board of directors.[1169] A vacancy is filled by the remaining members of the board for the unexpired term.[1170]

Rights and Powers of the District

To accomplish its purposes, the district has the rights, powers, privileges, authority and functions of a conservation and reclamation district, and those conferred by Chapter 54 of the Water Code.[1171] Specifically, the district has the power to impose an ad valorem tax to provide for a mass transit system.[1172] The district may do road projects.[1173] Also, a district may levy impact

---

[1161]   *Id.* § 375.068.
[1162]   *Id.* § 375.067.
[1163]   *Id.* § 375.068.
[1164]   *Id.* § 375.071 (West Supp. 2011).
[1165]   *Id.* § 375.072 (West 2005).
[1166]   *Id.* § 375.070.
[1167]   *Id.* § 375.069.
[1168]   *Id.* § 375.064 (West Supp. 2011).
[1169]   *Id.* § 375.065 (West 2005).
[1170]   *Id.* § 375.066.
[1171]   *Id.* § 375.091 (West Supp. 2011). *See* TEX. CONST. art. XVI, § 59.
[1172]   TEX. LOC. GOV'T CODE ANN. § 375.0921(b) (West Supp. 2011). *See* TEX, CONST. art. III, §§ 52, 52-a (Limitations on imposed ad valorem taxes for mass transit systems).
[1173]   TEX. LOC. GOV'T CODE ANN. § 375.0921(a). *See id.* § 375.0922 (Road standards and requirements for road projects).

fees pursuant to the state impact fee act in Chapter 395 of the Local Government Code.[1174] As mentioned above, to authorize the levy of property taxes or impact fees, or to propose the issuance of bonds, the board must obtain the written consent of at least two-thirds of the number of directors of the district.[1175]

Under certain circumstances, a district may levy special assessments against the benefitted property within the district.[1176] Special assessments may be used to pay for all or part of the construction or maintenance of the following types of improvements:

- landscaping;
- lighting, banners, and signs;
- streets and sidewalks;
- pedestrian skywalks, crosswalks, and tunnels;
- seawalls;
- marinas;
- drainage and navigation improvements;
- pedestrian malls;
- solid waste, water, sewer, and power facilities;
- parks, plazas, lakes, rivers, bayous, ponds, and recreation and scenic areas;
- historic areas;
- works of art;
- off-street parking facilities, bus terminals, heliports, and mass transit systems;
- theatres, studios, exhibition halls, production facilities and ancillary facilities in support of the foregoing;
- cost of any demolition in connection with providing any of the improvement projects; and
- other similar improvements.[1177]

The assessments may fund supplemental services for advertising, economic development, business recruitment, promotion of health and sanitation, public safety, traffic control, recreation and cultural enhancement.[1178] Also, these assessments may fund buying real property or an interest in real property in connection with an improvement, project or service associated with the district and any expenses in the establishment, administration, maintenance, and operation of the district or any improvement, project or service.[1179]

In order to use special assessments to finance a project or service, the district must receive a petition to make such improvements that is signed by:[1180]

[1174] *Id.* §§ 375.141-.142 (West 2005).
[1175] *Id.* § 375.071.
[1176] *Id.* §§ 375.111 (West 2005), .112 (West Supp. 2011).
[1177] *Id.* § 375.112 (a)(1)-(2) (West Supp. 2011).
[1178] *Id.* § 375.112(a)(4).
[1179] *Id.* § 375.112(a)(3), (5). *See* Tex. Transp. Code Ann. chs. 365, 441 (West 2007 & Supp. 2011), Tex. Water Code Ann. ch. 54 (West 2002 & Supp. 2011) (Authorization to acquire real property).
[1180] Tex. Loc. Gov't Code Ann. § 375.114 (West Supp. 2011).

- the owners of 50 percent or more of the assessed value of the property in the district subject to assessment, according to the most recent certified county property tax rolls, or

- the owners of 50 percent or more of the surface area of the district, according to the most recent certified county property tax rolls.[1181]

The area to be assessed may be the entire district or any part of the district.[1182] Before levying a special assessment, the district must provide notice of a public hearing on the proposed improvements and a public hearing on the advisability of the improvements and services and the proposed assessments.[1183] The notice must be published at least 30 days before the hearing in a newspaper with general circulation in the county in which the district is located.[1184] Also, notice must be sent by certified mail, return receipt requested or other method approved by the board to the owners subject to the assessment at least 30 days before the hearing.[1185] The notice must include:[1186]

1) Time and place of the hearing;

2) General nature of the proposed improvement project or service;

3) Estimated cost of the improvement, including interest during construction and associated financing costs; and

4) Proposed method of assessment.

At the conclusion of the hearing, the board must make a finding by resolution or order concerning the advisability and nature of the project or service, estimated cost, method of assessment and method and time for assessment payments.[1187] Also, the board must hear and rule on all objections to each proposed assessment.[1188] Once all objections are heard and action taken with regards to those objections, the board shall levy the special assessment, specify the method of payment of the assessment and may provide those assessment be paid in installments with interest.[1189]

The cost of the improvements shall be apportioned by any reasonable assessment plan that bases the assessment on the special benefits that accrue to the property because of the improvement or service.[1190] Governmental entities may contract with the district to provide for the payment of assessments on publicly owned property.[1191] Certain residential properties of lesser density than large apartment complexes are exempt from assessments and impact fees.[1192]

[1181] The surface area of the district does not include roads, streets, highways, and utility right-of-ways, other public areas, and any other property exempt from assessment under Section 375.162 or 375.163 of Chapter 375.

[1182] TEX. LOC. GOV'T CODE ANN. §§ 375.111, .117(a) (West 2005).

[1183] *Id.* §§ 375.113 (West 2005).

[1184] *Id.* § 375.115(a) (West Supp 2011).

[1185] *Id.* § 375.115(c).

[1186] *Id.* § 375.115(b).

[1187] *Id.* § 375.116 (West 2005).

[1188] *Id.* § 375.118(a).

[1189] *Id.* § 375.118(c).

[1190] *Id.* § 375.119.

[1191] *Id.* § 375.162.

[1192] *Id.* § 375.161.

A district may incur liabilities, borrow money, issue bonds and notes, and purchase, sell or receive real and personal property.[1193] The board may call a bond election on the written petition of the owners of 50 percent of the assessed value of the property in the district or by a petition of owners of at least 50 percent of the surface area of the district.[1194] Also, the approval of the governing body of the city must be obtained to issue bonds for an improvement project.[1195] Also, if the district is issuing bonds to provide water, sewage, or drainage facilities, the district must get the approval of TCEQ.[1196] Additionally, if a project involves the right-of-way of streets or the use of city land or easements, the district must receive the city's approval before undertaking such a project.[1197]

A district may own and operate facilities inside or outside of the district, and may enter into contracts for joint use of district facilities.[1198] It may charge rents or fees for use of constructed improvements owned or operated by the district.[1199] The district may hire or dismiss employees and consultants necessary to conduct the affairs of the district.[1200] Also, the district may do all things necessary to carry out the purpose of the district, except that a district may not exercise the powers of eminent domain.[1201]

A district has an obligation to attempt to stimulate the growth of disadvantaged businesses inside its boundaries by encouraging participation of these businesses during procurement and other district activities.[1202] The district is required to establish programs to increase the participation of disadvantaged business in public contract awards. The district must review its disadvantaged business programs and determine if each of those programs is the most effective method for remedying historical discriminatory actions and if disparities exist between the disadvantaged business qualified to undertake district work and the percentage of total district funds that are awarded to disadvantaged businesses.

The district must follow Subchapter I of Chapter 49 of the Water Code when entering into contracts for construction work, equipment, materials, or machinery.[1203] The board may adopt rules governing the receipt of bids and the award of the contract and provide a waiver of the competitive bid requirement if:

1. There is an emergency;

2. The needed materials are available from only one source;

3. In a procurement requiring design by the supplier, competitive bidding would not be appropriate and competitive negotiation, with proposals solicited from an adequate

---

[1193]   *Id.* § 375.092(d)-(e).
[1194]   *Id.* §§ 375.242-.243.
[1195]   *Id.* § 375.207(a).
[1196]   *Id.* § 375.208.
[1197]   *Id.* § 375.207(c).
[1198]   *Id.* § 375.092(f)-(g).
[1199]   *Id.* § 375.092(h).
[1200]   *Id.* § 375.096(a)(1)-(2).
[1201]   *Id.* § 375.092(a), (o); .094. *See* Op. Tex. Att'y Gen. No. GA-268 (2004).
[1202]   TEX. LOC.GOV'T CODE ANN. § 375.222 (West 2005).
[1203]   *Id.* § 375.221 (West Supp. 2011).

number of qualified sources, would permit reasonable competition consistent with the nature and requirements of the procurement; or

4. After solicitation, it is ascertained that there will be only one bidder.

Because the district is a political subdivision, it is subject to the Open Meetings Act, the Public Information Act, and Tort Claims Act.[1204]

Consolidation of Two or More Districts

Two or more districts may consolidate if none of the districts has issued bonds or notes secured by assessments or ad valorem taxes or has levied taxes.[1205] Consolidation is initiated when the district adopts a resolution proposing consolidation and delivers a copy of the resolution to the board of each district with which it proposed to consolidate. The districts become consolidated when each district adopts a resolution containing the terms and conditions for the consolidation. The terms and conditions of the consolidation must include:[1206]

1) adoption of a name for the consolidated district;

2) the number and apportionment of directors to serve on the board of the consolidated district;

3) effective date of the consolidated district;

4) an agreement on finances for the consolidated district, including disposition of funds, property, and other assets of each district; and

5) an agreement on governing the districts during the transition period, including selection of officers.

Each district must publish notice and hold a public hearing on the terms and conditions for consolidation.[1207] The notice of the hearing must be published once in a newspaper of general circulation in the area of each district at least seven days before the date of the hearing. After the hearing, each board by resolution may approve the terms and conditions of consolidation and enter an order consolidating the districts. The consolidation order shall be kept in the records of the consolidated district, filed with the county clerk in each of the counties in the consolidated district, and filed with the executive director of TCEQ.[1208]

Once the districts are consolidated, the debt of the original districts shall be protected and assured that it will not be impaired by the consolidated district.[1209] If the consolidated district has the taxing authority, it can pay the original debts of the original districts by levying taxes on the land in the original districts as if they were not consolidated or from contributions from the consolidated districts as agreed in the consolidation terms. Also, if the consolidated district has taxing authority and assumes the bonds, notes and other obligations of the original districts, taxes

---

[1204] *Id.* § 375.004(a) (West 2005). *See* TEX. GOV'T CODE ANN. chs. 551 (Open Meetings Act), 552 (Public Information Act) (West 2004 & Supp. 2011), Tex. Civ. Prac. & Rem. Ann. ch. 101 (Tort Claims Act).
[1205] TEX. LOC. GOV'T CODE ANN. § 375.351 (West Supp. 2011).
[1206] *Id.* § 375.352.
[1207] *Id.* § 375.353.
[1208] *Id.* § 375.357.
[1209] *Id.* § 375.355.

may be levied uniformly throughout the consolidated district. Also, a consolidated district with taxing authority must assess and collect taxes uniformly throughout the district for maintenance and operation of the district.[1210]

Dissolution of a District

The district may be dissolved in several ways:

- upon a majority vote of the board of directors;[1211]

- upon a petition of the owners of 75 percent or more of the assessed value of the property within the district;[1212]

- by petition of the owners of 75 percent or more of the surface area of the district:[1213] or

- upon a two-thirds vote of the governing body of a city in which the whole district is located adopting an ordinance dissolving the district.[1214]

If the dissolution is done by city ordinance, the city succeeds to the property and assets of the district and assumes all bonds, debts, obligations and liabilities of the district.[1215] The district may be dissolved by the board only after any remaining bonded indebtedness has been repaid or defeased in accordance with the order or resolution authorizing the issuance of the bonds.[1216]

Municipal Development Districts

In 2005, the Texas Legislature passed legislation enabling all cities to establish municipal development districts, which are governed by Chapter 377 of the Local Government Code. Prior to 2005, only cities which were located in two neighboring counties could take advantage of chapter 377. These districts are financed through an additional sales tax approved by the city's voters, a tax which is similar to the economic development sales tax discussed in Chapter I of this handbook.

There are two possible advantages of a municipal development district sales tax over an economic development sales tax: (1) the municipal development district tax need not be levied over the entire city, which is useful for cities that are at the two-percent sales tax "cap" in some portion of the city but not in others; and (2) it is the only municipal sales tax that may be levied in a city's extraterritorial jurisdiction (ETJ).

Creation of a Municipal Development District

A city may create a Municipal Development District comprising all or part of its city limits, all or part of its extraterritorial jurisdiction (ETJ), or any combination of all or part of these areas.[1217] To create a district, a city must call an election through an order that defines the

---

1210   *Id.* § 375.356.
1211   *Id.* § 375.261 (West 2005).
1212   *Id.* § 375.262(1).
1213   *Id.* § 375.262(2).
1214   *Id.* § 375.263(a) (West Supp. 2011).
1215   *Id.* § 375.263(b).
1216   *Id.* §§ 375.263(b), .264.
1217   *Id.* § 377.002.

proposed boundaries of the district.[1218] The ballot at this election must be printed to allow voting for or against the following proposition:[1219]

> **Authorizing the creation of the** *(insert name of district)* **Municipal Development District and the imposition of a sales and use tax at the rate of** *(insert one-eighth, one-fourth, three-eighths, or one-half, as appropriate)* **of one percent for the purpose of financing development projects beneficial to the district.**

In the order calling the election, the city may provide that the district boundaries will automatically conform to future changes in the city's boundaries, as when increased through annexation, and also to future changes in the city's ETJ, through annexation and population growth.[1220] If the voters turn down creation of the district, a subsequent election to establish a district may not be held within a year of the first election.[1221]

Sales Tax

Chapter 323 of the Tax Code generally governs the specifics of assessing and administering the tax.[1222] The district may not impose a sales and use tax that would result in a combined local tax rate of more than two percent in any location in the district.[1223] The sales tax rate adopted must be one-eighth, one-fourth, three-eighths, or one-half of one percent.[1224] The rate may be changed at a subsequent election.[1225] The ballot at this election must be printed to allow voting for or against the following proposition:[1226]

> **The adoption of a sales and use tax at the rate of** *(insert one-fourth, three-eights, or one-half, as appropriate)* **percent of one.**

The adoption of the tax or a change in its rate takes effect on the first day of the first calendar quarter occurring after the expiration of the first complete quarter occurring after the date the Comptroller receives notice of the election's results.[1227] Revenue from the sales tax must be deposited in the district's development project fund.[1228]

Rights and Powers of the District and its Board

The district must establish a development project fund, which may have separate accounts within the fund.[1229] The district must deposit the sales tax proceeds and all revenue from the sale of

---

[1218]   *Id.* § 377.021(a)-(b) (West 2005).
[1219]   *Id.* § 377.021(c).
[1220]   *Id.* § 377.021(g).
[1221]   *Id.* § 377.021(e) (Currently, this means that cities will have to wait through one election date, either in May or November, as there are only two uniform election dates).
[1222]   *Id.* § 377.102(a).
[1223]   *Id.* § 377.101(c).
[1224]   *Id.* § 377.103.
[1225]   *Id.* § 377.104(a).
[1226]   *Id.* § 377.104(c).
[1227]   *Id.* § 377.106.
[1228]   *Id.* § 377.108.
[1229]   *Id.* § 377.072(a).

bonds or other obligations into the fund.[1230] The money in the fund may be used to pay costs associated with development projects in the district, including maintenance and operation costs, as well as to pay costs relating to bonds or other obligations.[1231] A development project may consist of a Type B project as defined by the Development Corporation Act (see Chapter I of this handbook).[1232] Also, a project may include a convention center facility or related improvements, including parking facilities and civic center hotels.[1233]

The district may: [1234]

- accept grants or loans;

- buy, sell, and lease property;

- employ necessary personnel;

- enter into contracts with public and private parties;

- adopt rules to govern its operation; and

- perform any act necessary to the full exercise of the district's power.

It may not levy an ad valorem tax.[1235] It may issue bonds or other obligations to pay the costs of a development project after approval by the Texas Attorney General.[1236] The district is a political subdivision of Texas and the city that created it which makes it subject to the Open Meetings Act and the Public Information Act.[1237]

The district is governed by a board of at least four directors, although it would be best to have an odd number of directors to prevent tie votes.[1238] The board is appointed by the district-creating city council. Directors serve staggered two-year terms, so the initial terms must have about half the directors serving two-year terms and about half serving one- or three-year terms. Directors may be removed by the city council without cause. Directors must reside in the city or its ETJ. An employee or officer of the city or a member of the city council may serve as a director, but this person may not have a personal interest in a contract executed by the district. Board members are not compensated but may be reimbursed for actual and necessary expenses.[1239] Board meetings must be in the city that created the district, not in the ETJ or elsewhere.[1240]

[1230] *Id.* § 377.072(b).
[1231] *Id.* § 377.072(c)-(d) (A district located in a county with a population of 3.3 million or more [Harris County] may spend money on development projects in the ETJ of the city where the district is located).
[1232] *Id.* § 377.001(3)(A) (West Supp. 2011).
[1233] *Id.* § 377.001(3)(B).
[1234] *Id.* § 377.071(a)-(b) (West 2005).
[1235] *Id.* § 377.071(c).
[1236] *Id.* § 377.073.
[1237] *Id.* § 377.022.
[1238] *Id.* § 377.051.
[1239] *Id.* § 377.052.
[1240] *Id.* § 377.053.

Repeal of the Sales Tax

By order, the district can repeal the sales tax if a majority of the registered voters in the district vote at an election to repeal the sales tax.[1241] The ballot at this election must be printed to allow voting for or against the following proposition:[1242]

> **The repeal of the sales and use tax for financing development projects in the** *(insert name of district)* **Municipal Development District.**

The repeal of the tax takes effect on the first day of the first calendar quarter occurring after the expiration of the first complete quarter occurring after the date the Comptroller receives notice of the election's results.[1243] However, if the district has outstanding bonds or obligations at the time of the election, then the district continues to collect the tax until these bonds or obligations are paid, at which time the district should notify the Comptroller.[1244]

Neighborhood Empowerment Zones

A potential vehicle for economic development in Texas cities is a designated area within a city that is created to promote certain economic development activities.[1245] These designated areas are called Neighborhood Empowerment Zones. Neighborhood Empowerment Zones are governed by Chapter 378 of the Local Government Code.

Creation of a Neighborhood Empowerment Zone

To establish a Neighborhood Empowerment Zone, a city council must adopt a resolution containing the following:[1246]

1) a determination that the Neighborhood Empowerment Zone will promote:

    a. the creation of affordable housing, including manufactured housing within the zone;

    b. an increase in economic development within the zone;

    c. an increase the quality of social services, education or public safety provided to residents within the zone; or

    d. the rehabilitation of affordable housing within the zone;

2) a legal description that sufficiently describes the boundaries of the zone;[1247]

[1241]   *Id.* § 377.104(a).

[1242]   *Id.* § 377.104(d).

[1243]   *Id.* §§ 377.106, .107(c).

[1244]   *Id.* § 377.107(a)-(b).

[1245]   *Id.* § 378.002.

[1246]   *Id.* § 378.003(a).

[1247]   *See Parker v. Harris County Drainage Dist. No. 2,* 148 S.W. 351, 353 (Tex. Civ. App. - Galveston 1912, writ ref'd) (County line used as boundary line in petition was held sufficient. Petition need only contain a sufficient definite description of the boundaries of the proposed district to notify landowners that their lands were included within the district).

3) a finding by the city council that the creation of the zone benefits and is for the public purpose of increasing the public health, safety and welfare of the persons within the city; and

4) a finding by the city council that the zone satisfies the requirements contained in Section 312.202 of the Tax Code. This section lists the criteria to create a tax abatement reinvestment zone. To be designated a Neighborhood Empowerment Zone, the area must either be:[1248]

   a. an area whose present condition substantially arrests or impairs the city's growth, retards the provision of housing, or constitutes an economic or social liability to the public health, safety, morals or welfare because of one or more of the following conditions:

      i. a substantial number of substandard or deteriorating structures,

      ii. inadequate sidewalks or street layout,

      iii. faulty lot layouts,

      iv. unsanitary or unsafe conditions,

      v. a tax or special assessment delinquency that exceeds the fair market value of the land,

      vi. defective or unusual conditions of title, or

      vii. conditions that endanger life or property by fire or other cause;

   b. an area that is predominately open, and because of obsolete platting, deteriorating structures or other factors, substantially impairs or arrests the growth of the city;

   c. an area that is in a federally assisted new community located in a home rule city or in the area immediately adjacent to a federally assisted new community in a home rule city;

   d. entirely in an area that meets the requirements for federal assistance under Section 119 of the Housing and Community Development Act of 1974 (42 U.S.C. Section 5318);

   e. encompass signs, billboards, or other outdoor advertising structures designated by the city for relocation, reconstruction, or removal for the purpose of enhancing the physical environment of the city, which the legislature has declares to be public purpose; or

   f. reasonably likely as a result of the designation as a Neighborhood Empowerment Zone to contribute to the retention or expansion of primary employment or to attract major investment in the zone that would be a benefit to the property and that would contribute to the economic development of the city.

[1248] TEX. TAX CODE ANN. § 312.202(a)(1)-(6) (West 2008) (Lists the Tax Abatement Reinvestment Zone criteria. To create a Neighborhood Empowerment Zone the area must meet one of these six conditions contained in Section 312.202 of the Tax Code.).

A city is authorized to create more than one neighborhood empowerment zone.[1249] Further, an area may be included in more than one neighborhood empowerment zone.

Municipal Powers Within the Zone

Creation of a neighborhood empowerment zone vests a city with various development powers within the designated area. These powers include:

Building Fee Waiver: The power to waive or adopt fees related to the construction of buildings in the zone, including impact fees and fees for the inspection of buildings.[1250]

Municipal Sales Tax Refunds: For the purpose of benefitting the zone, the power to enter into municipal sales tax refund agreements. These agreements may be for a term not to exceed 10years, and apply to municipal sales taxes on sales made within the zone.[1251]

Property Tax Abatement: The power to enter into agreements abating municipal property taxes on property in the zone, subject to the 10 year duration limit for tax abatement agreements under Section 312.204 of the Tax Code.[1252]

Environmental Goals: The power to set baseline performance standards, such as the Energy Star Program as developed by the Department of Energy, to encourage the use of alternative building materials that address concerns relating to the environment or to building costs, maintenance or energy consumption.[1253]

North American Free Trade Agreement Impact Zones

General law cities and home rule cities are allowed to establish North American Free Trade Agreement (NAFTA) Impact Zones. The statute governing NAFTA Impact Zones is found in Chapter 379 of the Local Government Code. The permissible agreements and mechanics in creating these zones are very similar to those found in Neighborhood Empowerment Zones (discussed above).

Creation of NAFTA Impact Zone

To establish a NAFTA Impact Zone, a city council must adopt a resolution containing the following:[1254]

1) a determination that the NAFTA Impact Zone will promote:

   a. business opportunities for local businesses within the zone;

   b. an increase in economic development within the zone; or

   c. employment opportunities for residents within the zone;

[1249]   Tex. Loc. Gov't Code Ann. § 378.003(b) (West 2005).
[1250]   *Id.* § 378.004(1).
[1251]   *Id.* § 378.004(2).
[1252]   *Id.* § 378.004(3).
[1253]   *Id.* § 378.004(4).
[1254]   *Id.* § 379.003(a)(1)-(3).

2) a legal description that sufficiently describes the boundaries of the zone;[1255] and

3) a finding by the city council that the zone satisfies the requirements contained in section 312.202 of the Tax Code. Section 312.202 of the Tax Code lists the criteria to create a tax abatement reinvestment zone. To be designated a NAFTA Impact Zone, the area must either be: [1256]

    a. an area whose present condition substantially arrests or impairs the city's growth, retards the provision of housing, or constitutes an economic or social liability to the public health, safety, morals or welfare because of one or more of the following conditions:

        i.   a substantial number of substandard or deteriorating structures,

        ii. inadequate sidewalks or street layout,

        iii. faulty lot layouts,

        iv. unsanitary or unsafe conditions,

        v.   a tax or special assessment delinquency that exceeds the fair market value of the land,

        vi. defective or unusual conditions of title, or

        vii. conditions that endanger life or property by fire or other cause;

    b. an area that is predominately open, and because of obsolete platting, deteriorating structures or other factors, substantially impairs or arrests the growth of the city;

    c. an area that is in a federally-assisted new community located in a home rule city or in the area immediately adjacent to a federally assisted new community in a home rule city;

    d. entirely in an area that meets the requirements for federal assistance under Section 119 of the Housing and Community Development Act of 1974 (42 U.S.C. Section 5318);

    e. encompass signs, billboards, or other outdoor advertising structures designated by the city for relocation, reconstruction, or removal for the purpose of enhancing the physical environment of the city, which the legislature has declares to be public purpose; or

    f. reasonably likely as a result of designation as a NAFTA Impact Zone to contribute to the retention or expansion of primary employment or to attract major investment in the zone that would be a benefit to the property and that would contribute to the economic development of the city.

[1255]   *See Parker v. Harris County Drainage Dist. No. 2*, 148 S.W. 351, 353 (Tex. Civ. App. - Galveston 1912, writ ref'd) (County line used as boundary line in petition was held sufficient. Petition need only contain a sufficient definite description of the boundaries of the proposed district to notify landowners that their lands were included within the district).

[1256]   TEX. TAX CODE ANN. § 312.202(a)(1) - (6) (West 2008) (Lists the Tax Abatement Reinvestment Zone criteria. To create a Neighborhood Empowerment Zone the area must meet one of these six conditions contained in Section 312.202 of the Tax Code.).

A city is authorized to create more than one NAFTA Impact Zone. Further, an area may be included in more than one NAFTA Impact Zones.[1257]

Permissible NAFTA Impact Zone Agreements

Once property is located within a NAFTA Impact Zone, a city is granted certain powers. These powers include:

Building Fee Waiver: The city is authorized to waive or adopt fees related to the construction of buildings in the zone, including inspection and impact fees.[1258]

Municipal Sales Tax Refund and Abatement Agreements: For the purpose of benefitting the zone, the power to enter into municipal sales tax refund agreements. These agreements may be for a term not to exceed 10 years, and apply to municipal sales taxes on sales made within the zone.[1259]

Property Tax Abatement: The city can abate municipal property taxes on property located within the zone subject to the ten-year duration limit contained in Section 312.204 of the Tax Code.[1260]

Environmental Goals: The city may set baseline performance standards, such as the Energy Star Program as developed by the Department of Energy, to encourage the use of alternative building materials to address concerns related to the environment or to building costs, maintenance or energy consumption.[1261]

NAFTA Displaced Workers

If a business operating within a NAFTA Impact Zone enters into an agreement with the city for the waiver or adoption of building fees, inspection fees or impact fees, that business must make a good faith effort to hire individuals receiving NAFTA transitional adjustment assistance under 19 U.S.C. Section 2331.[1262] Similarly, if the business enters into an agreement with the city for a municipal sales tax refund, municipal sales tax abatement or municipal property tax abatement, the business must make a good faith effort to hire individuals receiving NAFTA transitional adjustment assistance. The business must report to the city council annually the percentage of the total number of individuals hired by the business who are receiving NAFTA transitional adjustment assistance.[1263]

Improvement Districts in Certain Counties

Chapter 382 of the Local Government Code allows certain counties[1264] to engage in economic development projects or create a public improvement district to oversee and manage economic

---

1257   TEX. LOC. GOV'T CODE ANN. § 379.003(b) (West 2008).
1258   *Id.* § 379.004(1).
1259   *Id.* § 379.004(2).
1260   *Id.* § 379.004(3).
1261   *Id.* § 379.004(4).
1262   *Id.* § 379.005(a).
1263   *Id.* § 379.005(b).
1264   *See id.* § 382.002 (West Supp. 2011).

development projects for the county.[1265] Upon the receipt of a proper petition, the commissioners court of an eligible county may establish by order either a project in a designated portion of the county, or, if the county determines it is in the best interest of the county, a district, but only in an area located in the extraterritorial jurisdiction of a city of that county.[1266] The petition must state:[1267]

1) the general nature of the proposed improvements;

2) the estimated cost of the improvements;

3) the boundaries of the proposed assessment district;

4) the proposed method of assessment, which may specify included or excluded classes of assessable property;

5) the proposed apportionment of cost between the public improvement district and the county as a whole;

6) whether the management of the district is to be by the county, private sector, or a partnership between the county and the private sector;

7) that the persons signing the petition request or concur with the establishment of the district; and

8) that an advisory body may be established to develop and recommend an improvement plan to the county.

The petition is sufficient if it meets two conditions. First, it must be signed by owners of more than 50 percent of the appraised value of taxable real property subject to assessment under the proposal.[1268] Second, the petition must also be signed by record owners of real property liable for assessment under the proposal who:[1269]

- Constitute more than 50 percent of all record owners of property that is liable for assessment under the proposal; or

- own taxable real property that constitutes more than 50 percent of the area of all taxable real property that is liable for assessment under the proposal.

The order must:[1270]

- Describe the territory in which the project is to be located or the boundaries of a district;

- Specifically authorize the district to exercise the powers of the district if the county has determined that creating a district is in the county's best interest; and

---

1265 *Id.* § 382.003(b).
1266 *Id.* §§ 382.006(a), .004.
1267 *Id.* § 382.006(a) (Refers to section 372.005 of the Local Government Code for the requirements of the petition). *See id.* § 382.006(a)-(b) (Specific requirements if a district is created under section 382.002(2) of this chapter).
1268 *See id.* § 372.005(b)(1) (West 2005).
1269 *See id.* § 372.005(b)(2).
1270 *Id.* § 382.006(c) (West Supp. 2011).

- State whether the petition requests improvements to be financed and paid for with taxes authorized by this law instead of or in addition to assessments.

Board of Directors

If the county elects to delegate its authority, it shall establish a board of directors to manage the project or to govern the district.[1271] The board of directors will consist of seven directors to serve staggered two-year terms, with three or four directors' terms expiring June 1st of each year. To serve as a director, a person must be at least 18 years old.[1272] However, if the population of the district is more than 1,000, to be eligible to be director, a person must:[1273]

1) be at least 18 years old; and

2) either be:

    a) a resident of the district;

    b) an owner of property in the district;

    c) an owner of stock, whether beneficial or otherwise, or a corporate owner of property in the district;

    d) an owner of a beneficial interest in a trust that owns property in the district; or

    e) an agent, employee, or tenant of a person covered by a, b or c above.

Each director shall execute a $10,000 bond payable to the district and conditioned on the faithful performance of the director's duties.[1274] Once the bond is approved by the board, the director shall take the oath of office prescribed by the constitution for public officers. The bond and the oath shall be filed with the district and retained in the records. Directors are compensated not more that $50 a day for each day that the director performs the duties of a director.[1275] Vacancies on the board are filled by the county.[1276] If a conflict of interest arises, Chapter 171 of the Local Government Code governs.[1277]

The county may authorize the board to adopt rules[1278]:

- To administer and operate the district;

- For the use, enjoyment, availability, protection, security, and maintenance of district property, including facilities;

- To provide public safety and security in the district; or

- To regulate the private use of public roadways, open spaces, parks, sidewalks, and similar public areas in the district, if the use is for a public purpose.[1279]

[1271] *Id.* § 382.051.
[1272] *Id.* § 382.052(a).
[1273] *Id.* § 382.052(b). *See id.* § 375.063 (West 2005) (Refers to the qualification of the directors).
[1274] *Id.* § 382.056 (West Supp. 2011). *See id.* § 375.067 (West 2005) (Refers to bond of the directors).
[1275] *Id.* § 382.055(b) (West Supp. 2011).
[1276] *Id.* § 382.053(a).
[1277] *Id.* § 382.054.
[1278] *Id.* § 382.106.

Also, the county may authorize a board to establish, revise, repeal, enforce, collect, and apply the proceeds from user fees or charges for the enjoyment, sale, rental, or other use of its facilities or other property, or for services or improvement projects.[1280]

Powers and Duties of the County or the District

The county or the board of directors of the district can exercise the powers and duties to operate the district set forth by the following:[1281]

- A county development district under Chapter 383 of the Local Government Code;

- A road district created by a county under Section 52, Article III of the Texas Constitution; and

- A city or county under Chapters 380 or 381, or under 372.003(b)(9) of the Local Government Code.

However, a county cannot delegate to a district the powers and duties of a road district or the power to provide water, wastewater, or drainage facilities unless both the city and county consent by resolution.[1282]

The district may not exercise the power of eminent domain.[1283] Some districts may annex or exclude land from the district as provided by Subchapter J of Chapter 49 of the Water Code.[1284] The district must obtain the consent of the county that created the district by a resolution of the commissioners court and the consent of a city in whose extraterritorial jurisdiction the district is located by a resolution adopted by the city council.[1285] Also, the board is not granted any right-of-way management authority over public utilities.[1286] To the extent that a project requires the relocation or extension of public utility facilities, the district shall reimburse the public utility for the all of the costs associated with the relocation, or extension of the facility. As for tax abatements, a county may not grant a tax abatement or enter into a tax abatement agreement for a district.[1287]

The district can only issue bonds or negotiable promissory notes with the approval of the commissioners court of the county that created the district.[1288] Bonds may only be issued with a majority vote of the voters of the district voting in an election held for that purpose.[1289] If the

---

[1279]   *Id.* § 382.108(a). *See id.* § 382.108(b)-(c) (Deals with conflict and providing safe and orderly use).

[1280]   *Id.* § 382.107.

[1281]   *Id.* § 382.101(a). *See* Chapter 4 of this handbook for information on County Development Districts, Chapter 5 for information on Chapter 380.(Section 372.003(b)(9) deals with the acquisition, construction, or improvement of water, wastewater, or drainage facilities or improvements that are authorized improvement projects for public improvement districts).

[1282]   TEX. LOC. GOV'T CODE ANN. § 382.101(c) (West Supp. 2011). *See id.* § 382.109 (Dealing with the county delegating authorization of road projects to the district).

[1283]   *Id.* § 382.112.

[1284]   *Id.* § 382.113(a)-(b). *See id.* § 382.002(1) (Describes which districts are able to annex or exclude land).

[1285]   *Id.* § 382.113(c).

[1286]   *Id.* § 382.110.

[1287]   *Id.* § 382.151.

[1288]   *Id.* § 382.152(a)-(b).

[1289]   *Id.* § 382.152(a).

commissioners court grants approval for bonds, notes or other district obligations, then the district may use district revenues, taxes or assessments, or any combination of taxes and revenue pledged to the payment of bonds to secure them.[1290]

Authority to Impose Assessments and Taxes

A county or district may accomplish its purposes and pay the cost of services and improvements by imposing:[1291]

- An assessment;

- An ad valorem tax;

- A sales and use taxes; or

- A hotel occupancy tax.

A district may impose an ad valorem tax, hotel occupancy tax, or sales and use tax to accomplish the economic development purposes prescribed by Article III, Section 52a of the Texas Constitution, if the tax is approved by the commissioners court of the county that created the district and a majority of the voters of the district voting at an election held for that purpose.[1292] The county must adopt an order providing to the district the authority to impose these taxes and provide the rate at which the district may impose the tax.[1293]

If the district imposes an ad valorem tax on property in the district, then it must do so in accordance with Chapter 257 of the Transportation Code.[1294] If the district imposes a sales and use tax, it must generally do so in accordance with Chapter 383 of the Local Government Code or Chapter 323 of the Tax Code.[1295] The rate of the sales and use tax may be imposed in increments of one-eighth of one percent up to a rate of two percent.[1296] The ballot for a sales tax election shall be printed to provide for voting for or against the proposition:[1297]

> **A sales and use tax at a rate not to exceed *(insert percentage rate)* in the *(insert name of district).***

> **or**

> **The adoption of a *(insert percentage rate)* sales and use tax in the *(insert name of district).***

A tax authorized at a sales and use tax election may be imposed at a rate less than or equal to the rate printed in the ballot proposition.[1298]

[1290]   *Id.* § 382.152(c).
[1291]   *Id.* § 382.153(a).
[1292]   *Id.* § 382.153(b).
[1293]   *Id.* § 382.153(c).
[1294]   *Id.* § 382.157.
[1295]   *Id.* § 382.156(b)
[1296]   *Id.* § 382.156(a)
[1297]   *Id.* § 382.156(c).
[1298]   *Id.* § 382.156(d).

If authorized by the county, a district shall impose a hotel occupancy tax as provided by Section 352.107 of the Tax Code.[1299] However, some districts that imposed a hotel occupancy tax may use it for a purpose described by Chapter 352 of the Tax Code or to encourage the development or operation of a hotel in the district, including economic development programs for or a grant, loan, service, or improvement to a hotel in the district.[1300] Hotel occupancy taxes may be used for any purpose authorized by Chapter 382 of the Local Government Code.[1301] However, hotel occupancy taxes can only be imposed if the owner of the hotel agrees to the imposition. Once an owner agrees, the agreement may not be revoked by the owner or any subsequent owners of the hotel.[1302]

Any tax authorized by a county to be imposed in the district may be used to accomplish any improvement project or road project, or to provide any service authorized by this chapter, or Chapter 372, 380, 381 or 383 of the Local Government Code.[1303]

Agreements and Contracts

There are various agreements or contracts that the county or the district may make to promote an economic development project. A county may enter into an economic development agreement, only on terms and conditions that the commissioners court and a board consider advisable, to make a grant or loan of public money to promote state or local economic development and to stimulate business and commercial activity in the area where the economic development project is located or in the district.[1304]

A district, if authorized by the county, may order an election to approve a grant or loan agreement.[1305] The grant or loan may be payable over a term of years and be enforceable on the district under the terms of the agreement and the conditions of the election. The terms of the agreement may include the irrevocable obligation to impose an ad valorem tax, sales and use tax, or hotel occupancy tax for a term not to exceed 30 years. If the voters approve the agreement, then the board may contract to pay the taxes to the recipient of the grant or loan in accordance with the agreement.

A county may enter into a development agreement with an owner of land in the territory designated for an economic development project or district.[1306] The terms of the development agreement may not exceed 30 years on any terms and conditions the county or the board consider advisable. The parties may amend the agreement.

[1299]   *Id.* § 382.155(b).

[1300]   *Id.* § 382.155(d). *See id.* § 382.002(1) (Description of districts able to use hotel occupancy tax in the additional way).

[1301]   *Id.* § 352.1555(a).

[1302]   *Id.* § 382.1555(b).

[1303]   *Id.* § 382.154.

[1304]   *Id.* § 382.103(a) (This includes grants or loans to induce the construction of a tourist destination or attraction in accordance with Chapter 380 or 381 of the Local Government Code).

[1305]   *Id.* § 382.103(b).

[1306]   *Id.* § 382.102.

A district may contract with any person or political subdivision to:[1307]

- accomplish any district purpose; and

- receive, administer, and perform the county's or district's duties and obligations under an improvement project or proposed improvement project.

This includes contracts to pay, repay or reimburse from tax proceeds or another specified source of money any costs, including reasonable interest, incurred by a person on the county's or the district's behalf, including all or part of the costs of an improvement project. State agencies, cities, counties, other political subdivisions, corporations or other persons may contract with the county or district to carry out the purposes of this law. Also, a district may contract for materials, supplies, and construction in accordance with the law applicable to counties or in the same manner as local government corporations created under Chapter 431 of the Transportation Code.[1308]

Annexation by a City

If a city annexes the entire territory of a district, the city assumes that district's assets, but not the district's debt or obligations.[1309] The district will remain in existence, even after annexation by a city, in order to collect any taxes or assessments.[1310] The taxes and assessment that are collected will be used solely for the purpose of satisfying any preexisting debt or obligation. After the debt or obligations have been discharged, or two years have expired since the date of the annexation, the district is dissolved and any outstanding debt or obligations are extinguished.

County Assistance Districts

County assistance districts are another tool for counties to use to fund economic development programs. Chapter 387 of the Local Government Code governs the creation of the district and the sales tax and the permissible uses of the sales tax revenue.

Initiating an Election for the Creation of a County Assistance District

The commissioners court of a county may call an election for the creation of a county assistance district.[1311] The commissioners court may create more than one county assistance district, but not more than one district can be created in a commissioners precinct.

The election order must:

- define the boundaries of the district to include any portion of the county in which the combined tax rate of all local sales and use taxes imposed, including the rate to be imposed by the district if approved at the election, would not exceed the maximum

---

[1307]   *Id.* § 382.104.
[1308]   *Id.* § 382.105.
[1309]   *Id.* § 382.201(a).
[1310]   *Id.* § 382.201(b). *See id.* § 382.202 (Deals with imposition of taxes in a district that is wholly or partly annexed by a city and how the legislature intends that the level of taxation of areas where the district and the city overlap do not exceed the level of taxation of fully annexed areas).
[1311]   *Id.* § 387.003(a) (West Supp. 2011).

combined rates of sales and use taxes imposed by political subdivisions of this state that is prescribed by Sections 321.101 and 323.101 of the Tax Code; and

- call the election to be held within those boundaries.[1312]

If the proposed district includes any territory of a city, the commissioners court shall send notice by certified mail to the city's governing body of its intent to create the district.[1313] If the city has created a Type A or Type B economic development corporation under the Development Corporation Act, the commissioners court shall also send the notice to the board of directors of the economic development corporation. The commissioners court must send the notice by the 60th day before the date the commissioners court orders the election. The governing body of the city may exclude the city's territory from the proposed district by sending notice of its desire to have the territory excluded to the commissioners court by certified mail no later than the 45th day after the city received the original notice from the commissioners court. City territory excluded in this manner may later be included in:

- the district in an election held by the commissioners court with the city's consent; or

- another district after complying with the notice requirements and after an election held by the commissioners court.

In addition, the following requirements must be met:

Potential Election Dates. The election must be held on a uniform election date as provided by Chapter 41 of the Election Code. There are uniform election dates in May and November. The current uniform election dates are:

- the second Saturday in May in an odd-numbered year;
- the second Saturday in May in an even number year, for an election held by a political subdivision other than a county; or
- the first Tuesday after the first Monday in November.[1314]

Time Frame for Ordering the Election. The city should order the election at least 71 days prior to the date of the election, unless the election is the general election for state and county officers.[1315] If the election is the general election for state and county officers, then the city should order the election at least 78 days prior to the date of the election.[1316] The Tax Code requires only that the city order the election at least 30 days before the date of the election.[1317] Nonetheless, it is advisable to provide at least 71 or 78 days' notice, since this is the requirement applicable to most other special elections in Texas and it allows time to comply with other Election Code requirements, such as early voting. In addition, the Election Code provision

---

[1312]   *Id.* § 387.003(b). *See* TEX. TAX CODE ANN. §§ 321.101 (West 2008), 323.101 (West Supp. 2011) (Defines which taxes are authorized by the municipal sales and use tax act and county sales and use tax act, respectfully).

[1313]   *Id.* § 387.003(b-1).

[1314]   TEX. ELEC. CODE ANN. § 41.0052 (West Supp. 2011).

[1315]   *Id* § 3.005(c)).

[1316]   *Id.*

[1317]   TEX. TAX CODE ANN. § 321.403 (West 2008).

governing time frames for ordering an election "supersedes a law outside this code to the extent of any conflict."[1318]

Notice to be Provided of Election. The city must publish notice of the election at least once in a newspaper of general circulation in the city.[1319] The notice must be published not more than 30 days and not less than 10 days before the date of the election. The notice must state the nature and date of the election, the location of each polling place, hours that the polls will be open, and any other election-related information required by law.[1320] The notice must also include the wording of all the ballot propositions.[1321] The entire notice must generally be provided in both English and Spanish.[1322]

Other Procedural Requirements. The city must follow all other applicable procedural requirements under the Election Code for elections. For further information about the requirements contained in the Election Code, contact the Secretary of State's Office, Elections Division, at (800) 252-8683.
Required Ballot Wording for County Assistance District Ballot. There is statutorily required wording for a county assistance district and sales tax proposition ballot. The wording that must be used is as follows:[1323]

> **Authorizing the creation of the *(insert name of district)* County Assistance District No.__ and the imposition of a sales and use tax at the rate of *(insert appropriate rate)* of one percent for the purpose of financing the operations of the district.**

The actual wording used on the ballot must indicate what rate is proposed for the county assistance district's sales tax. The voters then vote for or against the proposition.

Reporting Election Results of a County Assistance District's Tax.

If a majority of the voters approve the district and adopt the sales tax, the commissioners court by resolution entered in the minutes of the proceedings, must declare the results of the election. The order or the resolution should include statements showing:

- the date of the election;
- the proposition on which the vote was held;
- the total number of votes cast for and against the proposition; and
- the number of votes by which the proposition was approved.[1324]

[1318] TEX. ELEC. CODE ANN. § 3.005(b) (West Supp. 2011).
[1319] *Id.* § 4.003(a)(1), (c) (West 2010).
[1320] *Id.* § 4.004(a) (West Supp. 2011).
[1321] *Id.* § 4.004(b).
[1322] *See id.* ch. 272 (West 2010 & Supp. 2011).
[1323] TEX. LOC. GOV'T CODE. ANN. § 387.003(c) (West Supp. 2011).
[1324] *Id.* §§ 387.003(d) (West Supp. 2011), TEX. TAX CODE ANN. § 323.405 (West 2008). *See* TEX. LOC. GOV'T CODE ANN. § 387.008 (West 2005) (Making Chapter 323 of the Tax Code applicable to County Assistance District except where inconsistent with Chapter 387 of the Local Government Code).

If the election results change the application of the local sales tax, the county judge should send a certified copy of the order or the resolution, by U.S. certified or registered mail, to the Revenue Accounting, Tax Allocation Section of the Comptroller's office.[1325] The order or resolution should also include a map showing the boundaries of the district.

If more than one election to authorize a sales tax is held on the same day in the area of a proposed district and if the resulting approval by the voters would cause the imposition of a local sales tax in any area to exceed the maximum combined rate of sales taxes imposed by political subdivisions of this state that is prescribed by Sections 321.101 and 323.101 of the Tax Code, then only the county assistance sales tax can be imposed.[1326]

If a majority of votes received at the election are against the creation of the district, the district is not created. The county has the authority to call one or more elections to create one or more county assistance districts at any time after the failure of creating a district.[1327]

Effective Date of County Assistance District Sales Tax

After the voter approval of the district and adoption of the sales tax, the sales tax becomes effective on the first day of the first calendar quarter occurring after one complete calendar quarter has elapsed after the Comptroller received a copy of the order of the district's governing body adopting the tax.[1328] For example, if the county was to hold a successful election in May 2008 and the Comptroller received a copy of the order by June 2008, the sales tax would take effect October 1, 2008. The district would begin receiving sales tax allocations from the Comptroller starting in December 2008.

Allocation of the Sales Tax Proceeds by the Comptroller

Once the sales tax is effective, retailers collect it along with any other applicable sales taxes including the state sales tax, and remit the revenues to the Comptroller. The Comptroller remits the proceeds to the district. The County Sales and Use Tax Act (Chapter 323 of the Tax Code) governs the imposition, computation, administration and use of the tax, except where it is inconsistent with the County Assistance District Act (Chapter 387 of the Local Government Code).[1329]

Use of Revenue

The district, which is governed by either the commissioners court of the county or a governing body appointed by the commissioners court,[1330] may use the sales tax revenues to perform the following functions of the district:

[1325] TEX. TAX CODE ANN. § 323.405(b) (West 2008). *See* TEX. LOC. GOV'T CODE ANN. § 387.008 (West 2005) (Making Chapter 323 of the Tax Code applicable to County Assistance District except where inconsistent with Chapter 387 of the Local Government Code).

[1326] TEX. LOC. GOV'T CODE ANN. § 387.003(h) (West Supp. 2011). *See* TEX. TAX CODE ANN. §§ 321.101 (West 2008), 323.101 (West Supp. 2011) (Defines which taxes are authorized by the Municipal Sales and Use Tax Act and County Sales and Use Tax Act, respectfully).

[1327] TEX. LOC. GOV'T CODE ANN. § 387.003(e) (West Supp. 2011).

[1328] *Id.* § 387.012.

[1329] *Id.* § 387.008 (West 2005).

[1330] *Id.* § 387.005(a) (West Supp. 2011).

- the construction, maintenance, or improvement of roads or highways;

- the provision of law enforcement and detention services;

- the maintenance or improvement of libraries, museums, parks, or other recreational facilities;

- the provision of services that benefit the public welfare, including the provision of firefighting and fire prevention services; or

- the promotion of economic development and tourism.[1331]

Board of Directors

The commissioners court can decides to appoint a governing body for the district.[1332] The board of directors shall consist of five directors who serve staggered terms of two years.[1333] To be eligible to serve as a director, a person must be at least 18 years of age and a resident of the county in which the district is located. The initial directors shall draw lots to achieve staggered terms, with three of the directors serving one-year terms and two of the directors serving two-year terms. The members of the district's governing body are not entitled to compensation for service on the governing body of the district, but are entitled to reimbursement for actual and necessary expenses.[1334]

Powers of the District

A district is a political subdivision of the state.[1335] The district may:

- perform any act necessary to the full exercise of the district's functions;

- accept a grant or loan from the United States, state agencies, political subdivisions, or public or private persons;

- acquire, sell, lease, convey, or otherwise dispose of property under terms determined by the district;

- employ necessary personnel;

- adopt rules to govern the operation of the district and its employees and property; and

- enter into agreements with cities necessary or convenient to achieve the district's purposes, including agreements regarding the duration, rate, and allocation between the district and the city of sales and use taxes.[1336]

The district may contract with a public or private person to perform any act the district is authorized to perform.[1337] However, the district may not levy an ad valorem tax.[1338]

[1331] *Id.* § 387.003(a-1).
[1332] *Id.* § 387.005(a)(2).
[1333] *Id.* § 387.005(c).
[1334] *Id.* § 387.005(b).
[1335] *Id.* § 387.004 (West 2005).
[1336] *Id.* § 387.006(a) (West Supp. 2011).
[1337] *Id.* § 387.006(b).
[1338] *Id.* § 387.006(c).

Expanding the District and Excluding Area from the District

After creation of the district, it can be expanded if the commissioners court calls and holds an election for that purpose in the territory to be added to the district.[1339] A majority of voters in the territory to be added must approve the expansion.[1340] If more than one election to authorize a sales tax is held on the same day in an area proposed to be added to a district and if the resulting approval by the voters would cause the imposition of a local sales tax in any area to exceed the maximum combined rate of sales and use taxes imposed by political subdivisions on this state that is prescribed by Sections 321.101 and 323.101 of the Tax Code, then only the county assistance sales tax can be imposed.[1341]

Also, the expanding of the district can be initiated by a petition or petitions signed by the owners or owners of the majority of the land in the area to be included in the district.[1342] Once the district receives the petition, the district, by order, will include the area after an election is held in that area approving the inclusion of the area into the district. However, if there are not registered voters in the area to be included, then an election is not required.

The commissioners court by order may exclude an area from the district if the district has no outstanding bonds payable wholly or partly from the sales and use taxes and the exclusion does not impair any outstanding district debt or contractual obligations.[1343]

Decreasing, Repealing or Increasing the Tax Rate

The district may decrease the tax or repeal the tax, by order.[1344] The tax rate can be reduced or repealed without an election.[1345] However, the repeal or reduction of the tax cannot be below the amount pledged to secure payment of an outstanding district debt or contractual obligation. There is no statutory authorization for a voter-initiated petition to decrease or repeal the tax.

Also, the district can increase the tax by order and as long as the increase of the tax will not result in a combined tax rate of all local sales and use taxes that would exceed the maximum combined rate prescribed by Sections 321.101 and 323.101 of the Tax Code, in any location in the district.[1346] If the increased tax rate will not exceed the rate approved at the initial election, then the district can increase the rate without an election.[1347] If the increased tax rate would exceed the rate approved at the initial election, then the tax rate can only be increased after it is

---

[1339]   *Id.* § 387.003(f).

[1340]   *Id.* § 387.003(g).

[1341]   *Id.* § 387.003(h). *See* TEX. TAX CODE ANN. §§ 321.101 (West 2008), 323.101 (West Supp. 2011) (Defines which taxes are authorized by the Municipal Sales and Use Tax Act and County Sales and Use Tax Act, respectfully).

[1342]   *Id.* § 387.003(i) (West Supp. 2011).

[1343]   *Id.* § 387.003(j).

[1344]   *Id.* § 387.010.

[1345]   *Id.* § 387.010(a)(1)

[1346]   *Id.* § 387.010(a)(2)-(3). *See* TEX. TAX CODE ANN. §§ 321.101 (West 2008), 323.101 (West Supp. 2011) (Defines which taxes are authorized by the municipal sales and use tax act and county sales and use tax act, respectfully).

[1347]   *Id.* § 387.010(a)(2) (West Supp. 2011).

approved by a majority of the votes received in the district at an election held for that purpose.[1348]

The tax may be changed in one or more increments of one-eighth of one percent to a maximum of one-half of one percent.[1349] The ballot for an election to increase the tax shall be printed to permit voting for or against the proposition:[1350]

> **The increase of a sales and use tax for the *(insert name of district)* County Assistance District No.__ from the rate of *(insert appropriate rate)* to the rate of *(insert appropriate rate)*.**

If the voters approve the increase, then the increase will become effective on the first day of the first calendar quarter occurring after one complete calendar quarter has elapsed after the Comptroller received a copy of the order of the district's governing body increasing the tax.[1351]

[1348]   *Id.* § 387.010(a)(3).
[1349]   *Id.* § 387.010(b).
[1350]   *Id.* § 387.010(c).
[1351]   *Id.* § 387.012.

VIII. Public Disclosure of Economic Development Negotiations

Open Meetings and Public Information Acts

Local governments must comply with the requirements of both the Open Meetings Act and the Public Information Act in their quest to promote economic development. Economic development corporations, pursuant to a provision in the Development Corporation Act, are also subject to the requirements of the Open Meetings Act[1352] and the Public Information Act.[1353] Accordingly, cities, counties and development corporations must consider applicable open meetings and open records requirements when they deal with companies that request that certain financial information and the company's intent to relocate be kept confidential.

The Open Meetings Act and the Public Information Act permit certain economic development-related issues to be discussed in an executive session and provide a limited time period during which certain records regarding economic development prospects would be considered confidential.[1354] The Open Meetings Act allows a governmental body to conduct a closed session to discuss commercial or financial information that the governmental body has received from a business prospect.[1355] In order to hold a closed session under this exception, the business prospect must be one that the governmental body is seeking to have locate, stay or expand in or near the governmental body's territory. In addition, the business prospect must be one with which the governmental body is conducting economic development negotiations. If a business prospect meets both of these requirements, then the governmental body will also be authorized to conduct a closed session to deliberate the offer of an incentive to the business prospect.

The Public Information Act authorizes a governmental body to withhold information relating to economic development negotiations involving a governmental body and a business prospect.[1356] In order to be eligible for this exception, the business prospect must be one that the governmental body is seeking to have locate, stay or expand in or near the governmental body's territory. In addition, in order to be withheld, the information must relate to either: 1) a trade secret of the business prospect, or 2) commercial or financial information, the disclosure of which would cause substantial competitive harm to the person from whom the information was obtained. Information about a financial or other incentive being offered to the business prospect is also excepted from required public disclosure unless and until an agreement is made with the business prospect.

Once an agreement is made with the business prospect, information about the incentive becomes public. Even if an incentive is offered by a person other than the governmental body, information regarding that incentive would generally be open to the public if the incentive may directly or

---

1352   *Id.* § 501.072 (West Supp. 2011). *See also,* Tex. Att'y Gen. LO-96-104. *But see,* Op. Tex. Att'y Gen. No. JC-327 (2001) (As ruled under the former statute, the board of the Bryan - College Station Economic Development Corporation, formed under the Texas Non-Profit Corporation Act and not the Development Corporation Act of 1979, was held not to be subject to the Open Meetings Act).

1353   TEX. LOC. GOV'T CODE ANN. § 501.072 (West Supp. 2011).

1354   TEX. GOV'T CODE ANN. §§ 551.087 (West 2004), 552.131 (West Supp. 2011).

1355   *Id.* § 551.087 (West 2004).

1356   *Id.* § 552.131(West Supp. 2011).

indirectly result in the expenditure of public funds by a governmental body or in the reduction of revenue received by a governmental body. Finally, it is important to note that, when submitting its request for a ruling, a governmental body should assert all applicable exceptions to disclosure.[1357] All applicable exceptions must be asserted within ten business days. If the exceptions are not asserted timely, a governmental body could waive them.[1358]

[1357] *Id.* § 552.301.
[1358] *Id.* § 552.302.

IX. Synopses of Attorney General Opinions on Economic Development

Readers should be certain to check for any opinions issued by the Attorney General after the publication of this handbook and also make certain that the opinions mentioned below have not been overruled by legislative change, subsequent opinions or court cases.

Legislative Effect will be indicated by ▶ with reference to the Legislative Bill.

Type A Sales Tax

Please note that the Development Corporation Act was codified as of April 1, 2009 and can be found in the Local Government Code, Chapters 501 – 507.

GA-0819: Type A Sales Tax and Affordable Housing

It is for the board of directors of a development corporation to determine, in the first instance, whether a project or expenditure is authorized under the Development Corporation Act.

GA-0320: Infrastructure Expenses Allowed

An expenditure for road construction may qualify as a "project" under section 2(11)(A) of the Development Corporation Act of 1979, provided the board of directors of an industrial development corporation finds that the expenditure is "required or suitable for infrastructure necessary to promote or develop new or expanded business enterprises." *Tex. Rev. Civ. Stat. Ann. art. 5190.6, § 2(11)(A) (Vernon Supp. 2005).* Section 4(A)(i) of the Act does not preclude a 4A corporation from providing a transportation facility that benefits property acquired for another authorized project.

GA-0264: House Bill 2912 and Grandfathered Projects

House Bill 2912 significantly amended the Development Corporation Act of 1979, Tex. Rev. Civ. Stat. Ann. art. 5190.6, but contained a grandfather provision continuing former law for a project undertaken or approved before the bill's June 20, 2003 effective date. The Port Arthur Economic Development Corporation is now authorized to grant funds and refund sales taxes to a private corporation to promote economic development if former law authorized it to do so and if paying these funds constitutes a "project" "undertaken or approved" before June 20, 2003. The development corporation's board of directors must demonstrate that a project was "undertaken or approved" either by reference to some final official action taken by the board in an open meeting prior to June

20, 2003, or by reference to the terms of an election held under section 4A(r)-(s) of the Act prior to that date. The grant and sales tax refund were not a "project" under former law. Moreover, because development corporation's board of directors did not vote to make the grant or sales tax refund at an open meeting prior to June 20, 2003, it would not fall within the House Bill 2912 grandfather provision.

GA-0086: Section 4A Sales Tax and Promotional Expenditures

Whether a hippopotamus statue would serve a Hutto Economic Development Corporation ("HEDC") promotional purpose is a question of fact for the HEDC board of directors to resolve in the first instance, subject to judicial review and the supervisory authority of the Hutto City Council. The City Council may disapprove an HEDC expenditure for the statue. The HEDC may not spend more than 10% of its current annual revenues for promotional purposes in any given year. In addition, unexpended revenues specifically set aside for promotional purposes in past years may be expended for such purposes.

JC-0553: City Council Retains a Degree of Control over Disposition of Section 4A Assets Upon Dissolution

An industrial development corporation that is dissolving under article 5190.6, section 4A(k) of the Revised Civil Statutes must submit its dissolution plan to the corporation's creating unit for its review and approval. *See Tex. Rev. Civ. Stat. Ann. art. 5190.6, § 4A(k) (Vernon Supp. 2005)*. But the creating unit may not use its approval power to prevent the development corporation from performing its statutory duty to, "to the extent practicable, . . . dispose of its assets and apply the proceeds to satisfy" the corporation's obligations. *Id.* Neither article 5190.6 nor the Non-Profit Corporation Act preclude an industrial development corporation from establishing an escrow account to meet calculable future financial commitments.

JC-0547: Mayor May Simultaneously Serve as Paid Executive Director of EDC Corporation

Under current law, a mayor of a city that creates an industrial development corporation pursuant to article 5190.6, Revised Civil Statutes, is not prohibited from serving as a salaried executive director of the corporation. If, however, he receives more than ten percent of his gross income from his compensation as executive director, he must disclose that interest whenever the city council considers any matter involving the industrial development corporation, so long as the action contemplated will have an economic effect on the industrial development corporation that is different from its effect on the public. In such instance, he must file "an affidavit stating the nature and effect of the interest" and he must "abstain from further participation in the matter."

JC-0362: Section 4A Funds for Job Training

The City of Port Arthur Economic Development Corporation is authorized to expend sales and use tax proceeds to finance the Port Cities Rescue Mission's "rehabilitation and job training/educational facility" only if the Corporation's board of directors reasonably finds that such a facility promotes business development and otherwise complies with the Development Corporation Act of 1979, article 5190.6 of the Revised Civil Statutes. The Act does not expressly authorize a "grant" for the Mission's facility. Instead, any sales tax expenditure for such a facility must be made pursuant to a contract or other arrangement that ensures that the funds will be used for the authorized purpose and otherwise be in compliance with the Act.

► In 2003, the Texas Legislature amended sections 2(11)(A) and 38 of the Development Corporation Act of 1979. These sections address projects and job training. Consequently, primary job training facilities for use by institutions of higher education are an authorized project. Further, certain job training classes are permissible provided the business enterprise commits in writing to create new jobs that pay wages at least equal to the prevailing wage for the applicable occupation in the local labor market area. *See Tex. H.B. 2912, 78th Leg., R.S. (2003).*

JC-0349: Section 4A Board of Directors May be Reappointed to Subsequent Term

Directors of a corporation created under section 4A of article 5190.6, Revised Civil Statutes, serve a six-year term pursuant to section 11 of article 5190.6, subject to removal at any time by the governing body of the city that created the corporation, unless the articles of incorporation or bylaws of the corporation establish a shorter term of service. Neither article 5190.6 nor the Texas Non-Profit Corporation Act, article 1396 of the Revised Civil Statutes, bars a director of a corporation created under article 5190.6, section 4A from being reappointed as director. The governing body of the City of Copperas Cove may reappoint a director of the corporation to subsequent service as director, absent any contrary provision in the articles of incorporation or bylaws of the Copperas Cove Economic Development Corporation, or in the city charter, an ordinance, or a resolution of the City of Copperas Cove. Whether or not the city reappoints a particular individual as director is a matter for the governing body of the city, in the exercise of its reasonable discretion.

JC-0032: Prevailing Wage Law and Development Corporations

Chapter 2258 of the Government Code applies to a worker employed on a public work "by or on behalf of the state or a political subdivision of the state." *Tex. Govt. Code Ann. § 2258.021(a) (Vernon 2000).* Because a development corporation created under the Development Corporation Act of 1979 is not a political subdivision for purposes of the laws of this state, *see Tex. Rev. Civ. Stat. Ann. art. 5190.6, § 22 (Vernon Supp. 2005),* chapter 2258 does not apply to a worker employed by or on behalf of a development corporation. Chapter 2258 will apply to a worker on a project undertaken by a development corporation only if the development corporation undertakes the project on behalf of the state or a political subdivision of the state. In order for the project to be undertaken on behalf of the state or a political subdivision, the state or political subdivision must be a party to the construction contract.

LO-97-061: Donation of Section 4A Funds to Local College

Given the information provided, it appears that the board of directors of the Pampa Economic Development Corporation would have no basis on which to conclude that an expenditure of section 4A tax proceeds to support a Clarendon College center in Pampa, Texas would be consistent with the purposes of the Development Corporation Act of 1979. Furthermore, the act does not permit a section 4A development corporation to make gifts of public funds.

► In 2003, the Texas Legislature amended section 2(11)(A) of the Development Corporation Act of 1979 by removing "educational facilities" from the definition of project. Further, the Act was amended to allow funding of "primary job training facilities for use by institutions of higher education". *See Tex. H.B. 2912, 78th Leg., R.S. (2003)*.

LO-96-104: Economic Development Corporation is Subject to Open Meetings Act

The board of directors of the Beeville-Bee County Redevelopment Authority Corporation is subject to the Open Meetings Act, Gov't Code ch. 551, by virtue of section 11(b) of the Development Corporation Act of 1979, V.T.C.S. art. 5190.6.

LO-96-010: No Nepotism Prohibition

Because a member of the board of directors of an industrial development corporation, established under the Development Corporation Act of 1979, V.T.C.S. article 5190.6, receives only reimbursement for the member's expenses, the member is not "directly or indirectly compensated from public funds or fees of office." Thus, section 573.041 of the Government Code, which generally prohibits nepotistic appointments, is inapplicable.

No statute precludes one member of a city council from voting on removal of a member of the board of directors of an industrial development corporation, even where the city council member and director of the industrial development corporation are related within the second degree by affinity.

DM-0299: Industrial Development Corporations and Debt Prior to Restriction

Section 4A(q) of the Development Act of 1979, V.T.C.S. art. 5190.6, would violate article I, section 16 of the Texas Constitution if applied retroactively. A court would construe section 4A(q) only to apply to debts assumed by a development corporation after its enactment date.

LO-94-037: Section 4A Economic Development Sales Tax & Promotional Expenses

The Development Corporation of Abilene, which operates under section 4A of the Development Corporation Act, V.T.C.S. article 5190.6, may spend proceeds of the sales and use tax imposed under section 4A for "promotional purposes," subject to the proviso of subsection (b)(1) that no more than 10 percent of corporation revenue may be spent for such purposes, and so long as the expenditures are otherwise consistent with the provisions of the act and state law generally.

LO-93-104: Combined Proposition/Sales Tax for Property Tax Relief

For a simultaneous election on the imposition, under section 4A, V.T.C.S. article 5190.6, of a sales and use tax of one-fourth of one percent for economic development and the reduction of its previously adopted additional sales and use tax for the reduction of property taxes under Tax Code section 321.101(b) from a rate of one-half of one percent to one-quarter of one percent, the city should use the proposition language set out in section 4A(p), as follows:

The adoption of a sales and use tax within the city for the promotion and development of new and expanded business enterprises at the rate of one-fourth of one percent and the adoption of an additional sales and use tax within the city at the rate of one-fourth of one percent to be used to reduce the property tax rate.

LO-92-086: Use of Section 4A Tax Money for Technical College

The Marshall Economic Development Corporation may use proceeds of a sales and use tax collected pursuant to article 5190.6, section 4A, to finance bonds for the start-up costs of the Texas State Technical College System Extension Center in Marshall, Texas, so long as the funds are used solely for technical-vocational training purposes.

▶ In 2003, the Texas Legislature amended section 2(11)(A) of the Development Corporation Act of 1979 by removing "educational facilities" from the definition of project. Further, the Act was amended to allow funding of "primary job training facilities for use by institutions of higher education". *See Tex. H.B. 2912, 78th Leg., R.S. (2003).*

DM-0137: Economic Development Tax Reduction Application to Bonds Issued

Where, pursuant to subsections (n) and (o) of section 4A, article 5190.6, V.T.C.S., an election is held to reduce the sales and use tax rate collected by a municipality on behalf of an industrial development corporation, or to limit the length of time during which the tax may be collected, such reduction or limitation may not be applied to any bonds issued prior to the date of the election.

DM-0080: Economic Development Corporation Could Not Fund a Hospital

Hospitals are not "manufacturing or industrial facilities" or facilities "required or suitable for the promotion of commercial development" and may not be financed by bonds issued by industrial development corporations created pursuant to the Development Corporation Act of 1979, as amended.

Type B Sales Tax

Please note that the Development Corporation Act was codified as of April 1, 2009 and can be found in the Local Government Code Chapters 501 – 507.

GA-0522: Tax Exemption for Private Businesses May Be Unconstitutional

Under the terms of section 4B(k) of article 5190.6, Texas Revised Civil Statutes (the "Act"), land and improvements for the specifically listed purposes in section 4B(a)(2) of the Act constitute projects eligible for tax exemptions. Additionally, any other land and improvements that the Westworth Redevelopment Authority's (the "Authority") board of directors determines promote or develop business enterprises in accordance with section 4B(a)(3) of the Act are such eligible projects. But whether a particular property or improvement constitutes a "project" under the section 4B(a) standards is a question of fact. The Act grants the Authority's board of directors the discretion to make that determination in the first instance subject to judicial review for abuse of discretion. Under the terms of section 4B(k) of the Act, projects used for private commercial purposes would be eligible for tax exemption. A court could determine that section 4B(k), when applied to exempt from ad valorem taxes such projects that do not meet the established public purpose use test, is unconstitutional as applied. The Tax Code permits the Tarrant County Appraisal District and a taxing unit in which a particular property designated by the Authority as a section 4B(k) project is located to challenge the property's tax-exempt status.

► In 2007, the Texas Legislature, addressed the authority of an entity that acquires a leasehold interest from a development corporation to enter into subleases if it has an agreement with the development corporation that authorizes such subleases. *See Tex. H.B. 3440, 80th Leg., R.S. (2007).*

GA-0265: Voter Approval Allows 4B Funding of Youth Football Field

Consistent with the election proposition approved by the voters in 1997, the sales taxes collected in Gun Barrel City under section 4B of the Development Corporation Act of 1979 may be used to fund facilities for amateur sports, including children's sports, athletic, and public park purposes. The legislature has determined that section 4B(a)(2)(A) projects accomplish public purposes relating to economic development and the board of an economic development corporation is not required to make this finding for individual projects within this provision. Attorney General Opinion JC-0494 (2002), which was based on incorrect facts, is overruled to the extent it is inconsistent with this opinion.

GA-0004: Section 4B Corporation is Not Governmental Entity for Purposes of Section 272.001 (b)(5) of Local Government Code

Section 272.001(b)(5) of the Local Government Code exempts "a real property interest conveyed to a governmental entity that has the power of eminent domain" from the public notice and bidding requirements generally applicable to the sale or exchange of land owned by a political subdivision. The Euless Economic Development Corporation, a nonprofit industrial development corporation created under the Development Corporation Act of 1979, article 5190.6 of the Revised Civil Statutes, is not a "governmental entity" for the purposes of section 272.001(b)(5) of the Local Government Code. Furthermore, section 272.001(b)(5) does not authorize a political subdivision to transfer land to a private party by using a "governmental entity" as a pass-through.

JC-0547: Mayor May Simultaneously Serve as Paid Executive Director of EDC Corporation

Under current law, a mayor of a city that creates an industrial development corporation pursuant to article 5190.6, Revised Civil Statutes, is not prohibited from serving as a salaried executive director of the corporation. If, however, he receives more than ten percent of his gross income from his compensation as executive director, he must disclose that interest whenever the city council considers any matter involving the industrial development corporation, so long as the action contemplated will have an economic effect on the industrial development corporation that is different from its effect on the public. In such instance, he must file "an affidavit stating the nature and effect of the interest" and he must "abstain from further participation in the matter."

JC-0494: Consistent with Particular Ballot Proposition Section 4B Proceeds Could Only be Used for Projects Which Promote Business Development (overruled by GA-0265 due to new facts presented)

Consistent with the particular 1997 voter-approved election proposition, the sales taxes collected in Gun Barrel City under section 4B of the Development Corporation Act of 1979 may be used only for projects that promote business development. The Board of Directors of the Gun Barrel City Economic Development Corporation may not use the sales tax proceeds to fund a project that does not promote business development.

JC-0488: Section 4B Proceeds Could be Used for Access Road to Undeveloped Commercially Zoned Property

Under section 4B of the Development Corporation Act of 1979, the sales and use tax is levied for the benefit of the Lake Jackson Development Corporation established by the City of Lake Jackson under section 4B; and the Corporation, rather than the City, is authorized to expend the tax proceeds for authorized projects.

The 1995 sales and use tax election proposition approved by the voters of the City of Lake Jackson pursuant to section 4B does not prohibit the Lake Jackson Development Corporation from using the sales tax proceeds to build an access road to service undeveloped commercially zoned property that fronts a state highway if the expenditure will promote development of new or expanded business enterprises.

JC-0400: Section 4B Ballot Language and Use of Proceeds for Public Park or Nature/Birding Center

The Industrial Development Corporation of the City of Sonora, Texas is not precluded, as a matter of law, from using sales and use tax proceeds for a "nature/birding center" or a public park project that was not specifically approved by the voters when they authorized collection of the tax because it was within the scope of the purposes for which the voters approved the sales and use tax. The particular tax election ballot language submitted to the voters indicated that the tax proceeds would be used for projects authorized by section 4B of the Development Corporation Act of 1979; and, on the date of the tax election, the statute authorized public park projects. Additionally, the city published notice of the proposed project as required by section 4B, and no subsequent voter petition requesting an election on the project was submitted.

JC-0338: Section 4B May Not Approve Loan to Section 4B Director

The board of an economic development corporation may not approve a loan to a director of the corporation. An economic development corporation is not prohibited by law from entering into other transactions with a member of the board or with an entity in which a board member is interested if it complies with the provisions of the Texas Non-Profit Corporation Act governing transactions between corporations and directors, or, in the event the corporation bylaws impose a stricter standard, with the bylaws.

JC-0118: All Section 4B Incidental Costs Must be Related to a Project /May Not Expend Section 4B Sales Tax Proceeds for Promotional Purposes

Sales and use taxes levied under section 4B of the Development Corporation Act of 1979, TEX. REV. CIV. STAT. ANN. art. 5190.6 (Vernon Supp. 2005), may only be used for project costs; they may not be used for "promotional" costs unrelated to projects.

▶ In 2001, the Texas Legislature amended section 4B(b) of the Development Corporation Act of 1979 to allow 4B corporations to spend up to 10 percent of the sales tax revenue for "promotional purposes." *See Tex. H.B. 3298, 77th Leg., R.S. (2001).*

JC-0109: Section 4B Corporations Not Subject to Chapter 272 Sale of Property Requirements

A development corporation established under section 4B of article 5190.6 of the Revised Civil Statutes is not subject to section 272.001 of the Local Government Code, which establishes procedures political subdivisions must follow to sell land. However, a development corporation must ensure that it receives fair market value for any land, purchased with sales and use tax proceeds, that the development corporation sells for non-project purposes. Although article 5190.6 prohibits a city from granting a development corporation public money or free services, the Act does not preclude a city from providing funds or services to a development corporation in exchange for consideration from the development corporation, within certain limitations.

▶ In 2001, the Texas Legislature amended Section 21 of the Development Corporation Act of 1979 to allow a home-rule city to grant public money to a 4A or 4B corporation under a contract authorized by Section 380.002 of the Local Government Code. *See Tex. H.B. 782, 77th Leg., R.S. (2001).*

JC-0032: Prevailing Wage Law and Development Corporations

Chapter 2258 of the Government Code applies to a worker employed on a public work "by or on behalf of the state or a political subdivision of the state." Tex. Govt. Code Ann. § 2258.021(a) (Vernon 1999). Because a development corporation created under the Development Corporation Act of 1979 is not a political subdivision for purposes of the laws of this state, see Tex. Rev. Civ. Stat. Ann. art. 5190.6, § 22 (Vernon Supp. 1987), chapter 2258 does not apply to a worker employed by or on behalf of a development corporation. Chapter 2258 will apply to a worker on a project undertaken by a development corporation only if the development corporation undertakes the project on behalf of the state or a political subdivision of the state. In order for the project to be undertaken on behalf of the state or a political subdivision, the state or political subdivision must be a party to the construction contract.

LO-98-062; Section 4B Proceeds to Fund Maintenance and Operating Costs of a Project

Under V.T.C.S. article 5190.6, section 4B(a-2), section 4B tax proceeds may not be used to pay for maintenance and operating costs of a project unless the city publishes notice of this proposed use. If the proposed use is challenged by a petition of more than 10% of the voters within 60 days of the notice, the City of League City will be required to hold an election to obtain voter approval of the proposed use because such use has not been approved in a prior election.

LO-96-110; Joint Propositions for Economic Development Sales Tax

A city is not authorized to combine in a single proposition proposals for voting on adoption of an economic development tax under Section 4B, V.T.C.S. article 5190.6, and a sales and use tax for property tax relief under Tax Code Section 321.101(b).

▶ In 2005, the Texas Legislature enacted Section 321.409 of the Texas Tax Code, which enables a city to use a combined ballot proposition to lower or repeal any dedicated or special purpose sales tax and simultaneously raise or adopt another such tax, including the sales tax for property tax relief. *See Tex. H.B. 3195, 79th Leg., R.S. (2005).*

LO-96-104: Economic Development Corporation is Subject to Open Meetings Act

The board of directors of the Beeville-Bee County Redevelopment Authority Corporation is subject to the Open Meetings Act, Gov't Code ch. 551, by virtue of section 11(b) of the Development Corporation Act of 1979, V.T.C.S. art. 5190.6.

LO-96-010: No Nepotism Prohibition

Because a member of the board of directors of an industrial development corporation, established under the Development Corporation Act of 1979, V.T.C.S. article 5190.6, receives only reimbursement for the member's expenses, the member is not "directly or indirectly compensated from public funds or fees of office." Thus, section 573.041 of the Government Code, which generally prohibits nepotistic appointments, is inapplicable.

No statute that precludes one member of a city council from voting on removal of a member of the board of directors of an industrial development corporation, even where the city council member and director of the industrial development corporation are related within the second degree by affinity.

LO-95-072: Construction of Residential Sewer Lines

V.T.C.S. article 5190.6, section 4B authorizes the board of directors of a development corporation organized under V.T.C.S. article 5190.6 to determine whether the construction of sanitary sewer lines in an existing residential subdivision would promote or develop new or expanded business enterprises. Although it seems unlikely that the construction of sewer facilities in a residential subdivision would promote or develop new or expanded business enterprises, this office cannot exclude the possibility as a matter of law. The board's determination would be reviewed under an abuse of discretion standard.

City/County Venue Project Tax

GA- 0602: Venue Project Fund Money May Be Used To Pay Cost of Approved Venue Projects

A county, such as Terrell County, may use money in its venue project fund to pay any of the costs of constructing an approved venue project. The county may borrow money to pay such costs, to be repaid from the venue project fund, only by the "issuance of bonds… or other obligations."

GA-0156: City Must Spend Funds Consistent With Voter Approval

The terms of the election pursuant to which the Terrell County voters approved the venue-project tax for park improvements constitute a contract with the voters, and Terrell County is authorized to use venue-project funds for improvements outlined in the current Expenditure Plan only if the improvements are consistent with the election orders.

Improvements proposed by Terrell County constitute a "venue project," as defined by Local Government Code section 334.001(3), (4)(B), and (5), only if Terrell County intends to develop and construct a convention center facility and to undertake other improvements and infrastructure in conjunction with the development and construction of the convention center facility, and if the other improvements are related improvements located in the convention center facility's vicinity or infrastructure that relate to and enhance the convention center facility.

LO-98-074: City May Not Hold a Sales Tax Election Earlier Than One Year From Date of Previous Sales Tax Election

Section 321.406, Tax Code, which limits the frequency of sales tax elections held by a municipality, is applicable to elections held under chapter 334, Local Government Code. Thus, the city of Arlington may not hold a sales tax election under chapter 334 earlier than one year from the date of any previous sales tax election.

DM-0455: Houston's Ability to Participate in Sports Authority

The City of Houston is authorized to participate in the Harris County-Houston Sports Authority created pursuant to House Bill 92, Act of May 22, 1997, 75th Leg., ch. 551, 1997 Tex. Sess. Law Serv. 1929.

DM-0454: Houston's City Council Limited Authority over Harris County-Houston Sports Authority

The Houston City Council does not have either the formal power of appointment or the right of confirmation of directors of the Houston-Harris County Sports Authority (the "authority"). The city council is not empowered to approve change orders for authority contracts or to place restrictions on lease agreements negotiated by the authority, nor does it have general oversight responsibilities over the authority beyond the right to approve the issuance of bonds and other obligations.

DM-0453: Harris County Not Required to Hold a Second Election to Impose Hotel Occupancy and Short Term Car Rental Taxes

Harris County is not required to hold an election under the provisions of House Bill 92, Act of May 22, 1997, 75th Leg., R.S., ch. 551, 1997 Tex. Sess. Law Serv. 1929, 1929. The imposition of hotel occupancy and short-term car rental taxes does not, in the absence of a second election, contravene the due process clauses of the federal or state constitutions. Neither does House Bill 92 unconstitutionally discriminate against residents of Harris County on equal protection grounds. Section 7 of the bill is not a "local or special law" in contravention of article III, section 56, Texas Constitution.

Property Tax Abatement

GA-0734: Tax Abatement Period May Start In a Year After the Year the Tax Abatement Agreement Is Entered

The maximum ten-year abatement period authorized under Tax code section 312.204(a) may commence in a year subsequent to the year in which an agreement providing for the tax abatement is entered into by the taxing unit and the owner of the property subject to the agreement.

GA-0600: Abatement for Improvements Allowed if Governing Body Members Owns Only Real Property

A county may enter into a tax abatement agreement with the owner of taxable real property located in a reinvestment zone, and with the owner of a leasehold interest in or improvements on tax-exempt property located in a reinvestment zone. Assuming that the "fixtures and improvements" owned by a wind turbine company constitute "improvements on tax-exempt real property that is located in a reinvestment zone" under section 312.402 of the Tax Code, the mere fact that a member of a commissioners court owns the real property on which the fixtures and improvements will be located does not prohibit fixtures and improvements from being the subject of a tax abatement agreement.

A member of a commissioners court generally must abstain from a vote on a matter if it is reasonably foreseeable that an action on the matter will have a special economic effect on the value of the property distinguishable from its effect on the public. Whether a vote on a particular tax abatement agreement will have such a special economic effect is generally a question of fact that cannot be resolved in an attorney general opinion.

GA-0304: Successive Tax Abatements for Personal Property on Same Real Property Parcel Allowed

Under the Property Redevelopment and Tax Abatement Act, chapter 312 of the Tax Code, a prior tax abatement agreement concerning specific property does not preclude a municipality from agreeing to abate taxes on different business personal property at the same location. A new abatement agreement must fully comply with chapter 312 requirements.

GA-0134: Tax Abatement Agreements May Not Retroactively Extinguish Existing Tax Liability

Section 312.208 of the Tax Code, permitting amendment of tax abatement agreements, does not modify the rule established by section 11.42(a) of the Tax Code that a "person who does not qualify for an exemption on January 1 of any year may not receive the exemption that year." Tex. Tax Code Ann. §11.42(a) (Vernon Supp. 2005). In addition, a retroactive amendment of a tax abatement agreement that extinguishes an existing tax liability violates article III, section 55 of the Texas Constitution.

JC-0300: Tax Abatement Agreements Must be Executed With Owner of Real Property

Section 312.206(a) of the Tax Code authorizes a commissioners court to enter into a tax abatement agreement only with the "owner of taxable real property." The owner of a leasehold interest in tax-exempt real property is not such an "owner of taxable property."

▶ In 2001, sections 312.204(a) and 312.402 (a) of the Tax Code were amended to allow taxing units to also enter into tax abatement agreements with "the owner of a leasehold interest" in real property. *See Tex. H.B. 1448, 77th Leg., R.S. (2001) and Tex. S.B. 985, 77th Leg., R.S. (2001).*

JC-0236: Newly Elected Councilmember Loses Benefit of Tax Abatement Agreement on Date Councilmember Assumes Office

Attorney General Opinion JC-0155 (1999) determined that property owned or leased by a member of a municipality's governing body is not eligible for a tax abatement agreement authorized by the Property Redevelopment and Tax Abatement Act, chapter 312 of the Tax Code. Attorney General Opinion JC-0155 is clarified by determining when the property loses the tax exemption granted by the tax abatement agreement.

If the owner of property subject to the tax abatement agreement is elected to the municipality's governing body, the tax exemption created by the agreement is lost on the date the property owner assumes office as a member of the governing body. The tax due on the property for the year is determined according to the method set out in section 26.10 of the Tax Code.

► In 2001, section 312.204 (d) of the Tax Code was amended to allow a tax abatement agreement to continue in effect if the property owner becomes a member of city council or a member of the zoning or planning commission. *See Tex. H.B. 1194, 77th Leg., R.S. (2001).*

JC-0155: Property Owner Subject to Tax Abatement Agreement Becomes Ineligible to Continue to Receive Tax Abatement Once Elected to City Council

The Property Redevelopment and Tax Abatement Act, chapter 312 of the Tax Code, does not bar a property owner from serving on the city council that granted a municipal tax abatement to the property owner. However, the owner's position on the council makes his property ineligible to continue to receive a tax abatement. Section 171.004 of the Local Government Code bars him from participating in a vote on a matter involving the property if he has a substantial interest in the property or in the business that owns the property, and if it is reasonably foreseeable that an action on the matter would confer a special economic benefit on the property that is distinguishable from the effect on the public. Votes made in violation of section 171.004 of the Local Government Code are voidable only if the measures on which the property owner voted would not have passed without his vote.

► In 2001, section 312.204 (d) of the Tax Code was amended to allow a tax abatement agreement to continue in effect if the property owner becomes a member of city council or a member of the zoning or planning commission. *See Tex. H.B. 1194, 77th Leg., R.S. (2001).*

JC-0133: Tax Abatement Agreements May Not Exceed Ten Years

A tax abatement agreement made pursuant to chapter 312 of the Tax Code, the Property Redevelopment and Tax Abatement Act, may not exceed ten years. A governmental entity may not grant a tax abatement for property that previously received a ten-year tax abatement. In order for property to receive more than ten years of tax abatement, the agreement for the abatement must have been made prior to September 1, 1989.

► In 2001, section 312.204 (a) of the Tax Code was amended to allow a tax abatement agreement to take effect on January 1 of the next tax year after the date the improvements or repairs are substantially completed. *See Tex. H.B. 3001, 77th Leg., R.S. (2001).*

JC-0106: Tax Abatement May Apply to Relocated Beach Property

The movement of a structure from one location on a piece of property in a reinvestment zone to another location on the property may constitute a "specific improvement or repair" to the property for purposes of a tax abatement agreement under Property Redevelopment and Tax Abatement Act, chapter 312 of the Tax Code, if it improves or repairs the property in the ordinary sense and if the improvement or repair is consistent with the purpose of the reinvestment zone designation.

JC-0092: County Provision of an Economic Development Grant to a Private Company

Chapter 312 of the Tax Code neither precludes nor authorizes a commissioners court agreement to make payments of county funds to a private company that are the economic equivalent of an abatement of real property taxes. However, section 381.004 of the Local Government Code, which Dallas County cites as the basis for its authority to make such payments, neither expressly or impliedly authorizes a commissioners court to enter into an agreement of this kind. The legislative history indicates that the legislature did not intend section 381.004 to implement article III, section 52-a of the Texas Constitution and, moreover, confirms that the legislature did not intend section 381.004 to authorize county economic development loans and grants.

► In 2001, the Texas Legislature added subsection 381.004(g) of the Local Government Code. This subsection now allows the county commissioners court to develop and administer a permissible Chapter 381 program that includes entering into a tax abatement agreement with an owner or lessee of a property interest. *See Tex. H.B. 2870, 77th Leg., R.S. (2001).*

LO-98-001: Commissioners Court May Enter Into Tax Abatement Agreement Despite Ownership Interest

Tax Code Section 312.402 (d) does not preclude a commissioners court from entering into a tax abatement agreement with a corporation merely because a commissioners court member owns a very small percentage of shares in the corporation or the corporation's parent or because a commissioners court member invests in the corporation by way of a mutual fund.

LO-97-096: City Cannot Meet in Executive Session to Discuss a Tax Abatement Agreement

A city council or county commissioners court is not authorized to meet in executive session under the Open Meetings Act to discuss a proposed city or county property tax abatement for an existing industry.

▶ In 1999, the Texas Legislature added section 551.086 of the Texas Government Code, now renumbered to section 551.087 of the Texas Government Code. This section allows governmental bodies to meet in executive session to deliberate or discuss certain commercial or financial information or to deliberate the offer of a financial or other incentive to a business prospect.

DM-0456: County Not Authorized to Delete Land From Existing Reinvestment Zone

A county is not authorized to amend a Tax Code chapter 312 tax abatement agreement by deleting land from an existing reinvestment zone. A county reinvestment zone under chapter 312 must be contiguous and may not consist of only a portion of a building. The legislature intended to leave the substance of criteria for tax abatement agreements to the discretion of each county commissioners court, subject to very general constraints and certain specific limitations imposed by chapter 312.

LO-95-090: City Cannot Abate Delinquent Taxes

Neither Local Government Code section 380.001 nor Tax Code section 312.204 authorizes a municipality to abate delinquent taxes owed by a taxpayer who participates in the municipality's enterprise zone. Moreover, article III, section 55 of the Texas Constitution expressly forbids the abatement of delinquent taxes.

DM-0090: Day Opt in Period for Tax Abatement Agreements

The authority of the Chambers-Liberty Counties Navigation District to enter into a tax abatement agreement pertaining to land that is the subject of a county tax abatement agreement expired 90 days after the date of the execution of the county agreement.

▶ In 2001, the Texas Legislature amended section 312.206(a) of the Tax Code removing the 90-day period for other tax entities to enter into a tax abatement agreement on property located within a city. *See Tex. S.B. 1710, 77th Leg., R.S. (2001).*

Tax Increment Financing

GA-0725: Council Member's Reservation In Conveyed Property Does Not Exclude Property From Tax Increment Financing

Tax Code section 312.204(d) excludes real property owned by a member of a city's governing body from tax increment financing. It is unlikely that a city council member who in a deed conveying real property reserves to himself the sale proceeds of the property, if and when the property is sold, is the owner of the property under section 312.204(d) by virtue of the reservation. Thus, such a reservation does not by itself appear to operate to exclude property from tax increment financing under section 312.204(d).

GA-0549: School Value to Deduct Includes Only Increment Actually Paid

Section 403.302(d)(4) of the Government Code requires the Texas Comptroller of Public Accounts to deduct the total dollar amount of only the percentage of the captured appraised value of school district property located in a tax increment reinvestment zone that corresponds to the percentage of the tax increment actually paid into the tax increment fund by the school district.

▶ In 2007, the Texas Legislature changed how to determine the total dollar amount of the captured appraised value of the school district property located in a tax increment reinvestment zone. *See Tex. S. B. 1908, 80th Leg., R.S. (2007).*

GA-0514: TIF Area Must Be Blighted Despite No Use of Bonds

A city may not designate an area as a reinvestment zone under Tax Code section 311.005(a)(5) unless the area is "unproductive, underdeveloped, or blighted," within the meaning of article VIII, section 1-g(b) of the Texas Constitution, even if the area's plan of tax increment financing does not include issuance of bonds or notes.

GA-0474: Homestead Preservation District Anomalies

Local Government Code chapter 373A enacted in 2005 provides for the creation of homestead preservation districts and homestead reinvestment zones. Section 373A.108's tax exemption applies to land trust real property owned by a community housing organization or a housing finance corporation operating as a land trust in a homestead preservation district only if the real property is inside the district. The exemptions provided by Tax Code sections 11.182 and 11.1825 and by Local Government Code section 394.905 do not apply to such property inside the district.

A city creating a homestead reinvestment zone is not authorized to establish a termination date for the zone. Additionally, a city and a participating county are not authorized to execute an agreement that requires the county to deposit its tax increments into the zone's tax increment fund for a period exceeding one year and under which the county does not have the right to annually reconsider its participation in the zone. Finally, the tax increment fund revenues may be used only to purchase real property, construct or rehabilitate housing units in the zone, and pay zone and housing-related administrative expenses.

A family's income eligibility to receive a benefit from a homestead preservation reinvestment zone tax increment fund under Local Government Code section 373A.157(b) may be determined in accordance with the United States Department of Housing and Urban Development's family income eligibility rules codified at part 5 of title 24 of the Code of Federal Regulations. Additionally, the section 373A.157(b) median family income eligibility determination is required only for the year in which the family is granted a housing benefit from the tax increment fund.

▶ In 2007, the Texas Legislature passed legislation that addressed the issue discussed in this opinion. *See Tex. H.B. 470, 80th Leg., R.S. (2007).*

GA-0305: Competitive Bidding Statute Applies to Increment Fund Expenditures

A city may use a Tax Code chapter 311 tax increment fund to pay a private developer for environmental remediation, renovation, or facade preservation costs if the costs constitute "project costs" within the scope of section 311.002(1). A tax increment fund is a municipal fund within the meaning of chapter 252 of the Local Government Code, and chapter 252's competitive bidding requirements may apply to expenditures from the tax increment fund. Whether a particular expenditure is subject to competitive bidding will depend upon whether the expenditure falls within the terms of section 252.021 and whether the expenditure is exempt from chapter 252 under section 252.022. If a municipal expenditure is subject to chapter 252, the city would be precluded from reimbursing a person for costs incurred for work not performed pursuant to a competitively bid contract.

▶ In 2005, the Texas Legislature amended section 311.010(g) to except any dedications, pledges, or other uses of revenue in the increment fund from chapter 252.

GA-0276; City May Not Extend Original Termination Date of Reinvestment Zone

A home-rule city may not extend a Tax Code, chapter 311 reinvestment zone's termination date beyond the date provided in the ordinance designating the zone.

GA-0169: Councilmember May Serve on Reinvestment Zone Board

A city council member is not prohibited from simultaneously serving as a member of the board of directors of a tax increment reinvestment zone created by his or her municipality under chapter 311 of the Tax Code.

JC-0373: Tax Increment Financing Under The Texas Urban Renewal Law

Section 403.302 of the Government Code requires the Comptroller to conduct annual studies to determine the total value of taxable property within Texas school districts. Subsection 403.302(d)(8) of the Government Code requires the Comptroller to deduct from the market value of property taxable by a school district any property value that is subject to a tax increment financing agreement entered into under Local Government Code, chapter 374, subchapter D. The deduction is not optional, but is required by statute.

The predecessor of Local Government Code, chapter 374, subchapter D was unconstitutional when adopted. It was not impliedly validated by the 1981 adoption of article VIII, section 1-g of the Texas Constitution authorizing tax increment financing, but it was validated in 1987 when the predecessor statute was reenacted in the codification of laws relating to local government. A municipality may not adopt tax increment financing under Local Government Code, chapter 374, subchapter D unless it holds an election as required by section 374.031(a) of that statute.

JC-0152: Petitioned-For Tax Increment Financing Reinvestment Zones Must Also be Unproductive, Underdeveloped or Blighted

A city may not designate an area as a tax increment financing reinvestment zone, including an area subject to a petition under section 311.005(a)(5) of the Tax Code, unless the area is "unproductive, underdeveloped, or blighted" within the meaning of article VIII, section 1-g(b) of the Texas Constitution. An area that satisfies the criteria of section 311.005(a)(1), (a)(2), or (a)(3) comports with this constitutional requirement. A city must determine that an area subject to a petition under section 311.005(a)(5) is "unproductive, underdeveloped, or blighted" either according to the criteria set forth in subsection (a)(1), (a)(2), or (a)(3) of section 311.005 or according to its own, similar criteria. This determination is for the city to make in the first instance, in good faith, exercising reasonable discretion, subject to judicial review.

Section 403.302 of the Government Code defines the "taxable value" of school district property for purposes of school-finance funding equalization formulas. Subsections (d) and (e) of section 403.302, which exclude from the definition of "taxable value" the value of property located within certain chapter 311 reinvestment zones, do not as a matter of law violate the constitutional mandate that the legislature establish and maintain an "efficient system of public free schools," Tex. Const. art. VII, § 1.

JC-0141: City May Not Use Unexpended Tax Increment Funds After Termination of Reinvestment Zone For Improvements Outside of Reinvestment Zone

Under chapter 311 of the Tax Code, a city is not authorized to undertake or complete a reinvestment zone project in a manner that is not consistent with the reinvestment zone board of directors' project and financing plans, which must provide for projects within the zone. Therefore, as a general matter, a city may not use unexpended tax increment fund money after termination of a reinvestment zone to build an improvement outside the zone. The city may do so only if, prior to the zone's termination, the reinvestment zone board of directors agreed to dedicate revenue from the tax increment fund to replace areas of public assembly, and if construction of the improvement is a cost of replacing an area of public assembly under section 311.010(b) of the Tax Code, as added by, Act of May 24, 1989, 71st Leg., R.S., ch. 1137, § 22, sec. 311.010, 1989 Tex. Gen. Laws 4683, 4690.

DM-0390: City Which Terminates a Tax Increment Financing Reinvestment Zone May Create a New Reinvestment Zone With Identical Geographic Boundaries

A municipality that terminates a reinvestment zone by ordinance pursuant to section 311.017(a) of the Tax Code may then create a new reinvestment zone with geographic boundaries identical to those of the original zone. A municipality's loan to the first reinvestment zone may not be treated as a "project cost" of the second reinvestment zone pursuant to section 311.002(1) of the act, nor may such a loan be assumed by the second reinvestment zone. There is no mechanism for adjusting the tax increment base of a reinvestment zone to account for a severe decrease in the total appraised value of the real property in the reinvestment zone. See Tax Code § 311.012(c).

LO 96-138: City May Be Permitted to Condemn Property in a Reinvestment Zone as a Group

Section 311.008(a) of the Tax Increment Financing Act authorizes but does not require a city to exercise the powers listed, including the power to condemn property, to implement a reinvestment zone redevelopment plan. A city may be permitted to condemn property as a group under certain circumstances at the discretion of the court.

Texas Economic Development Act

GA-0686: Comptroller May Include More Information Then Required in its Value Limitation Agreement Report

In preparing the report on limitation agreements under the Texas Economic Development Act, the Comptroller of Public Accounts may include more information than is required by sections 313.008 and 313.032 of the Tax Code if the information is reasonably necessary to assess the progress of such agreements.

The Comptroller may use in the report information provided by recipients of limitations, regardless of whether the information is marked as confidential by the recipients, so long as the information is not confidential by law. The Comptroller must, in the first instance, determine whether information is confidential by law.

GA-0665: Owner of Qualified Property Is Eligible To Apply for a Limitation on Appraised Value

Tax Code section 313.025(a) authorizes "the owner of qualified property" to apply to a school district for a limitation on the appraised value of the qualified property for the purposes of school district-imposed maintenance and operation property taxes. Under Tax Code section 313.021(2), land, building or other improvement, and tangible personal property each constitute "qualified property." Accordingly, a person that owns a building or other improvement or tangible personal property is an "owner of qualified property" under section 313.025(a). Thus, a person meeting the other requirements of chapter 313 who owns such qualified property--building or other improvement or tangible personal property--is eligible to apply for a limitation on the appraised value of the person's qualified property irrespective of whether the person owns or leases the land on which the qualified property is to be placed.

Adopting the Freeport Exemption

DM-0463: Freeport Exemption for Component Parts

Article VIII, section 1-j of the Texas Constitution establishes an exemption from ad valorem tax for "freeport" goods, that is, certain property destined for shipment out-of-state within 175 days after the date the property was acquired in or imported into the state. The freeport exemption is available to property where it is acquired or imported in this state by a person who detains it in the state "for assembling, storing, manufacturing, processing, or fabricating purposes," even though the property is not sold or transported out of the state by that person, but is instead sold to an in-state purchaser who uses the property in manufacturing other items which are then transported out of state within 175 days of the time the first owner acquired it.

Whether the freeport exemption applies to specific property owned by one person and sold to another involves questions of fact, which cannot be addressed in the opinion process.

Local Hotel Occupancy Tax

GA-0851: Restrictions on Use of Reserve Funds Originally Generated from Hotel Occupancy Tax

Hotel occupancy tax revenues collected under chapter 351, Tax Code, must be expended only as authorized by the chapter. Chapter 351 prohibits hotel occupancy tax revenues, including any surplus funds, from being expended for general city purposes.

GA-0682: Hotel Occupancy Tax Revenue Can Pay for Administrative Cost if they Are Incurred Directly From Authorized Promotion and Servicing Expenditures

Tax Code section 352.1015(c) allows hotel occupancy tax revenue to be expended for administrative costs only if they are incurred directly for the promotion and servicing expenditures authorized by the provision applicable to the particular county, and the expenditure is otherwise consistent with chapter 352 of the Code. Whether expenditures for "key person insurance" premiums constitute an authorized administrative cost is for the commissioners court to determine in the first instance, subject to judicial review.

GA-0408: Tax in Extraterritorial Jurisdiction May Cause Total Tax to Exceed 15 Percent if Adopted Before County Tax

Section 351.0025(b) of the Tax Code prohibits a municipality with a population of fewer than 35,000 from adopting and imposing a hotel occupancy tax in its extraterritorial jurisdiction when the combined rate of state, county, and municipal taxes would exceed 15 percent. The section does not, however, prohibit a municipality from imposing its tax if the combined rate did not exceed 15 percent when the municipality adopted its tax but exceeds that rate after the county adopts a county tax.

GA-0124: Use of Hotel Occupancy Tax Revenue Towards County Senior Center

Under section 351.101 of the Tax Code, a municipality may expend its municipal hotel occupancy tax revenue "only to promote tourism and the convention and hotel industry" and only for the specific uses listed in the statute. *Tex. Tax Code Ann. § 351.101(a) (Vernon Supp. 2004)*. Whether a particular proposed expenditure of municipal hotel occupancy tax revenue is a permissible use and will "directly enhanc[e] and promot[e] tourism and the convention and hotel industry" is for a municipality's governing body to determine in the first instance.

JC-0105: City Which Collected More Than $2 Million in Hotel Occupancy Tax Revenue in Calendar Year Is Not Bound By Allocation Formula of Section 351.103(a) of the Tax Code

Pursuant to section 351.103(b) of the Tax Code, the allocation restriction of section 351.103(a) of the Tax Code does not apply to a municipality that has collected in excess of $2 million in hotel occupancy tax revenue in the most recent calendar year.

LO 97-005: City May Not Collect a Municipal Hotel Occupancy Tax in a Municipal Utility District Annexed For Limited Purposes

A city may not collect a municipal hotel occupancy tax in a municipal utility district annexed for limited purposes pursuant to a strategic partnership agreement under Local Government Code section 43.0751. A city with a population of less than 35,000, however, may impose a hotel occupancy tax in the city's extraterritorial jurisdiction pursuant to Tax Code section 351.0025 irrespective of city annexation of the area.

LO 96-113: Committee of Chamber of Commerce Not Subject to Open Meetings Act

A committee of the chamber of commerce that is expending funds raised by the local hotel tax under contract with the city is not a governmental body under the Open Meetings Act.

DM-0394: Use of Hotel Occupancy Tax Funds as Proposed for George Bush Presidential Library Was Impermissible

The City of College Station may, without violating article III, section 52 of the Texas Constitution, spend public funds on the George Bush Library to be established by Texas A&M University only if there is a city purpose for the expenditure, if the city receives adequate consideration for the expenditure, and if sufficient controls are attached to the transaction to ensure that the public purpose will be carried out. Hotel-motel occupancy taxes raised by the city under chapter 351 of the Tax Code may be spent only for the purposes expressly set out in section 351.101 of the code. No showing has been made that the tax funds proposed for allocation to the George Bush Library will be used for any purpose stated in section 351.101.

LO 93-55: Convention and Visitors Bureau Funded with Hotel Tax Monies Not Subject to Open Meetings Act

Neither the Greater San Marcos Chamber of Commerce, the Greater San Marcos Economic Development Council, nor the San Marcos Convention and Visitors Bureau are governmental bodies subject to the Texas Open Meetings Act, V.T.C.S. article 6252-17.

LO 92-51: City May Expend Municipal Hotel Tax Funds to Improve Visitors Information Center

A city may expend municipal hotel tax funds for the improvement of a visitors information center. The city must insure that the expenditure fulfills one or more of the specific purposes authorized by section 351.101 of the Tax Code. Section 351.103 of the Tax Code governs the allocation of tax receipts.

LO 92-16: Municipal Hotel Tax Funds Generally May Not be Used for General Landscaping and Sidewalk Improvements

Hotel occupancy tax funds may only be expended in conformity with chapter 351 of the Tax Code.

LO 89-103: City May Not Use Municipal Hotel Occupancy Tax for Reconstruction of Municipal Tennis Courts

Of the purposes for which Clarendon hotel tax funds may be spent under the applicable provisions, we think only that of "improvement" or "equipping" of a convention center facility under section 351.101(a)(1) might conceivably include reconstruction of municipal tennis courts. We assume from your letter that the courts are not part of a convention center. Therefore, we think that the city of Clarendon lacks authority to spend municipal hotel tax funds on tennis court reconstruction.

JM-1080: Federal Employee Travelling on Official Business is Not Exempt From Local Hotel Occupancy Tax

A federal employee travelling on official business whose travel expenses are reimbursable by his employer, either on a per diem or actual expenses basis, is not exempt from a local hotel occupancy tax imposed under chapters 351 or 352 of the Tax Code when he rents hotel accommodations.

▶ Sections 156.103(a) and 351.006(a) of the Tax Code now exempt federal employees from payment of the local hotel occupancy tax "when traveling on or otherwise engaged in the course of official duties" for the governmental entity.

JM-0972: State Officials Traveling on State Business Are Not Exempt from Local Hotel Occupancy Tax

State officials or employees traveling at state expense on state business are not exempt from the hotel occupancy tax provided for in chapters 156, 351 and 352 of the Tax Code.

▶ Sections 156.103(b), (c), (d) and 351.006 (b), (c), (d) of the Tax Code now exempt certain state officials from payment of the local hotel occupancy tax. Other state employees must still pay the hotel occupancy tax when paying their bill, but the state agency may request a refund from the city.

JM-0965: Municipality May Not Use Hotel Tax to Supplement Recreational Budget

Section 351.101 of the Tax Code sets out the exclusive purposes for which the municipal hotel tax may be used. The tax may not be used for the operation of general recreational facilities.

JM-0865: No Authority for Exemptions from Hotel Occupancy Tax

Neither a county nor a home rule city possesses the authority to grant an "exception" for religious, charitable or educational purposes from the hotel occupancy tax absent constitutional and statutory authority to do so.

JM-0690: Limited Use of Hotel and Motel Tax

Subsection 3c(a)(3) of article 1269j-4.1, V.T.C.S., does not authorize the use of hotel/motel occupancy tax funds for advertising which is not related to attracting conventions, visitors, or tourists..

JM-0184: Hotel Occupancy Tax May Not Be Used for Golf Course

The county of El Paso may not use revenues from a county hotel occupancy tax collected pursuant to article 2372-8, V.T.C.S., to purchase golf carts or finance general improvements for a county-operated golf course.

County Development District Tax

JC-0291: County Development District Not Authorized to Levy Ad Valorem Taxes

A county development district created under chapter 383 of the Local Government Code is not authorized to levy ad valorem taxes. A county development district may undertake a project only if it is consistent with the purpose of chapter 383 - "providing incentives for the location and development of projects in certain counties to attract visitors and tourists." *Tex. Loc. Gov't Code Ann. § 383.002 (Vernon 1999) (statement of legislative intent)*.

Loans Under Local Government Code Chapter 380

GA–0529: City May Fund Housing that Promotes Economic Development

Texas Constitution article III, section 52-a and Local Government Code section 380.001 authorize a city to make a loan for a housing project if the project will promote economic development within the meaning of these provisions.

GA-0137: Municipal Sales Tax Agreements

House Bill 3534, which amended sections 321.002(a)(3) and 321.203 of the Tax Code, prevents certain outlets, offices, facilities or locations from qualifying as a "place of business of the retailer" for municipal sales tax purposes. House Bill 3534 does not invalidate existing municipal sales tax rebate contracts nor prohibit municipalities and businesses from executing new contracts.

GA-0071: Municipal Sales Tax Rebates

If a business collects and remits municipal sales taxes as required by law, the city's rebate of those taxes to the business does not violate article III, section 55 of the Texas Constitution. *See* Tex. Const. art. III, § 55 (prohibiting the legislature and political subdivisions from "releasing or extinguishing, in whole or in part, the indebtedness, liability or obligation of any corporation or individual" to the state or political subdivision).

LO 95-090: City Cannot Abate Delinquent Taxes

Neither Local Government Code section 380.001 nor Tax Code section 312.204 authorizes a municipality to abate delinquent taxes owed by a taxpayer who participates in the municipality's enterprise zone. Moreover, article III, section 55 of the Texas Constitution expressly forbids the abatement of delinquent taxes.

DM-0185: Economic Development Program

Section 380.001 of the Local Government Code, which the legislature enacted pursuant to article III, section 52-a of the Texas Constitution, is constitutional. The legislature intended section 380.001 to authorize municipalities to offer a range of incentives designed to promote state or local economic development. It is outside the scope of the opinion process to determine, however, whether a particular incentive or combination of incentives constitutes a "program . . . to promote state or local economic development" for purposes of section 380.001 of the Local Government Code.

A home-rule municipality may issue bonds to fund an economic development program that the municipality has established in accordance with section 380.001, but only if two conditions are met.

First, the bonds must be in an amount and to the extent allowed by the city charter. Second, a majority of the duly qualified property tax-paying voters must approve the bond issuance at an election held to consider the issue.

Public Improvement Districts

GA-0724: City Can Contract with Another Local Government to Collect Special Assessment s Imposed by the Public Improvement District

A special assessment to finance a public improvement is imposed only upon the property that is specially benefitted by the improvement, and its amount is based on the special benefits accruing to the property. A special assessment is imposed under the taxing power, but it is not an ad valorem property tax within the Texas Constitution, nor does the term "taxation" in statutes ordinarily include special assessments.

Tax Code section 6.24 authorizes contracts between a municipal governing body and another taxing unit or an appraisal district board to collect ad valorem taxes, but it does not authorize contracts to collect special assessments imposed under the Public Improvement District Assessment Act, Local Government Code chapter 372, subchapter A.

Pursuant to the Interlocal Cooperation Act, a municipal governing body may contract for the collection of a special assessment it imposes in a public improvement district with another local governmental entity that is authorized to collect assessments for public improvements.

GA-0528: City Must Have Interest in Land it Funds

Texas Constitution article III, section 52(a) requires a city that builds a seawall on privately-owned land to maintain sufficient control over it to ensure that the public purpose is accomplished and to protect the public's interest in it. To carry out this duty, a city must have an appropriate interest in the land on which a seawall funded from assessments levied pursuant to Local Government Code, chapter 372, subchapter A or B will be located.

GA-0237: Homestead is Subject to Forced Sale for Nonpayment of Public Improvement District Assessments Relating to Lien Created Before Property Used as Homestead

A public improvement district assessment may be enforced by foreclosure of a homestead provided that the statutory lien created by section 372.018(b) of the Local Government Code predates the date the property became a homestead and the amounts to be collected fall within the lien's scope.

JC-0386: Homestead is Not Always Subject to Forced Sale for Nonpayment of Public Improvement District Assessment

Chapter 372 of the Local Government Code authorizes a city to levy special assessments on real property to aid in funding improvements in public improvement districts. The municipal governing body is authorized by statute to collect these assessments according to the procedures for collecting an ad valorem tax on real property, except for procedures applicable to the forced sale of homestead property to collect ad valorem taxes.

Assessments are not "taxes" as that term is used in the Texas Constitution, and a homestead may not be subjected to forced sale for nonpayment of a public improvement district assessment under the "taxes due thereon" clause of article XVI, section 50 of the Texas Constitution.

A homestead may not be subjected to forced sale for nonpayment of a public improvement district assessment under the "improvement thereon" clause of article XVI, section 50, absent a written, signed contract between the owner of the homestead property and the supplier of materials and labor for an improvement on the homestead property.

LO 96-129: City Must Receive a Petition From Property Owners First to Establish a Public Improvement District

The petition referenced in section 372.002 of the Local Government Code and described in section 372.005 of the Local Government Code is a prerequisite for the establishment of a public improvement district.

Municipal Management Districts

GA-0386: Member of Legislature May Not Be District Employee

Article XVI, section 40(d) of the Texas Constitution prohibits an employee of a municipal management district operating under chapter 375 of the Local Government Code from simultaneously serving as a member of the Texas Legislature. This constitutional provision does not prohibit an individual who works as an independent contractor for a municipal management district from simultaneously serving as a member of the Legislature. Attorney General Letter Opinion 90-55A is overruled.

GA-0307: Dual Office Holding Forbids Holding Two Board Positions

Under the conflicting loyalties aspect of the common-law doctrine of the incompatibility, an individual may not simultaneously serve as trustee of the New Caney Independent School District and director of the East Montgomery County Improvement District.

GA-0268: Municipal Management Districts Generally Do Not Have Power of Eminent Domain

A municipal management district (MMD) created under chapter 375 of the Local Government Code has no power of eminent domain. A municipal management district created under chapter 376 has eminent domain power only if the power is conferred expressly or implicitly. Those districts whose enabling statutes expressly withhold eminent domain power do not have such power. Harris County Improvement District No. 3 does not have eminent domain power. The enabling statute of any other municipal management district must be analyzed to consider whether the statute confers expressly or implicitly the power of eminent domain. A municipal management district with the power of eminent domain may use the power to acquire property for a use consistent with the district's legitimate purposes even if exercise of the eminent domain power may interfere with a transaction between private parties. Whether property is being condemned, in any particular circumstance, for a legitimate purpose of the condemning municipal management district is a question of fact.

▶ SB 224 (2005) clarified that most MMD's have no eminent domain power.

GA-0150: Special Districts with Municipal Management District Powers May Not Provide General Law Enforcement Services

The Town Center Improvement District of Montgomery County (with powers of a MMD) may not enter into a contract with a city to provide general law enforcement services outside the city's jurisdiction in unincorporated areas of Montgomery County.

County Economic Development Powers

JC-0092: County Provision of an Economic Development Grant to a Private Company

Chapter 312 of the Tax Code neither precludes nor authorizes a commissioners court agreement to make payments of county funds to a private company that are the economic equivalent of an abatement of real property taxes. However, section 381.004 of the Local Government Code, which Dallas County cites as the basis for its authority to make such payments, neither expressly or impliedly authorizes a commissioners court to enter into an agreement of this kind. The legislative history indicates that the legislature did not intend section 381.004 to implement article III, section 52-a of the Texas Constitution and, moreover, confirms that the legislature did not intend section 381.004 to authorize county economic development loans and grants.

► In 2001, the Texas Legislature added subsection 381.004 (g) of the Local Government Code. This subsection allows the county commissioners court to develop and administer a permissible Chapter 381 program, which includes entering into a tax abatement agreement with an owner or lessee of a property interest. *See Tex. H.B. 2870, 77th Leg., R.S. (2001).*

LO 98-007: County Lacks Authority to Fund Small Business Development Program

Section 381.004 of the Local Government Code does not authorize a commissioners court to appropriate funds to a small business development program that was not developed by the county and is not administered either by the county or by another entity under contract with the county.

LO 96-035: Donation of County Tax Funds to a Nonprofit Organization

Article III, section 52 of the Texas Constitution prohibits a county commissioners court from making a donation of county tax funds pursuant to Local Government Code section 381.001(f) to a nonprofit organization whose purpose is to assist industrial development.

Public Disclosure of Economic Development Negotiations

ORD-639: Adopting Two-Prong Test for Confidentiality of Commercial or Financial Information; Overruling Open Records Decision No. 592

National Parks & Conservation Association v. Morton, 498 F.2d 765 (D.C. Cir. 1974), which established a two-prong test for the confidentiality of commercial or financial information, is a "judicial decision" for the purpose of Section 552.110 of the Government Code. Information is confidential if disclosure is likely to either impair the government's ability to obtain necessary information in the future or cause substantial harm to the competitive position of the person from whom the information was obtained.

Miscellaneous Opinions Concerning Economic Development

GA 0687: TxDOT Does Not Have Authority to Transfer Trust Money to Subaccount

Section 228.012 of the Transportation Code does not provide authority for the Texas Department of Transportation to transfer monies held in trust in a particular subaccount of the state highway fund to a regional transportation authority.

GA-0653: Regional Transportation Authority's Different Tax Rates for Different Subregions Could Be Constitutional

Article VIII, section 1(a) of the Texas Constitution, requires that all taxation be equal and uniform. Article VIII, section 1(a) authorizes the classification of persons and property for taxation when the tax classification is not unreasonable, arbitrary, or capricious and when the tax operates equally on all persons or property within the class.

Chapter 452 of the Transportation Code authorizes a Regional Transportation Authority ("RTA") consisting of more than one subregion to collect a sales and use tax at different rates in the different subregions. For any RTA organized under chapter 452 that has more than one subregion and that collects the sales and use tax at different rates from the different subregions, the difference in tax rates could be upheld under article VIII, section 1(a) if the tax falls equally on people and property within each subregion and the different tax treatment by each subregion is reasonable.

GA-0634: "Fair Market Value" Does Include the Values of a Lease

The Brazos River Authority (the "Authority"), a special law conservation and reclamation district under Texas Constitution article XVI, section 59, owns real property surrounding Possum Kingdom Lake that is leased to private parties at below-market lease rates. The Authority is formulating procedures to offer to sell the property to the lessees of the property.

The first question presented is whether the leased property must be valued as unencumbered by the leases or encumbered by the unexpired terms of the existing leases for the purposes of determining the sales price if the property is offered for sale to the lessees. If the property is offered for sale to the lessees, the Authority would sell the property pursuant to section 49.226 of the Water Code. Section 49.226(a) generally provides that surplus real or personal property owned by a water district may be sold in a private or public sale or be exchanged. Section 49.226(a) requires that the surplus property be exchanged for "like fair market value." The Authority and the lessees assume that this fair market provision applies to the sale of the Authority's property. The lessees contend that the fair market value provision in section 49.226 requires the Authority to value the property as encumbered by the leases. Because section 49.226(a) does not explicitly state that a lease may not be considered, fair market value as used in the statute has the meaning established by the Texas courts, which meaning includes the value of a lease. Thus, application of the established judicial definition of fair market value requires the Authority to value the property as encumbered by the leases.

The second question presented is whether using the discounted sales price resulting from valuing the Authority's property as encumbered by the leases would violate Texas Constitution article III, section 52(a), which prohibits gratuitous transfers of public funds to individuals or private parties. Using a discounted sales price--resulting in this particular instance from valuing the property as encumbered by the existing leases-- would not violate article III, section 52(a).

GA-0603: Private Entity that is Supported or Spends Public Funds is Subject to the Public Information Act

A private entity that is supported in whole or in part by public funds or that spends public funds is in whole or in part a governmental body subject to the Public Information Act. Whether a private entity, such as a non-profit economic development foundation that receives partial funding from "quasi-public" utilities, is a governmental body requires a determination regarding the public nature of the funds and whether the public funds are spent or received by the entity in return for specific, measurable services or as general support. Such a determination involves the resolution of facts and is inappropriate for the attorney general opinion process.

Private entities that are in whole or in part governmental bodies under section 552.003 of the Government Code are subject to the Public Information Act and must make public information available to the public. Whether information is public information required to be disclosed or information otherwise excepted from disclosure is a matter for an attorney general decision under the Public Information Act.

GA-0472: Hospital District Status Defined

The Sabine County Hospital District, which intends to maintain an ambulance only for transporting patients between hospitals, is not required by law to dispatch its ambulances for emergency calls, even if there are no other ambulances operating within the District.

The District may provide financial incentives in a contract to induce a doctor to move to the District so long as the District finds that such an incentive is necessary for the direct accomplishment of a legitimate public purpose, that the District receives adequate consideration for its expenditure, and that appropriate controls are in place to assure that the public purpose will be carried out. Furthermore, the Professional Services Procurement Act, Government Code chapter 2254, which governs a hospital district's contract for professional services, requires that payment for services rendered under the contract be fair and reasonable, that they be consistent with and not higher than the recommended practices and fees published by the applicable professional associations, and that they not exceed any maximum provided by law. The act does not permit the contract to be competitively bid.

The District may meet under Government Code section 551.071 in a closed meeting to discuss legal issues raised in connection with the contract for the doctor's professional services. The District may not meet under Government Code section 551.087 in a closed meeting to deliberate economic development negotiations.

GA-0206: Business Council Not Subject to Open Meetings Act

The Bryan Business Council, Inc. is not a "governmental body" within the terms of the Open Meetings Act, chapter 551 of the Government Code.

JC-0567: Enterprise Zone May Not Receive an Additional Designation

Under chapter 2303 of the Government Code and section 151.429 of the Tax Code, a business entity located in an enterprise zone and presently designated an "enterprise project" and allocated the maximum jobs and related tax benefits may not receive an additional and concurrent enterprise project designation in the same enterprise zone and an additional maximum job allocation and the related tax benefits.

▶ In 2003, the Texas Legislature added section 2303.406(e) to the Government Code. This section allows the "department [to] designate multiple concurrent enterprise projects in the same enterprise zone. . ." *See, Tex. H.B. 2424, § 92, 78th Leg., R.S. (2003).* Additionally, the Texas Legislature amended section 151.429 of the Tax Code. This section now allows a maximum refund of $500,000 to a "double jumbo enterprise project" and a maximum refund of $750,000 to a "triple jumbo enterprise project" in each state fiscal year. *See Tex. S.B. 275, §§ 3.51 to 3.53, 78th Leg., R.S. (2003).*

JC-0327: Non Profit Corporation Not Subject to Open Meetings Act

The board of the Bryan-College Station Economic Development Corporation, an EDC organized under the Texas Non-Profit Corporation Act and not incorporated under the Development Corporation Act of 1979, is not subject to the Open Meetings Act.

LO 98-082: Meaning of the Phrase "Fair Market Value of the Land"

Under Local Government Code section 272.001(h), the fair market value of a municipality's interest in land is the amount that a willing buyer, who desires but is not obligated to buy, would pay a willing seller, who desires but is not obligated to sell. Unless evidence to the contrary is produced, the leasehold estate merges into the fee simple estate when the lessee purchases the land he or she currently leases. A lessee who purchases the whole of the city's interest in a lakeside lot under section 272.001(h) must pay for both the city's right to future rent payments and the city's reversionary interest.

A municipality may not instruct an appraiser as to whether to value the land as encumbered or unencumbered.

LO 96-073: Withdrawing from Transit Tax to Adopt Sales Tax for Economic Development

Should the City of Richardson decide by election to withdraw from the Dallas Area Rapid Transit (DART), it would be able--presuming it met the qualifications of article V.T.C.S. 5190.6, section 4B and Tax Code section 321.101(f) for the ceiling on its sales and use taxes--to adopt a section 4B sales and use tax. However, the city would not be eligible to adopt a sales and use tax under V.T.C.S. article 5190.6, section 4A, or the "additional sales and use tax" created by Tax Code section 321.101(b).

LO 95-085: Private Entity Included in Qualified Hotel Project

The term "qualified hotel project," as defined by House Bill 2282, Act of May 11,1993, 73rd Leg., R.S., ch. 231, 1993 Tex. Gen. Laws 480, includes a private entity selected by a municipality.

DM-0188: Public Property Leases and Taxation

Property owned by the City of Amarillo consisting of an airport maintenance hangar that is leased to a private party for operation is exempt from ad valorem taxation if the property is used in direct support of the operation of the airport by the city. Buildings that are owned by the city are not tax-exempt if they are owned purely for the purpose of renting them to private commercial interests. An office complex owned by the Amarillo Independent School District and partially leased to private parties and other political subdivisions remains tax-exempt if the facility was acquired in its entirety for the purpose of conserving school district funds. Property acquired by the Amarillo Junior College District for purposes of future expansion and temporarily leased to private persons for storage units is tax-exempt. Property rented to students and employees of the junior college for residential housing also remains tax-exempt, but property rented for these purposes to persons who are not students or employees is subject to property taxation.